The Foundations of
Philosophical Semantics

The Foundations of Philosophical Semantics

John L. Pollock

Princeton University Press
Princeton, New Jersey

All Rights Reserved
Library of Congress Cataloging in Publication Data will be
found on the last printed page of this book

ISBN 0-691-07283-3

Publication of this book has been aided by the Whitney Darrow
Fund of Princeton University Press

This book has been composed in Linotron Times Roman
Clothbound editions of Princeton University Press books are
printed on acid-free paper, and binding materials are chosen for
strength and durability

Printed in the United States of America by
Princeton University Press
Princeton, New Jersey

THIS BOOK IS DEDICATED TO
MY DAUGHTER KATHERINE
(who asked me to dedicate a book to her)

Contents

Contents

Preface

This book seeks to meld into a coherent whole the results of a number of different research projects in philosophical logic that were originally undertaken separately. The purpose is to create a general account of philosophical semantics. I had intended to include much of this material in *Language and Thought*, but that book became too long and it seemed advisable to separate out the more formal parts of the book and provide them with a different vehicle of publication. The resulting material does still presuppose some of the conclusions defended in *Language and Thought*, so it has proven necessary to begin the present book with a sketch of the theory of language presented there. That sketch is contained in Chapter Two, which also contains a further development of the theory of modalities begun in *Language and Thought*. The theory of possible worlds contained in Chapter Three was originally intended for publication in *Language and Thought*, but was later excised from it. A very early version of some of the material in Chapter Three appeared as an article entitled "Plantinga on possible worlds" (in *Profiles: Plantinga*), although some of the most important conclusions of Chapter Three are diametrically opposed to conclusions drawn in that article. Chapter Four continues my perennial project of trying to get the analysis of counterfactuals right. It is based closely on my article "A refined theory of counterfactuals" (*The Journal of Philosophical Logic*), but corrects certain aspects of the theory presented in that article. The new material is concerned primarily with the analysis of counterfactuals at nondeterministic worlds. Chapter Five tries again to analyze causation in terms of counterfactuals. The first part of Chapter Five is approximately the same as the first part of my article "Causes, conditionals, and times" (*Pacific Philosophical Quarterly*), but the second part, which deals with the role of time in causation, is completely new. It became apparent to me shortly after the publication of "Causes, conditionals, and times" that the assumptions about time upon which the second part of that article was based were indefensible. Chapter Five replaces those false assumptions with what I hope are true assumptions and then rebuilds the theory on that basis. Chapter Six attempts to sort out the philosophical significance of formal (model-theoretic) semantics. This material was originally slated for publication in *Language and Thought*, but later deleted from that book. Although the formal results were obtained in approximately their present form as early as 1978, they have not previously been published.

This book has profited enormously from the helpful comments I have received from several philosophers. The chapter on possible worlds has evolved out of many long discussions I have had on that subject with Al Plantinga. On a number of important occasions, he has convinced me of the error of my ways. (I do not seem to be as successful in convincing him of the error of his ways, but perhaps he is just getting even with me for my sybaritic lifestyle in southern Arizona.) As is evident from the footnotes, the material on counterfactuals has been improved in response to objections raised by Donald Nute and Pavel Tichý to earlier versions of the material. The analysis of causation reflects in large measure the successful attacks Glenn Ross made on my earlier analysis. Finally, the entire book has profited from the diligent refereeing Donald Nute and Tom McKay did for Princeton University Press. Their work was extraordinarily careful, and their remarks were very helpful and constructive.

Tucson, Arizona
March 1983

The Foundations of
Philosophical Semantics

I
Introduction

Philosophical semantics has become a thriving branch of philosophy, and the accomplishments of philosophical semantics have had repercussions throughout philosophy. We can probably regard philosophical semantics as having begun with Rudolph Carnap in the forties.[1] It took a great leap forward in 1959 with Saul Kripke's publication of the first completeness theorem in modal logic.[2] Perhaps the next major step was Richard Montague's development of intensional logic in the late sixties and early seventies.[3] The publication of Alvin Plantinga's *The Nature of Necessity* in 1974 brought philosophical semantics to the attention of the general philosophical populace. The work on counterfactuals by Robert Stalnaker[4] and David Lewis[5] in the late sixties and early seventies, together with David Kaplan's underground manuscript *Demonstratives*,[6] began the now widespread application of philosophical semantics to topics other then modal logic. Current work in philosophical semantics applies it to the philosophy of language, ethics, epistemology, probability, and the philosophy of mind.

The principal tool of philosophical semantics is the concept of a possible world. Carnap began it all by talking about state descriptions. Kripke talked about possible worlds in his 1959 completeness proof for modal logic, but it is arguable that possible worlds served only heuristic purposes there. Possible worlds were taken more and more seriously with each advance

---

[1] See Carnap [1942], [1943], and [1947].
[2] Kripke [1959].
[3] See the collection of papers in Thomason [1974].
[4] Stalnaker [1968].
[5] Lewis [1972] and [1973].
[6] Kaplan [1976].

in philosophical semantics. Plantinga and Lewis take them very seriously indeed. Today talk of possible worlds is taken literally, and it is maintained that possible worlds are real entities that actually exist and to which we can appeal in philosophical analysis.

There are two importantly different kinds of philosophical semantics: realistic and formal. *Realistic semantics* makes explicit appeal to possible worlds, proposing logical analyses framed directly in terms of possible worlds. The simplest example of such an analysis is that identifying necessary truth with truth at all possible worlds. For a more complicated example, consider Lewis's theory of counterfactuals.[7] Taking possible worlds and the relation of "comparative similarity" as basic, Lewis proposes the following truth conditions for counterfactuals:

(1.1) $(P > Q)$ is true at a world w iff there is a world at which $(P\&Q)$ is true that is more similar to w than is any world at which $(P\&{\sim}Q)$ is true.

Realistic semantical theories abound, including competing theories of counterfactuals, theories of meaning, theories of personal identity, and theories of probability.

In contrast, *formal semantics* does not make explicit appeal to possible worlds. Possible worlds loom faintly in the background, guiding the hand of the formal logician, but formal semantical theories are not framed directly in terms of possible worlds. Formal semantics is carried on entirely within set theory. The basic tool of formal semantics is the concept of a model, which is a kind of set-theoretic structure. Consider, for example, the simplest of all formal semantical theories— the truth-functional semantics for the propositional calculus. We begin by contructing a logical notation based upon a set At of atomic formulas and the logical constants $\neg$ and $\wedge$. We define a model to be any function mapping At into $\{0,1\}$. Truth-in-a-model M is then defined recursively as follows:

(a) If P is atomic the P is true in M iff $M(P) = 1$;

[7] See Lewis [1973].

4

(b) $\neg P$ is true in M iff P is not true in M;

(c) $(P \wedge Q)$ is true in M iff P and Q are both true in M.

We say that a formula is *truth-functionally valid* iff it is true in every model.

It is important to realize that although this definition uses common semantical words like 'true', it uses them in a special way, with the result that it makes truth-functional validity a purely mathematical concept defined abstractly within set theory. But validity is supposed to have more than purely mathematical significance. The truth-functionally valid formulas are supposed to represent a certain body of necessary truths. In precisely what sense do they represent necessary truths? When asked this question, logicians typically wave their hands and mutter something about possible worlds. Models are said to "correspond to" possible worlds, and truth in all models "corresponds to" truth in all possible worlds. It is not at all clear, however, what this alleged correspondence amounts to.

Despite its popularity and apparent fruitfulness, the foundations of philosophical semantics are in doubt. Although philosophers of widely differing persuasions make free use of possible worlds, there is less than complete agreement about the nature of possible worlds and how they are related to, for instance, necessary truth, propositions, and meaning. These questions bear most directly on realistic semantics, and they will occupy our attention throughout most of this book. In the final chapter we will take up the foundations of formal semantics, which will turn out to be a morass. There are established techniques used in formal semantics, but it is not clear what to make of the results obtained by these techniques. It is remarkable that few practitioners of formal semantics have even raised the question of its significance. I will attempt to answer this question by drawing precise connections between formal semantics and realistic semantics.

The purpose of this book is to clarify the foundations of both realistic and formal semantics. Realistic semantics is based upon the concept of a possible world, so our most basic task will be to make that concept clear. Before we can do that, however, we must examine a number of other logical concepts that are presupposed by theories of possible worlds. These include the concepts of proposition, statement, and state of affairs. I have recently developed a theory of these concepts,[8] and parts of that theory will be presupposed by the present book. Chapter Two will sketch as much of that theory as will be required for understanding. Chapter Three will turn to the analysis of possible worlds, and various accounts will be examined and a preferred account proposed. The use of possible worlds in realistic semantics will be illustrated in Chapters Four and Five, where analyses will be proposed for counterfactuals and causation. Although the topics of Chapters Four and Five are of general philosophical interest, their role in the present book is illustrative. The reader who is not interested in these topics and does not feel the need for illustrations can proceed directly to Chapter Six, where an investigation of formal semantics is undertaken. The material in Chapter Six is more technical than the rest of the book, but conversely the rest of the book can be understood without assimilating the material in Chapter Six.

[8] Pollock [1982].

II
Sketch of a Theory of Language

Although the basic tool of philosophical semantics is the concept of a possible world, philosophical semantics also makes indispensable appeal to other philosophical entities. In particular, philosophical semantics presupposes certain views about the nature of language and the relation between language and various logical entities like propositions. An adequate theory of philosophical semantics must be based, at least loosely, on an adequate account of language. The purpose of this chapter is to sketch, and in some ways expand upon, a theory of language that I developed and defended in detail in my book *Language and Thought*.

1. Propositions

1.1 *Fine-Grained Objects of Belief*

Philosophers have used the term 'proposition' in a variety of ways, so to avoid confusion we must settle upon a single precise use of the term. As I shall use the term, propositions are possible objects of belief or disbelief. That is, in order for φ to be a proposition, it must be possible for there to be a person who either believes φ or disbelieves φ.[1] This is a nec-

---

[1] The point of stating the requirement disjunctively is that there may be propositions (e.g., explicit contradictions) that cannot be believed, but only disbelieved. We avoid taking a stand on that question by requiring only that propositions be possible objects of belief *or* disbelief. I am indebted to Jose Benardete for this way of avoiding the problem. In connection with this requirement, I assume that there are no *necessary* restrictions on the complexity of propositions entertained by persons. This is required for the class of propositions to be closed under conjunction, negation, etc.

essary condition for being a proposition, but as I shall use the term it is not a sufficient condition, for the reasons I will now explain.

Roughly, propositions are supposed to be what people believe, and we want it to be the case that people believe the same thing (i.e., have the same belief) iff they believe the same proposition. There is an obstacle to imposing this requirement on propositions, however, and that is that under different circumstances we adopt different criteria for believing the same thing. For example, suppose I believe that there is a typewriter on my desk, and I believed that yesterday too. Then we may be willing to say that I believed the same thing yesterday as I do today. But there is also a reason for insisting that what I believed yesterday was not the same thing as what I believe today. What I believed yesterday was about a different time (viz., yesterday) from what I believe today is about. As such, what I believed yesterday might well have been false, while what I believe today is true. But then it seems to follow that they are not the same thing after all. We can accommodate both of our conflicting inclinations by distinguishing between two different kinds of propositions: *transient propositions*, whose truth values can vary with time, and *nontransient propositions*, which are about fixed times and whose truth values cannot change with time. Given this distinction, we can say that yesterday I believed the same transient proposition that I believe today, but a different nontransient proposition.

Although the distinction between transient and nontransient propositions is helpful, it does not fully account for the variation in our criteria for believing the same thing. For example, suppose Susan and I each believe that Herbert has a mustache. In believing this, we may be thinking of Herbert in quite different ways, but it may still be granted that we believe the same thing. On the other hand, if we are thinking about Herbert in different ways then our thoughts are distinguishable, and this may incline us to insist that we are really believing two different things. Although our beliefs are both about Herbert, they *could* have been about different individuals and could even have had different truth values. Again, we can handle this sort of case by distinguishing between two different objects of belief. When I think about Herbert, I must think about him *in some particular way*, i.e., under some particular mode of representation. We can either take that mode of representation to contribute to the identity of the proposition believed, or we can ignore the mode of representation and say that we believe the same proposition just as long as we believe the same thing of the same object (regardless of how we are thinking of that object). Propositions of the latter sort have been called *directly referential propositions*; we might call those of the first sort *indirectly referential propositions*.

It seems that there is a finest possible criterion for deciding whether two people (or one person in two possible situations) believe the same thing. This requires them to be thinking of objects in the same way, to be holding the beliefs at the same time, and in some cases (e.g., in first-person belief) to be the same person; there may also be additional requirements. Objects of belief or disbelief individuated by this criterion are maximally fine-grained.[2] I propose to reserve the term *proposition* for these maximally fine-grained objects of belief or disbelief. That is the way the term will be used throughout this book.

The decision to reserve the term 'proposition' for maximally fine-grained objects of belief should not be taken to impugn the integrity of less fine-grained objects of belief. We believe coarse-grained objects of belief *by* believing fine-grained objects of belief. For example, I believe the directly referential proposition that Herbert has a mustache by thinking of Herbert in some particular way and believing a fine-grained object of belief that encodes that mode of representation. Coarse-grained objects of belief can be characterized by describing the range of propositions *by* believing which one believes the coarse-

---

[2] It is important to recognize that this criterion combines both internal criteria (having to do with psychological states in the narrow sense of Putnam [1975]) and external criteria fixing indexical parameters (such as speaker identity and the time of the thought). Otherwise we would encounter twin-earth-type difficulties. For further discussion of this, see *Language and Thought*, 11.

grained object of belief. We might very reasonably identify coarse-grained objects of belief with sets of propositions. For example, the directly referential proposition that Herbert has a mustache would be identified with the set of all propositions ascribing having a mustache to Herbert under different modes of representation.

It is commonly (but not universally) supposed that propositions have structures and constituents. For example, the proposition that all philosophers are wise has a structure that might be symbolized as

$$(\forall x)(\mathbf{P}x \rightarrow \mathbf{W}x)$$

where **P** is the concept of being a philosopher and **W** is the concept of being wise. The doctrine of propositional structure and constituents is problematic. I assume that it is to be spelled out in terms of the corresponding notion of the structure of our thoughts, but I will not have much to say about that here. I will simply assume that propositions can be individuated in terms of their structure and constituents and attribute to propositions however much structure that requires.

1.2 *Concepts*

The most familiar kind of propositional constituent is a *concept*. When we believe a proposition that is about a particular object, we believe something *of* that object. Concepts are what can be believed or disbelieved of objects. Objects "fall under" or *exemplify* concepts. Just as for objects of belief, on different occasions we employ finer- or coarser-grained criteria for believing the same thing of an object. I will take concepts to be individuated by the finest-grained criteria for deciding whether we believe the same thing of an object. That is required for concepts to be constituents of propositions.

1.3 *Propositional Designators*

If we are to describe propositions in terms of their structure and constituents, we need more than just concepts as constituents. We also need a variety of logical operators (e.g, conjunction and negation), and we need some kind of constituent that picks out the objects a proposition is about. I will call the latter *propositional designators*. Thought about an object always involves some mode of representation, and these modes of representation are encoded in propositions by propositional designators. The most familiar kind of propositional designator is a definite description (built out of concepts—not out of linguistic descriptions). Just what else should be included in an inventory of propositional designators is a matter of some dispute. A once-popular view was that definite descriptions are the only propositional designators there are. However, Kripke [1972] and Donnellan [1972] argued vigorously against the thesis that in order to refer to an object one must be able to supply an identifying description of that object, and their arguments seem best interpreted as indicating that one can think about an object without thinking about it under a description. I have recently argued that we most commonly think about an object with which we are quite familiar in terms of a nondescriptive kind of designator I call a *de re designator*.[3] In *Language and Thought* I argued that there are other nondescriptive designators as well. Everyone has a nondescriptive way of thinking of himself, and I called the corresponding propositional designators *personal designators*. We also think of the present time nondescriptively, in terms of *temporal designators*. The details of this inventory are debatable, but I offer it now only to illustrate the possible variety of kinds of propositional designators. Precisely what kinds of propositional designators there are will not be of great importance for the present investigation.

Given concepts, propositional designators, and various logical operators, we can describe many propositions in terms of their structure. For this purpose I will use & for conjunction, $\lor$ for disjunction, $\sim$ for negation, $\rightarrow$ for the material conditional, $\leftrightarrow$ for the material biconditional, $(\forall x)$ for the universal quantifier, $(\exists x)$ for the existential quantifier, and $\approx$ for identity. I will write the simple proposition that results from predicating the concept α of the propositional designator δ as

---

[3] In Pollock [1980] and [1982].

II. Sketch of a Theory of Language

$\ulcorner(\alpha:\delta)\urcorner$. More generally, if α is an n-place concept we can write $\ulcorner(\alpha:\delta_1,\ldots,\delta_n)\urcorner$. Thus, we might describe a proposition as having the form

$$(\forall x)(\exists y)[(\alpha:x,y) \leftrightarrow ((\beta:x) \lor (\gamma:y))].$$

If we leave free variables in such a formula, we have instead described a complex concept in terms of its structure.

1.4 *Propositional Modalities*

Two important modal properties of propositions are *necessary truth* and *a priori truth*. There are, of course, numerous philosophical problems associated with these modal properties, but for now I will simply assume that the notions make sense, without endorsing any particular theory regarding them.[4] Where φ is a proposition, let us abbreviate $\ulcorner\varphi$ is necessarily true$\urcorner$ as $\ulcorner\mathrm{Nec}(\varphi)\urcorner$. We can define possibility and entailment and equivalence relations in terms of this modality:

(1.1) $\mathrm{Poss}(\varphi)$ iff $\sim\mathrm{Nec}(\sim\varphi)$.

(1.2) φ entails θ iff $\mathrm{Nec}(\varphi \to \theta)$.

(1.3) φ is equivalent to θ iff $\mathrm{Nec}(\varphi \leftrightarrow \theta)$.

Until fairly recently, it was generally believed that a proposition is necessarily true iff it is *a priori* true, but that now seems doubtful. It is still generally supposed that all *a priori* truths are necessary,[5] but it is no longer regarded as certain that all necessary truths are *a priori* true. For example, Fermat's conjecture is the following proposition:

$$(\forall x)(\forall y)(\forall z)[(n > 2 \ \& \ x > 0 \ \& \ y > 0) \to x^n + y^n \neq z^n].$$

If Fermat's conjecture is true, every instance of this general-

---

[4] A number of traditional objections to these notions were discussed and dismissed in *Language and Thought*. A theory of *a priori* truth was proposed in Pollock [1976], Chapter Ten, and some tentative proposals were made regarding the relationship between these two modal properties.

[5] Kripke [1972] denied this, but his arguments have not generally been accepted. I would urge that his putative example of a contingent *a priori* truth is not really *a priori*.

ization is provable by simple numerical calculation, but there may be no way to prove the generalization itself. If every instance is provable, all the instances are *a priori* and hence necessary; and if every instance is necessary, the generalization is necessary. But the generalization may not be *a priori*. Thus there may be necessary truths that are not *a priori*.

Necessity and possibility are *properties* of propositions. We also employ necessity and possibility as modal *operators*. For example, the proposition that it is necessary that $2+2 = 4$ is a modal proposition. The proposition $\Box\varphi$ is about whatever φ is about, as opposed to the proposition that φ is necessary, which is about φ. Given necessity as a property, how is necessity as an operator to be understood? It is natural to try to define the one in terms of the other by taking $\Box\varphi$ *to be* the proposition that φ is necessary. But what proposition are we talking about when we talk about "the proposition that φ is necessary"? We can refer to φ in many different ways, such as John's favorite proposition or the first proposition entertained by Bertrand Russell on the morning of April 7, 1921. How we refer to φ makes a difference to what proposition is referred to as 'the proposition that φ is necessary'. For example, even if John's favorite proposition is the same proposition as the first proposition entertained by Bertrand Russell on the morning of April 7, 1921, the following two propositions are distinct:

(1) the proposition that John's favorite proposition is necessary;

(2) the proposition that the first proposition entertained by Bertrand Russell on the morning of April 7, 1921, is necessary.

If we are to identify $\Box\varphi$ with some proposition to the effect that φ is necessary, we must seize upon a particular propositional designator δ that designates φ and then, letting **N** be the concept of being necessarily true, identify $\Box\varphi$ with (**N**:δ). But what designator might δ be? Clearly, δ cannot be the same designator as in either (1) or (2) above. (1) is about John, and (2) is about Bertrand Russell, but $\Box\varphi$ is about neither. Similar difficulties arise for any designator that designates φ in terms of contingent properties it happens to have. If this general proposal for the analysis of □φ is to work, it must proceed in terms of some kind of propositional designator that designates φ necessarily. Is there such a designator, and does it make the analysis plausible?

The answer to this question turns upon our having a special way of thinking about propositions. There is a difference between entertaining a proposition and thinking *about* it. If I think to myself that 2+2 = 4, I am entertaining the proposition that 2+2 = 4. But I can also think to myself that the proposition that 2+2 = 4 is true. This is to entertain a proposition *about* the proposition that 2+2 = 4. When I do this, I do not normally think of the proposition that 2+2 = 4 in terms of some contingent description of it. I think of it in terms of its content. This is a special way of thinking of a proposition. If we could not think of propositions in this way, we would have no way of judging that a proposition is true or necessary. Suppose I think about φ in this special way, perhaps believing that φ is true. I thereby entertain a proposition about φ, so the proposition I entertain contains a propositional designator designating φ. That designator corresponds to my special way of thinking about φ. Let us call such designators *logical designators*. I will write the logical designator for φ as [⟨φ⟩]. There must be analogous logical designators for concepts. My proposal is now that we can identify modal propositions with propositions employing logical designators:

(1.4) □φ = (**N**: ⟨φ⟩).

(1.5) ◇φ = ~□~φ

I earlier distinguished between □φ and the proposition that φ is necessary by saying that □φ is about whatever φ is about, while the proposition that φ is necessary is about φ itself. (1.4) seems to fly in the face of that distinction. But it does so only partially. To think of φ in terms of ⟨φ⟩ is to think of φ in a very special way—in terms of its content. Thus there is a sense in which, although $(\mathbf{N}: \langle \varphi \rangle)$ is about φ, it is about φ in terms of whatever φ is about, and so can also be viewed as being about whatever φ is about. My suggestion is then that it is the existence of logical designators that makes modal propositions and modal operators possible.

1.5 *De Re Necessity*

The necessity of a proposition is *de dicto necessity*. To be contrasted with this is *de re necessity*, which is a relation between an object and a concept. For example, Wilfrid Sellars is necessarily such that he is not the number two, and the number two is necessarily such that it is the square root of four. If α is a concept, let us abbreviate $\ulcorner x$ is necessarily such that it exemplifies $\alpha\urcorner$ as $\ulcorner \text{Nec}[x,\alpha]\urcorner$. Let $\ulcorner \text{Poss}[x,\alpha]\urcorner$ mean $\ulcorner \sim\text{Nec}[x,\sim\alpha]\urcorner$. The notion of *de re* necessity is universally acknowledged to be problematic. The preceding examples are clear cases of *de re* necessity, but more interesting cases are invariably contentious. Still, as there are clear cases, the notion must make sense, and it plays an essential role in philosophical semantics. We will find that it is presupposed by the notion of a possible world.

We can define a *de re modal operator* just as we defined a *de dicto modal operator*. This operates on concepts to generate modal concepts. Let $\mathbf{N}_{dr}$ be the two-place concept expressed by $\ulcorner x$ is necessarily such that it is $y\urcorner$. Then if α is a concept, we can define a modal concept as follows:

(1.6) $\quad \Box\alpha = (\mathbf{N}_{dr}{:}x,\langle\alpha\rangle).$

This has the result that x exemplifies $\Box\alpha$ iff $\text{Nec}[x,\alpha]$.

We have used '$\Box$' for symbolizing both *de dicto* and *de re* necessity. That is the normal convention, but ambiguity threatens when we consider relational cases of *de re* necessity (i.e., cases in which an n-tuple of objects has a property necessarily). For example, Kripke [1972] alleges that a person is necessarily such that he has the parents he does—he could not have had different parents. According to such "geneological essentialism", if x and y are the parents of z, then $\langle x,y,z \rangle$ is necessarily such that if z exists then x and y are the parents of z. Let us liberalize our notation as follows:

(1.7) $\text{Nec}[x_1,\ldots,x_n,\alpha]$ iff $\text{Nec}[\langle x_1,\ldots,x_n\rangle,\alpha]$;

(1.8) $(\Box\alpha{:}x_1,\ldots,x_n) = (\mathbf{N}_{dr}{:}x_1,\ldots,x_n,\langle\alpha\rangle)$.

Our notation becomes ambiguous when we combine this with our way of symbolizing the structures of complex concepts. For example, suppose β is a two-place concept and δ and δ^* are propositional designators. We can form a one-place concept by filling one of the argument places in β by δ: $(\beta{:}x,\delta)$. From this we can form the modal concept $\Box(\beta{:}x,\delta)$ and apply it to δ^*, yielding the *de re* modal proposition $(\Box(\beta{:}x,\delta){:}\delta^*)$. This notation is awkward, and it is tempting to simplify it by writing $(\Box\beta{:}\delta^*,\delta)$. But this does not come to the same thing. In $(\Box(\beta{:}x,\delta){:}\delta^*)$ the necessity is only *de re* with respect to δ^*, but in $(\Box\beta{:}\delta^*,\delta)$ the necessity is *de re* with respect to both δ^* and δ. For example, let $(\beta{:}x,y)$ be the concept expressed by 'if x and y exist then they are identical', and let δ and δ^* both be the designator expressed by 'the tallest man in the world'. Then $(\Box\beta{:}\delta^*,\delta)$ is the proposition that the tallest man in the world is necessarily such that if he exists then he is self-identical. This proposition is true. But $((\Box\beta{:}x,\delta){:}\delta^*)$ is the proposition that the tallest man in the world is necessarily such that if he exists then he is the tallest man in the world. This proposition is false. We can avoid this ambiguity while still simplifying our notation by subscripting the modal operator with the designators with respect to which it is *de re*:

(1.9) $(\Box_{\delta_1,\ldots,\delta_i}\alpha{:}\delta_1,\ldots,\delta_n) =$
$\qquad (\Box(\alpha{:}x_1,\ldots,x_i,\delta_{i+1},\ldots,\delta_n){:}\delta_1,\ldots,\delta_i)$.

There is a certain ambiguity in the English locutions we ordinarily use in ascribing *de re* necessities. Suppose it is claimed that a particular table is necessarily such that it is made of wood. $\ulcorner x$ is made of wood$\urcorner$ implies $\ulcorner x$ exists$\urcorner$, so it seems that $\ulcorner x$ is necessarily such that it is made of wood$\urcorner$ should imply $\ulcorner x$ exists necessarily$\urcorner$; but of course it does not imply that. $\ulcorner x$ is necessarily such that it is made of wood$\urcorner$

means ⌜x is necessarily such that if it exists then it is made of wood⌝. Most attributions of *de re* necessity are to be understood analogously as attributing the necessity of something conditional on existence. However, there are some attributions that cannot be understood in that way. For example, ⌜x exists necessarily⌝ does not mean ⌜x is necessarily such that if it exists then it exists⌝. The English expression ⌜x is necessarily such that it is F⌝ must be recognized as ambiguous in this respect, and we must treat it with corresponding care. As it is used here, '□' does not symbolize necessity conditional on existence. Thus if we are to symbolize ⌜x is necessarily such that it is made of wood⌝, we must write ⌜$\Box_x((\mathbf{E}{:}x) \rightarrow (\mathbf{W}{:}x))$⌝ (where $\mathbf{E}$ is the concept of existing).[6]

The principal philosophical difficulty regarding *de re* modalities appears to be in explaining their source. Various theories have been proposed for the source of *de dicto* necessity, the main ones being conventionalism and logical intuitionism, but those theories cannot be generalized to *de re* necessity, and there are no other very plausible theories waiting in the wings. This is the main reason philosophers are suspicious of *de re* necessity. They feel that they do not understand this notion. On the other hand, as this book progresses we will find that there are an enormous number of common philosophical purposes for which *de re* necessity is indispensable and in which its use has generally gone unnoticed. *De re* necessity enjoys much more frequent use than philosophers commonly realize. One locus of such use concerns abstract entities of various sorts. For example, where α is a cardinal number, the assertion that it is possible for there to be α many physical objects in the world is *de re* with respect to α. Philosophers have tended to use modal operators freely in connection with abstract entities, perhaps supposing that *de re* modalities involving abstract entities can always be replaced by *de dicto* modalities. That can always be done for *de re* modal claims involving propositions, concepts, or propositional designators,

---

[6] Plantinga [1974] objects to this notion of *de re* necessity, maintaining instead that all *de re* necessity should be conditional on existence. This is discussed below in Chapter Three, section five.

because we can always reformulate them as *de dicto* modal claims involving the logical designators $\langle\varphi\rangle$. However, there is no good reason to suppose that *de re* necessity relative to sets, possible worlds, and cardinal numbers can be eliminated in similar ways. A second area in which the common use of *de re* necessity has been overlooked is in the formulation of logical analyses. It is generally supposed that logical analyses can be formulated in terms of the *de dicto* necessity of the universal closure of a biconditional. For instance, a logical analysis of a concept α would have the form

$$\Box(\forall x)((\alpha{:}x) \leftrightarrow \varphi x)$$

where $\ulcorner\varphi x\urcorner$ is some open formula expressing the analysans. But I will argue in Chapter Three (section five) that logical analyses cannot be adequately formulated in this way. Instead, they require both *de dicto* and *de re* necessity and have the form:

$$\Box(\forall x)\Box_x((\alpha{:}x) \leftrightarrow \varphi x).$$

Our use of the subscript notation $\ulcorner\Box_x\urcorner$ will bring forcefully to our attention just how often we employ *de re* necessity in philosophical logic. This is not a problem we can ignore. It thus becomes very important to have a reasonable theory of *de re* necessity. Unfortunately, I do not have such a theory to propose. A few remarks can be made concerning the relationship between *de re* necessity and *de dicto* necessity, but the major problems remain unresolved.

Although *de re* necessity and *de dicto* necessity are different modalities, there are interconnections. One of the most important is that *de dicto* necessity provides one source of *de re* necessity. The following holds in general:

(1.10) If $\text{Nec}((\forall x)(\alpha{:}x))$ then for any object z,
$\text{Nec}[z,((\mathbf{E}{:}z) \rightarrow (\alpha{:}z))]$.

In light of (1.10), it cannot be denied that there are any *de re* necessities. The strongest claim that can be made is that (1.10) provides the only source of *de re* necessity, and hence *de re* necessity is reducible to *de dicto* necessity. I doubt, however, that such a conservative view of *de re* necessity can be correct. There seem to be other sources of *de re* necessity as well. For example, I would tentatively propose that objects can be classified in terms of "basic sortals" and that if any object exemplifies a particular basic sortal then it does so necessarily. E.g., if Michael is a person, then Michael is necessarily a person (and hence necessarily not a number). A second source of *de re* necessity lies in identities. Although this was once a matter of considerable dispute, it is now generally agreed that:

(1.11) If $a = b$ then $\text{Nec}[a,b,((\mathbf{E}{:}x) \rightarrow (x \approx y))]$.[7]

There are no doubt other sources of *de re* necessity as well. Thus, I consider it extremely doubtful that *de re* necessity is reducible to *de dicto* necessity.

Conversely, however, it is plausible to suppose that *de dicto* necessity is definable as *de re* necessary truth for propositions. Letting **T** be the concept of *being true*, the proposal is:

(1.12) $\text{Nec}(\varphi)$ iff $\text{Nec}[\varphi, \mathbf{T}]$.

In other words, for φ to be necessarily true is for φ to be necessarily such that it is true. The ready availability of this reduction of *de dicto* necessity to *de re* necessity suggests that *de re* necessity is the basic kind of necessity, and it may be fruitless to look for independent theories of *de dicto* necessity.

2. Statements

2.1 *The Diagram of a Statement*

Statements are products of assertion, i.e., they are what we assert when we state something.[8] What is no doubt the most popular contemporary view identifies statements and propositions. The central thesis of *Language and Thought* was that

---

[7] The earlier resistance to this principle seems to have stemmed from a confusion of *de re* necessity with *de dicto* necessity.

[8] 'Statement' is ambiguous in English between the act of stating and what is stated. I am using it only in the latter sense.

this dogma of contemporary philosophy of language is false. In retrospect, much of the recent work on proper names and demonstratives points firmly in that direction, but this has not generally been appreciated. The view associated with Frege and Russell (perhaps unfairly) is that when one makes a statement by uttering a sentence containing a proper name, the function of the name is to express a definite description that becomes a constituent of the proposition asserted. But Kripke [1972] and Donnellan [1972] have argued persuasively that one can rarely find a definite description that is a plausible candidate for the sense of a use of a proper name. They have instead championed the *historical connection theory*, according to which the referent of the name is determined by a chain of historical connections between particular uses of the name. They coupled this view of reference with the semantical thesis that sentences containing proper names are used to express directly referential propositions. The latter view is the *denotation theory*.

Directly referential propositions are not propositions in my sense; they are coarse-grained objects of belief. The claim that proper names are used to state directly referential propositions is really the claim that it makes no difference how the speaker and his audience are thinking about the referent of the name—members of the audience have fully understood the speaker just as long as they come to think of the correct object as the referent and understand what the speaker is saying about that object. In making a statement, one is ordinarily "putting thoughts into words". The speaker entertains a certain proposition, utters a sentence appropriately related to it, and if the communication is successful then the members of the audience come to entertain propositions related in certains ways to the speaker's proposition. Let us call the proposition entertained by the speaker his *sent proposition* and those entertained by the members of the audience the *received propositions*. The traditional view was that in order for communication to be successful, the sent and received propositions must be the same. The denotation theory can be regarded as relaxing this requirement, insisting that successful communication occurs just as long as the sent and received propositions are about the same object and attribute the same thing to it.

Although I am convinced that the denotation theory is false, it constitutes an important advance over the traditional theory. No reasonable theory of communication could require the sent and received propositions to be the same. The ways in which speaker and hearers think about an object will typically reflect their idiosyncratic relationships to the object, and neither will know precisely how the other is thinking of the object. That cannot preclude successful communication. There must be some connection between the sent and received propositions, but they need not be identical. The nature of the required connection is a function of what statement is being made. For example, if a speaker uses a definite description attributively to refer to an object, saying ⌜The F is G⌝, then both he and his audience must be thinking of the object as "the F", and it is plausible to suppose that the sent and received propositions must be the same in this case.[9] On the other hand, if the speaker uses a proper name to refer to his object, it is quite implausible to suppose that the sent and received propositions must be the same. For example, if I say 'Richard Feynman is a famous physicist', I may be thinking of him as 'whoever Kripke was talking about in "Naming and necessity"'. If Feynman's mother happened to be in my audience, my utterance would lead her to entertain a proposition (her received proposition) wherein she thinks of Richard Feynman quite differently. But surely that does not imply that I have not successfully communicated with her. In connection with proper names, it is initially plausible to follow the denotation theory and say that the sent and received propositions need only be about the same object—the only constraint on the propositional designators contained in those propositions is that they designate the same object.

[9] As becomes apparent in *Language and Thought*, this is only true if F is a "conceptual" predicate.

II. Sketch of a Theory of Language

The statement that is being made is what determines the range of possible sent and received propositions. Furthermore, having specified this range of propositions, we seem to have completely characterized the content of the communication and thereby determined what statement is being made. This indicates that a statement can be described by describing this range of propositions. The possible sent and acceptable received propositions for a statement may vary with the circumstances under which the statement is being made. For example, the possible sent and acceptable received propositions for the directly referential statement that an object x is F will be a function in part of what descriptions happen to be satisfied by x (because the speaker and hearers can think of x in terms of those descriptions). Different features of the circumstances of utterance may be involved in determining the possible sent and acceptable received propositions for different statements. Let us call these the *dynamic parameters* of the statement. A statement can then be described by describing the possible sent and acceptable received propositions for each person relative to each possible assignment of values to the dynamic parameters. This is encoded in what I call the *diagram* of the statement. Let **S** be the function that assigns to each person S the set $\mathbf{S}(S)$ of possible sent propositions for that person, and let **R** be the function which assigns the set of acceptable received propositions for that person.[10] **S** and **R** may vary depending upon the values of the dynamic parameters. The diagram of the statement is then the function that yields the ordered pair $\langle \mathbf{S}, \mathbf{R} \rangle$ of functions when applied to each assignment of values to the dynamic parameters. The diagram of a statement can be regarded as giving us the information content of the statement. The more narrowly the possible sent propositions are constrained, and the more similar the acceptable received propositions are to the possible sent propositions, the more closely the audience's thoughts must resemble the speaker's and hence

---

[10] For some kinds of statements the possible sent and acceptable received propositions are the same, but for other kinds of statements (e.g., first-person statements) they are different. See *Language and Thought* for details.

the greater the information conveyed by making the statement. For example, a statement involving a definite description contains more information than the corresponding directly referential statement.

In *Language and Thought* I developed an entire theory of language based upon this conception of statements and their diagrams. To illustrate, consider proper names. According to the denotation theory, when a speaker utters a sentence containing a proper name, the statement he makes is directly referential. I argued at length in *Language and Thought* that that account of proper names is inadequate. The reader is referred to *Language and Thought* for the whole story, but the simplest objection to the denotation theory is that it makes it impossible to make a statement by using a nonreferring proper name. For example, a person who does not know any better might make a statement by saying 'Bourbaki is a famous French mathematician'.[11] It is undeniable that the person is making a statement, but that would be impossible according to the denotation theory because without a referent there would be no possible sent or acceptable received propositions—there would be nothing for the speaker or his audience "to think". For this and other reasons, the denotation theory must be replaced by a more elaborate theory.

Donnellan, Kaplan, and Kripke have all recommended combining the historical connection theory with the denotation theory. The idea is that the historical connection theory provides a theory of reference, and the denotation theory provides the corresponding theory of meaning. In fact, however, these two theories are incompatible. They are competing theories rather than complementary ones. The reason for this is that the denotation theory already entails a theory of reference. The speaker's sent proposition contains a propositional designator that designates the referent, and this designator determines the

[11] A group of French mathematicians published their work collectively under the fictitious name 'Bourbaki', and many people were initially taken in by this and assumed that 'Bourbaki' was the name of an individual mathematician.

referent of the name. There is no room left for the referent to be determined by any kind of historical connection.[12]

I believe that the intuitions behind the historical connection theory are actually semantical intuitions, and the theory should not be taken as a theory of reference at all. In *Language and Thought* I proposed a theory of meaning for proper names that can be regarded as a semantical version of the historical connection theory. Given that the denotation theory is false, it follows that there must be more serious constraints on the propositional designators contained in the sent and received propositions than their merely designating the same object. It is the nature of these constraints that the historical connection theory is really getting at. There are various kinds of "parasitic connections" between the propositional designators involved in different sent propositions. For example, in saying 'Richard Feynman is a famous physicist', a speaker may be thinking of Richard Feynman as 'the person Jones was just talking about'. Such parasitic (or historical) connections as this enable us to string together the sent propositions of different speakers, and when they can be connected in this way, they are sent propositions for the same statement. This can be turned into a precise account of the diagram of the statement made by uttering a sentence containing a proper name.[13]

This discussion of proper names has been very sketchy, but it is intended merely to illustrate the account of statements in terms of their diagrams. The details of the analysis of proper names will not be relevant to the present book, but this brief sketch should make it clear how much power we gain by

[12] Tom McKay has suggested to me that this incompatibility can be avoided by taking the historical connection theory to be a theory about what determines the designatum of the speaker's sent designator rather than as a theory directly about linguistic items in public language. I have never understood the theory in that way, but we can understand it in that way and it becomes an interesting theory. Diana Ackermann ([1979], [1979a], and [1980]) has proposed a theory of this general sort. My own feeling is that it succumbs to the considerations adduced in *Language and Thought*, 60–81, in connection with *de re* belief, but that is a different sort of objection than the one suggested in the text.

[13] See *Language and Thought* for the details.

adopting this view of statements. It becomes possible to construct linguistic theories that could not even be formulated if we insisted upon identifying statements with propositions.

2.2 *Attributes*

I have remarked that the notion of propositional structure is problematic. But as we will now see, if we accept the notion of propositional structure, we can make sense of statemental structure too. Statements can be viewed as constructed out of various statemental constituents. The simplest kind of statemental constituent is an *attribute*. We can characterize attributes as what can be stated of objects. For example, we can state of Herbert that he has a mustache. Just as we can talk about sent and received propositions for statements, we can talk about sent and received concepts for attributes. The most prevalent view of attributes has identified them with concepts. But if we consider an attribute like that expressed by 'brother of Robert', it is apparent that it cannot be a concept because of the way in which 'Robert' functions. If a speaker makes a statement by saying 'John is a brother of Robert', he could be sending different propositions (with different propositional designators corresponding to 'Robert'), and members of his audience could be receiving different propositions. In each of these propositions, what corresponds to 'brother of Robert' will be a concept of the form $(\beta{:}x,\delta)$, but different propositions may contain different designators δ and hence different concepts corresponding to 'brother of Robert'. Thus, the attribute expressed by 'brother of Robert' cannot be identified with any of these concepts.

If we turn to simple attributes like that of *being aluminum* or *being a tiger*, it is initially more plausible to suppose that the traditional view is correct and that these attributes are concepts. One way of interpreting the views of Kripke [1972] and Putnam [1975], however, is as urging that these attributes are not concepts. For example, Putnam [1975] has noted that he thinks of aluminum quite differently than a metallurgist does, but that he and the metallurgist can both make the same statement by saying 'This kettle is made of aluminum'. Putnam and the metallurgist think of aluminum in terms of concepts, but they employ different concepts. Despite their associating different concepts with the word 'aluminum', they can still use it in making the same statement. The concepts in terms of which they think of aluminum are their sent concepts. Or if one of them makes a statement about aluminum to the other, the hearer will think of aluminum differently than the speaker and so will employ a received concept different from the speaker's sent concept. These sent and received concepts comprise the diagram of the attribute of *being aluminum*. In general, the diagram of an attribute **A** is a function that assigns to each set of values of the dynamic parameters the ordered pair $\langle S,R \rangle$ of functions where for each person S, $S(S)$ is the set of possible sent concepts for **A** for S under those circumstances and $R(S)$ is the set of acceptable received concepts for **A** for S under those circumstances.

In *Language and Thought* I constructed a theory of predicates and attributes that I will sketch here without argument.[14] Some predicates literally have definitions, in something like the traditional sense. Such predicates express attributes constructed logically out of simpler constituents. Most syntactically simple predicates are not like this, however; they are instead handled as follows. Objects are classified as being of various *kinds*. Some kinds, like *electron*, can be described in a number of different ways, and none of those descriptions is more central to the kind than any other. What makes different descriptions equally appropriate is that it is a physical law that anything satisfying one of the descriptions will also satisfy the others, or as I will say, the descriptions (and the concepts expressed by them) are *nomically equivalent*. A class of nomically equivalent concepts can be taken to make up a *nomic kind*; for example, the nomic kind *electron* is comprised of the set of all nomically equivalent descriptions of electrons. I urged that predicates like 'aluminum' and 'tiger' "connote" nomic kinds.[15] I called predicates connoting nomic kinds *syn-*

[14] Chapters Five through Seven.
[15] The relation of connoting is made precise in *Language and Thought*, 154ff. Our *putative social knowledge* regarding something is the set of state-

thetic predicates. The attributes expressed by synthetic predicates are determined by the nomic kinds they connote. Roughly speaking, when one uses a synthetic predicate one makes a statement that is directly referential with respect to the nomic kind. More accurately, if I say 'That kettle is made of aluminum', the possible sent and acceptable received propositions for my statement have the form ⌜δ is made of κ⌝ where κ is *any* propositional designator designating the nomic kind connoted by 'aluminum'. Thus, I may think of aluminum as 'the stuff most kettles are made of' and a metallurgist may think of aluminum as 'the element of atomic weight 26.98', and yet we can both be making the same statement.

Because a nomic kind is constituted by the set of concepts describing it, the kind is necessarily such that it is described by those concepts. Thus, for example, it becomes a necessary truth that water is H_2O, and accordingly the statement that water is H_2O is necessarily true. I will say more about this below.

Given attributes and logical operators, we can describe the structures of many statements. For example, the statement that every kettle is made of aluminum can be said to have the structure

$$(\forall x)[(\mathbf{K}{:}x) \rightarrow (\mathbf{A}{:}x)]$$

where $\mathbf{K}$ is the attribute of being a kettle and $\mathbf{A}$ is the attribute of being aluminum. To describe the statement in this way is to give a shorthand description of its diagram. To say that the statement has this form is just to say that a proposition φ is a possible sent (or acceptable received) proposition for the statement iff φ has the form

$$(\forall x)[(\kappa{:}x) \rightarrow (\alpha{:}x)]$$

where κ is a possible sent (or acceptable received) concept for $\mathbf{K}$ and α is a possible sent (or acceptable received) concept

---

ments about it that are accepted as known by society at large. For example, it is regarded as known that electrons are negatively charged. Then, roughly, the nomic kind connoted by a predicate is the kind that maximally satisfies our putative social knowledge involving that predicate.

for **A**. Thus, talk of statemental structure is reduced to talk of propositional structure. To describe a statement in terms of its structure is to describe its diagram in terms of the structure of its possible sent and acceptable received propositions.

2.3 *Statemental Designators*

Consider the statement that Herbert has a mustache. The sent propositions for this statement have the form

$$(\mu:\delta)$$

where μ is a possible sent concept for the attribute of having a mustache and δ is the propositional designator in terms of which the speaker is thinking of Herbert. The received propositions have the same form, where δ is now a propositional designator the hearer is receiving by virtue of the speaker using the name 'Herbert'. The propositional designators thus associated with the name can be collected together into the diagram of a statemental constituent we can call a *statemental designator*. The propositional designators are the sent and received designators for the statemental designator. Then we can describe the statement that Herbert has a mustache as having the form

$$(\mathbf{M}:\partial)$$

where **M** is the attribute of having a mustache and ∂ is the statemental designator expressed by the speaker's use of 'Herbert'. To say that the statement has this form is just to say that the possible sent and acceptable received propositions have the corresponding form

$$(\mu:\delta)$$

where μ is any possible sent (or acceptable received) concept for the attribute **M** and δ is any possible sent (or acceptable received) designator for ∂.

I suggested above that when one makes a statement by uttering a sentence containing a proper name, the possible sent and acceptable received propositions are tied together by various parasitic relations between the ways the speakers and hearers may be thinking of the referent. These parasitic relations comprise constraints on the possible sent and acceptable received designators for the statemental designator expressed by the use of the proper name. I call statemental designators of this sort *hereditary designators*.

2.4 *Statemental Modalities*

Thus far we have taken necessary truth and *a priori* truth to be propositional modalities, but these propositional modalities can be used to generate similar statemental modalities. Statements are not objects of belief in the same sense as propositions are, so they cannot literally be known *a priori*. Instead, epistemic attitudes toward statements must be cashed out in terms of epistemic attitudes toward the sent and received propositions for the statements. Thus it is very natural to define apriority for statements as follows:

(2.1) If ψ is a statement, ψ is *a priori* true iff ψ is necessarily such that the possible sent and acceptable received propositions for ψ are all *a priori* true.

We can define an analogous notion of necessary truth:

(2.2) If ψ is a statement, ψ is *internally necessary* iff ψ is necessarily such that the possible sent and acceptable received propositions for ψ are all necessarily true.

There is another natural way to define necessity for statements, viz., as *de re* necessary truth:

(2.3) If ψ is a statement, ψ is *externally necessary* iff ψ is necessarily such that it is true.

One would naturally expect internal and external necessity to coincide. Interestingly enough, they do not. Their divergence reflects the fact that, because of their characterization in terms of their diagrams, statements have more structure than propositions. For example, the propositions $((x \approx y):\delta,\delta)$ and $((x \approx x):\delta)$ are the same proposition, namely, the proposition that might be written more simply as $(\delta \approx \delta)$. But where ∂ is a statemental designator, the statements $((x \approx y):\partial,\partial)$ and

$((x \approx x):\partial)$ are distinct. The sent and received propositions for $((x \approx x):\partial)$ all have the form $((x \approx x):\delta)$ (i.e., $(\delta \approx \delta)$) where δ is a possible sent or acceptable received designator for ∂. Consequently, the statement

(2.4) $(\mathbf{E}:\partial) \rightarrow ((x \approx x):\partial)$

is both internally and externally necessary. On the other hand, the sent and received propositions for the statement

(2.5) $((\mathbf{E}:x) \rightarrow ((x \approx y):\partial,\partial)$

have the form

(2.6) $(\mathbf{E}:x) \rightarrow ((x \approx y):\delta,\delta^*)$

where δ and δ^* may be distinct possible sent or acceptable received designators for ∂. If δ and δ^* are distinct, then (2.6) need not be necessary, and hence (2.5) will not normally be internally necessary. On the other hand, (2.5) is externally necessary. This is because although the sent and received propositions for this statement need not be necessary, they must always be true, i.e., δ and δ^* are sent or received designators for the same statemental designator ∂ and hence must designate the same object. A statement is true iff its sent and received propositions are true, so because it is necessary that all the sent and received propositions for (2.5) are true, it is necessary that this statement is true. Thus (2.5) is externally necessary. But as we have seen, it is not internally necessary.

If we accept the general account of proper names as expressing hereditary designators, this surprising divergence of internal and external necessity can be illustrated as follows. Consider a child whose tutor tells him about Thales both as 'that crazy philosopher who thought everything was made out of water' and as 'that early entrepreneur who cornered the grain market'. But suppose the child mistakenly thinks that these were two different men, each called 'Thales'. The child's use of the name 'Thales' is parasitic on its use by his tutor, but the tutor is using the name to express the same hereditary designator when he talks about Thales as a philosopher and when he talks about Thales as an entrepreneur. Thus, without realizing it, the child is also using the name to express the same hereditary designator in both contexts. If the child were to say 'If he existed, then Thales was Thales', with the intention to be talking about the philosopher with the first occurrence of the name and the entrepreneur with the second, the child would regard himself as making a false statement. The statement he would be making would not be *a priori* true and would not be internally necessary, but unbeknownst to the child, it would be externally necessary.

In *Language and Thought* I argued that similar considerations can be used to explain and partially defend the view of Kripke [1972] and Putnam [1975] that no distinction can be made between physical necessity and logical necessity as they apply to "natural kinds". For example, they have urged that if water is in fact H_2O (as a matter of physical necessity), then there are no possible worlds in which water is not H_2O. As I noted above, on my analysis of synthetic predicates in terms of nomic kinds, physically necessary statements about nomic kinds are externally necessary. But they are not internally necessary. For example, one possible sent proposition for the statement that water is H_2O is the contingent proposition that the stuff that comes out of the tap is H_2O. This simultaneously explains the intuitions of Kripke and Putnam and the intuitions of their detractors. The latter have urged that it "could have turned out" that water is not H_2O, and hence the statement that water is H_2O cannot be necessary. Kripke responded that it is "epistemically possible" for water not to have been H_2O, but not "metaphysically possible". The observation that it is epistemically possible for water not to have been H_2O really just amounts to the observation that the sent and received propositions for the statement are not themselves necessary. Thus, as Kripke uses the term, epistemic necessity might reasonably be identified with internal necessity and metaphysical necessity with external necessity. Consequently, the characterization of statements in terms of their diagrams enables us to make sense of this perplexing dispute.

The internal and external necessity of statements are species of *de dicto* necessity. We can define analogous notions of *de re* internal and external necessity. Where **A** is an attribute, an object is *internally necessarily* such that it is **A** iff the object necessarily exemplifies every possible sent or acceptable received concept for **A**:

(2.7) $\text{Nec}_I[x,\mathbf{A}]$ iff **A** is necessarily such that if α is any possible sent or acceptable received concept for **A** then $\text{Nec}[x,\alpha]$.

On the other hand, an object is *externally necessarily* such that it is **A** iff it is necessarily such that it exemplifies **A**:

(2.8) $\text{Nec}_E[x,\mathbf{A}]$ iff x and **A** are necessarily such that x exemplifies **A**.

Just as there are externally necessary statements that are not internally necessary, there are cases of objects being externally necessarily such that they exemplify certain attributes without being internally necessarily such that they exemplify those attributes.

2.5 *Statemental Modal Operators*

In discussing propositions we introduced necessity both as a property and as an operator. It must also be possible to introduce an operator for statements. This is because the most common use of 'necessary' in English is as a sentence operator, and it seems clear that the statement expressed by ⌜It is necessary that P⌝ ought to be of the form $\Box\psi$ where $\Box$ is a statement operator. It is not possible to introduce an operator on statements in the same way as we did the operator on propositions. That would require us to have something like logical designators for statements, but there do not seem to be such designators. We are unable to think of statements in the kind of direct fashion in which we can think of propositions. We tend instead to think of statements in terms of descriptions like 'what Mary said'. Lacking logical designators for statements, we must introduce statemental modal operators in some other way. I suggest that this can be done in terms of the diagrams of statements, taking $\Box\psi$ to be a statement for which the sent and received propositions are those of the form $\Box\varphi$ where φ is a sent or received proposition for ψ:

> (2.9) If ψ is a statement, $\Box\psi$ is a statement whose possible sent (or acceptable received) propositions (for any values of the dynamic parameters) are those of the form $\Box\varphi$ where φ is a possible sent (or acceptable received) proposition for ψ.

In other words, when one states $\Box\psi$, what one is thinking (i.e., the sent proposition) is a proposition of the form $\Box\varphi$ where φ is a possible sent proposition for ψ.

If there is to be such a statement as $\Box\psi$ satisfying (2.9), there must be certain constraints on the diagrams of statements. An obvious constraint is that all of the possible sent and acceptable received propositions for a given statement (relative to the actual values of the dynamic parameters) must have the same truth value. It is by believing these propositions that the speakers and hearers accept a statement. If they could differ in truth value, it could happen that some of the speakers and hearers are right in accepting the statement and that others are mistaken in accepting the same statement. That is clearly absurd. An analogous constraint on the diagram of an attribute is that all of the sent and received concepts must have the same extension. Similarly, all of the sent and received designators for a statemental designator must designate the same object.

Given the above truth constraint on the diagram of a statement, it follows that if there is to be such a statement as $\Box\psi$, then relative to any assignment of values to the dynamic parameters of ψ, if any of the possible sent or acceptable received propositions for ψ are necessary then they must all be necessary. Otherwise the truth constraint would be violated for $\Box\psi$, because some of its possible sent or acceptable received propositions relative to those values of the dynamic parameters would be true and some of them would be false. In *Language and Thought* I took this to indicate that there must be a modal constraint on the diagrams of statements to the effect that relative to any assignment of values to the dynamic parameters of a statement, if any of the possible sent or acceptable received propositions for that statement are necessary then they are all necessary. There appear, however, to be clear counterexamples to this. Consider the following statement:

(2.10) $(\mathbf{E}:\partial) \rightarrow ((x \approx y):\partial,\partial)$.

Some of the possible sent propositions for this statement have the form

(2.11) $(\mathbf{E}:\delta) \rightarrow ((x \approx y):\delta,\delta)$

and hence are necessary, but others have the form

(2.12) $(\mathbf{E}:\delta) \rightarrow ((x \approx y):\delta,\delta^*)$

where δ and δ^* are distinct propositional designators, and hence they need not be necessary. It must be concluded that the modal constraint is not always satisfied. But if a statement ψ does not satisfy the modal constraint, there can be no such statement as $\Box\psi$. Thus, application of a modal operator to a statement does not always yield a statement. This is a surprising conclusion, but not unintuitive when we consider specific examples. Recall the example of the child who thought that Thales the philosopher and Thales the entrepreneur were two different men, and imagine him saying, 'Necessarily, Thales (the philosopher) was Thales (the entrepreneur)'. Would you understand what he was saying? I would not. *De dicto* (as opposed to *de re*) necessity does not seem to be applicable in such a context.

Satisfaction of the modal constraint is a necessary condition for there to be such a statement as $\Box\psi$, but it is not sufficient. It seems clear that $\Box\psi$, if it exists, cannot be a contingent statement. That is, if $\Box\psi$ is true then it must be necessarily true, i.e., externally necessary. This implies that ψ satisfies a stronger modal constraint requiring that if there is an assignment of values to the dynamic parameters relative to which some possible sent or acceptable received proposition for ψ is necessary, then all possible sent and acceptable received propositions for ψ relative to all assignments of values to the dynamic parameters must be necessary. Otherwise, $\Box\psi$ could be true in one possible situation (with one set of values for the dynamic parameters) and false in another. Given this strong modal constraint, it follows that there is a simple relationship between our *de dicto* statemental operator and internal necessity:

(2.13) If ψ is a statement, $\square\psi$ is true iff ψ is internally necessary.

In many ways, external necessity is a more natural modality than internal necessity. Can we construct a modal operator $\boxplus$ that bears the same relationship to external necessity as $\square$ bears to internal necessity? It is interesting that there does not seem to be any way to do it. In order for there to be such a statement as $\boxplus\psi$, it must be possible to characterize it in terms of its diagram, but there seems to be no way to construct a diagram for $\boxplus\psi$ that would have the result that $\boxplus\psi$ is true iff ψ is externally necessary. This will be of some importance when we consider the relationship between possible worlds and statemental modalities. Note that it has the consequence that although the statement that water is H_2O is externally necessary, the modal statement that it is necessary that water is H_2O is false.

We can construct a *de re* statemental modal operator on analogy to our construction of our *de dicto* statemental modal operator. This is an operator that operates on an attribute **A** to convert it into the modal attribute $\square$**A**. $\square$**A** can be described in terms of its diagram:

(2.14) If **A** is an attribute, $\square$**A** is an attribute whose possible sent (or acceptable received) concepts (for any values of the dynamic parameters) are those of the form $\square\alpha$ where α is a possible sent (or acceptable received) concept for **A**.

We saw that the existence of the statement $\square\psi$ required there to be a modal constraint on the diagram of ψ. The existence of the modal attribute $\square$**A** requires a similar modal constraint on the diagram of **A**. If ($\square$**A**:∂) is true, the designatum of ∂ must be necessarily such that it exemplifies **A**. Consequently, if there is an assignment of values to the dynamic parameters for which some object x is necessarily such that it exemplifies some possible sent or acceptable received concept for **A** relative to those values of the dynamic parameters, then x is necessarily such that it exemplifies all possible sent and acceptable received concepts for **A** relative to all possible assignments of values to the dynamic parameters. This modal constraint has the consequence that:

(2.15) x exemplifies $\Box$**A** iff $\text{Nec}_I[x,\textbf{A}]$.

I noted above that the modal statement that it is necessary that water is H_2O is false, despite the fact that the statement that water is H_2O is necessary. That is a bit puzzling, because given the necessary truth of the statement that water is H_2O, one is strongly inclined to think he could be saying something true by saying 'It is necessary that water is H_2O'. The explanation for this is that English modal locutions do not distinguish very clearly between *de re* and *de dicto* necessity. One *could* be saying something true, but it would be the *de re* modal statement that water and H_2O (the nomic kinds) are necessarily such that everything of the first kind is also of the second kind.

3. Sentences

3.1 *The Meaning of a Sentence*

A few years ago, the most prevalent view of meaning identified the meaning of a (declarative) sentence[16] with the proposition asserted by uttering that sentence. Given the distinction between statements and propositions, a natural modification of that view would identify the meaning of a sentence with the statement made by uttering the sentence. In recent years, however, philosophers have become increasingly aware of the phenomenon of indexicality. To say that a sentence is indexical is to say that, without any change in meaning, it can be

[16] Throughout, when I say 'sentence' I mean 'declarative sentence'. For a discussion of nondeclarative sentences, see *Language and Thought*, 253–265.

used to make different statements under different circumstances, with the statement made being a function (at least in part) of the circumstances of utterance. It is obvious that a sentence like 'He is here' is indexical. This sentence can be used to make many different statements about different individuals and different places. Upon reflection, it appears that almost all sentences are indexical. Even a sentence like 'The Empire State Building is in New York' is indexical. The statement made by uttering this sentence is at least a function of the time of utterance. When one says 'The Empire State Building is in New York', one means that it is *now* in New York. There may come a time when that is false. For example, it might be moved to Lake Havasu, Arizona, and re-erected alongside the London Bridge. There might be a few sentences that can only be used to make a fixed statement (e.g., '$2+2 = 4$'), but these are rare exceptions.

If a sentence is indexical, there is no unique statement expressible by the sentence and hence no single statement with which the meaning of the sentence can be identified. It seems, however, that the meaning of the sentence determines what statements can be made by using it under various circumstances. Furthermore, once one has described what statements can be made by uttering a sentence under all possible circumstances, one has described the meaning. So rather than taking the meaning of a sentence to be a single statement, it seems more reasonable to regard it as consisting of all the different statements it can be used to make under different circumstances. Let us call those features of the circumstances determining what statement is made by uttering a sentence *the pragmatic parameters of the sentence*. Then the meaning of a sentence can be described by describing what statements can be made by uttering it when the pragmatic parameters have different values. Let the *S-intension* of the sentence be the function that assigns to each set of values of the pragmatic parameters the statement made by uttering the sentence in circumstances in which the pragmatic parameters have those values. The meaning of the sentence is then comprised by its *S*-intension.

It is useful to distinguish between (1) the meaning of a sentence and (2) its *sense* on a particular occasion. The sense of a sentence on a particular occasion is the statement made by using it on that occasion. The meaning of a sentence (i.e., its *S*-intension) is the function that determines its sense on each possible occasion of its use.[17]

3.2 *Predicates*

The normal role of a predicate in a sentence is to select an attribute to be incorporated into the statement by uttering the sentence. That attribute will be called *the sense* of the predicate on that occasion of utterance. The meaning of the predicate determines its sense on different occasions, so it seems reasonable to regard the meaning as a function from pragmatic parameters to attributes. This is the *A-intension* of the predicate. For some predicates, such as 'brother of John', the sense will obviously vary from circumstances to circumstances, but it is apt to seem that for most simple predicates the senses will be the same on all occasions. For example, it may be proposed that the sense of 'tiger' is always the attribute of being a tiger.[18] If that is correct, this account accomodates it by taking the *A*-intension of 'tiger' to be a constant-valued function.

3.3 *Singular Terms*

The normal role of a singular term (e.g., a proper name, definite description, or demonstrative) in a sentence is to select a statemental designator for incorporation into the statement one makes by uttering the sentence. This statemental designator is the sense of the singular term on that occasion. Then, once again, the meaning of the singular term will be

---

[17] The distinction between meaning and sense is, I believe, the same as the distinction Kaplan ([1976] and [1979]) has recently been drawn between content and character. The distinction is not a new one, going back at least to P. F. Strawson [1950] and Richard Cartwright [1962]. I learned it from Cartwright in the early sixties. It has been "rediscovered" at least twice, first by Richard Montague and then by David Kaplan.

[18] I argued in *Language and Thought* that this is inaccurate. The sense of 'tiger' is always the attribute of being a tiger, but what attribute that is may change. The change is a function of changes in our putative social knowledge about tigers (see n. 13).

comprised by the *D-intension* of the term, which is a function mapping the pragmatic parameters to the sense of the term. For example, I suggested above that the sense of a proper name is a statemental designator whose possible sent and acceptable received designators are tied together by historical or parasitic connections. Advocates of a directly referential theory of proper names would instead take proper names to express ''directly referential statemental designators'', the latter requiring of their possible sent and acceptable received designators only that they all designate the same object. Either theory is readily accommodated within the present account of meaning.

3.4 *Sentence Modalities*

The notion of an analytic sentence has played an important, though controversial, role in philosophy. It has probably assumed more importance than it should because of the misguided desire of many philosophers to avoid propositions and statements and to frame their theories in terms of sentences. Be that as it may, we are now in a position to define four different sentence modalities. Any one of these is a reasonable candidate for the traditional notion of an analytic sentence, but I have chosen to reserve that term for the first of them:

(3.1) If P is a declarative sentence and Δ is its S-intension, then P is (1) analytic, (2) internally necessary, (3) externally necessary, or (4) weakly analytic; iff Δ is necessarily such that if π is any possible assignment of values to the pragmatic parameters, then $\Delta(\pi)$ is (1) *a priori* true, (2) internally necessary, (3) externally necessary, or (4) true.

Given the assumption that *a priori* propositions are necessary, it follows that *a priori* statements are internally necessary, and hence analytic sentences are internally necessary. Internally necessary statements are also externally necessary, and externally necessary statements are true, so it follows that internally necessary sentences are externally necessary and externally necessary sentences are weakly analytic. In other words, our sentence modalities form a heirarchy in the order listed. In addition, two of the inclusions are proper inclusions, and the third may also be a proper inclusion. The sentence 'I exist' is weakly analytic (i.e., it can only be used to make a true statement) but not externally necessary (i.e., the statement it is used to make is not necessarily true). We have already seen that sentences employing predicates connoting nomic kinds can be externally necessary without being internally necessary. And if Fermat's conjecture is necessary but not *a priori*, a sentence expressing it will be internally necessary but not analytic.

I have already remarked that the most common use of 'necessary' in English is within the sentential modal operator 'it is necessary that', with this phrase being equivalent to the adverb 'necessarily' used in its *de dicto* sense. In philosophy, this is abbreviated as '$\square$', and its use is very common. It is of considerable importance to understand how these operators work. It now seems clear that modal sentences are used to express modal statements:

(3.2) If P is a declarative sentence then $\Delta_\square$ is an S-intension of $\ulcorner$It is necessary that $P\urcorner$ iff there is an S-intension Δ of P such that for any possible assignment π of values to the pragmatic parameters, if $\Delta(\pi) = \psi$ then $\Delta_\square(\pi) = \square\psi$

Philosophers have often felt that modal predicates should be less problematic than modal operators, and so they have tried to reduce the latter to the former.[19] There is no way to do that at the level of sentences. In particular, the following is false:

(3.3) For any values of the pragmatic parameters, $\ulcorner\square P\urcorner$ expresses a true statement iff P is internally necessary.

In order for P to be internally necessary, $\ulcorner\square P\urcorner$ must express a true statement given *any* values of the pragmatic parameters. The reason (3.3) fails is that there are sentences that sometimes express internally necessary statements and other times

---

[19] See particularly Quine [1953] and Skyrms [1978] for positive views on the matter, and Montague [1963] and Otte [1982] for negative views.

express contingent statements. An example is 'That is so', which can be used to express any statement at all. Even if (3.3) were true, it could not give us the *meaning* of '$\Box$' because the statement that P is internally necessary is a metalinguistic statement (it is about the sentence P) whereas the statement expressed by $\ulcorner\Box P\urcorner$ is not normally a metalinguistic statement. $\ulcorner\Box P\urcorner$ is about whatever P is about.

I concur with the view that modal predicates are more basic than modal operators. That is, in fact, the way the present analysis has proceeded. But the reduction cannot proceed at the level of either statements or sentences; it must occur at the level of propositions. In order to make the translation from modal predicates to modal operators, we must have the logical designators $\langle\varphi\rangle$, and these only exist for propositions and propositional constituents.

The adverb 'necessarily' occurs in English as a *de re* modal operator when we say 'Two is necessarily the square root of four' or 'Wilfrid Sellars is necessarily not the number two'. Here it is functioning as an operator converting predicates into modal predicates. It can be described as follows:

(3.4) If F is a predicate then $\Delta_\Box$ is an A-intesion of $\ulcorner\Box F\urcorner$ (or $\ulcorner$necessarily $F\urcorner$) iff there is an A-intension Δ of F such that for any possible assignment π of values to the pragmatic parameters, if $\Delta(\pi) = \mathbf{A}$ then $\Delta_\Box(\pi) = \Box\mathbf{A}$.

Thus, for example, if the sense of $\ulcorner N$ is $F\urcorner$ is the statement $(\mathbf{A}{:}\partial)$ then the sense of $\ulcorner N$ is necessarily $F\urcorner$ is $(\Box\mathbf{A}{:}\partial)$, or equivalently $\Box_\partial(\mathbf{A}{:}\partial)$.

English provides us with devices for distinguishing between *de dicto* and *de re* necessity. For example, we can express *de re* necessity by saying $\ulcorner t$ is necessarily such that it is $F\urcorner$ and *de dicto* necessity by saying $\ulcorner$It is necessary that t is $F\urcorner$. Unfortunately, we do not always adhere to this distinction, often using the latter to express *de re* necessity instead of *de dicto* necessity. One of the main reasons for introducing an artificial logical notation is to avoid ambiguities like this that are present in natural language. It is quite surprising to note, then, that the standard logical notation in modal logic is subject to this same ambiguity, only more so. If we write $\ulcorner(\forall x)\Box Fx\urcorner$, we know that '$\Box$' is symbolizing *de re* necessity and that the sense of the sentence is $(\forall x)\Box_x(\mathbf{A}:x)$. But if we write $\ulcorner\Box Ft\urcorner$, it is unclear whether the necessity is to be *de dicto* (in which case the sense of the sentence is $\Box(\mathbf{A}:\partial)$) or *de re* (in which case the sense of the sentence is $\Box_\partial(\mathbf{A}:\partial)$). The ambiguity can easily be resolved by extending our subscript notation to sentences and writing the *de re* sentence as $\ulcorner\Box_t Ft\urcorner$. I will follow this practice of attaching subscripts to modal operators whenever there is danger of a *de re/de dicto* ambiguity.

Once it has been pointed out, the distinction between $\ulcorner\Box Ft\urcorner$ and $\ulcorner\Box_t Ft\urcorner$ is so obvious that one would suppose it could not have confounded professional logicians. It is rather amazing to observe that standard modal logic provides us with no way to make this distinction, and eminent logicians have been led astray by not making the distinction. For example, it was once common to find logicians arguing that

$$(\forall x)(\forall y)[x = y \rightarrow \Box\, x = y]$$

always expresses a truth, and then "explaining" that this should not be confused with the unquantified sentence

$$t_1 = t_2 \rightarrow \Box\, t_1 = t_2$$

which need not express a truth. This led to obvious problems concerning universal instantiation in modal logic. What should have been said here is that

$$(\forall x)(\forall y)[x = y \rightarrow \Box(x \text{ exists} \rightarrow x = y)]$$

and

$$t_1 = t_2 \rightarrow \Box_{t_1,t_2}(t_1 \text{ exists} \rightarrow (t_1 = t_2)$$

express true statements, but

$$t_1 = t_2 \rightarrow \Box(t_1 \text{ exists} \rightarrow t_1 = t_2)$$

need not.

III
Possible Worlds

1. Introduction

The central tool of philosophical semantics is the concept of a possible world. It has become customary to "explain" necessary truth as truth at all possible worlds. Possible worlds are employed in providing foundations for modal and intensional logics, analyzing counterfactual conditionals and law statements, establishing a framework for probability theory, and much more. But it has never been entirely clear just what possible worlds are supposed to be. David Lewis [1973] says that possible worlds are "ways things could have been". Saul Kripke [1972] describes possible worlds as "counterfactual situations". Although there is much intuitive appeal to such notions, there is also considerable disagreement about how the concept of a possible world is to be defined or analyzed. It *might* be insisted that the notion is primitive and unanalyzable,[1] but that makes it rather mysterious and of questionable utility in the clarification of other concepts. The two most popular moves have been to identify possible worlds with maximal consistent sets of propositions, and to identify them with maximal possible states of affairs. I will consider these two alternatives in detail in sections two and three.

The best way to judge a proposed concept of a possible world is in terms of what is supposed to be accomplished by appealing to possible worlds. There are two major desiderata and two minor desiderata:

(1) *De dicto* necessity is supposed to be analyzable in terms of possible worlds as follows:

(1.1) Nec(φ) iff φ is true at all possible worlds.

---

[1] That is the position of David Lewis [1973].

Traditionally, in (1.1) φ was taken to be a proposition. We might also require the truth of (1.1) when φ is a statement, in which case we must consider whether it is to hold for internal necessity or external necessity. For the time being, however, it is best to hold this question in abeyance. This makes it convenient to have a single term that can be interpreted variously as meaning 'proposition', 'statement', or 'proposition or statement', depending upon the outcome of our investigations. I will use the term 'assertion' for this purpose. Much of our account of possible worlds can be constructed without deciding which meaning we should give to 'assertion'. We will then return to the question of how we should understand 'assertion' in various contexts. It is also convenient to have a term that is neutral between 'concept', 'attribute', and 'concept or attribute', and for this purpose I will use 'quality'. I will use the term 'designator' as neutral between 'propositional designator', 'statemental designator', and 'propositional or statemental designator'. Given these conventions, we can state our first desideratum for possible worlds as requiring that (1.1) hold for any assertion φ, leaving open what assertions are.

(2) The second major desideratum is that *de re* necessity should be analyzable in terms of possible worlds as follows:

(1.2) Nec[x,α] iff x exemplifies α at all possible worlds.

Here we take α to be a quality, remaining noncommittal on what qualities are. Note that if we take qualities to include attributes, we must distinguish between internal and external necessity in (1.2).

The two preceding desiderata are the most important ones, but there are also two minor desiderata:

(3) The truth conditions for quantified modal assertions are supposed to be expressible as first-order conditions involving quantification over possible worlds. For example, the following is supposed to hold:

(1.3) $\square(\exists x)\square(\alpha:x)$ is true iff $(\forall w)$[if w is a possible world then there is an object x existing in w such that x exemplifies α at every possible world].

This third desideratum can be regarded as a generalization of the first two. At least if we are talking about internal necessity, (1.1) and (1.2) appear to be equivalent, respectively, to:

(1.4) $\Box\varphi$ is true iff φ is true at all possible worlds.

(1.5) $\Box_\delta(\alpha{:}\delta)$ is true iff δ designates some object x that exemplifies α at all possible worlds.

(4) The fourth desideratum is a generalization of the third. It can only be stated rather vaguely as the requirement that possible worlds are to be generally useful in the analysis of various logical concepts such as modal operators, counterfactual conditionals, and probability. It may also be required that possible worlds be of use in a general theory of meaning,[2] and that they provide a basis for formal semantics and formal logic.

2. Possible Worlds as World Books

The simplest conception of possible worlds is as world books. World books are maximal consistent sets of assertions. Making this precise:

(2.1) A set of assertions is *consistent* iff it is possible for all of its members to be true together.

(2.2) A *world book* is any consistent set of assertions B that is such that if φ is any assertion not in B then φ cannot be consistently added to B (i.e., $B\cup\{\varphi\}$ is inconsistent).

Given any assertion φ, either it or its negation must be true. Thus, the following holds:

(2.3) Necessarily, the set of all true assertions is a world book.

Consequently, any reasonable construal of possible worlds must have the result that the set of assertions true at a particular world constitutes a world book. Let us define:

[2] As, for example, in Lewis [1972a] and Montague [1970] and [1973].

(2.4) If w is a possible world, B is the *world book for* w iff B is the set of all assertions true at w.

This suggests identifying possible worlds with their world books.[3] This is one way of understanding possible worlds as "ways things could have been".

It will follow from the discussion below that world books satisfy the first desideratum for possible worlds, i.e., an assertion is necessary iff it is true at all possible worlds. This is probably the main reason the identification of possible worlds with world books has seemed so attractive. The satisfaction of the second desideratum is extremely problematic, however; it requires that $Nec[x,\alpha]$ iff x exemplifies α at every possible world. But if possible worlds are just sets of assertions, what does it mean to say that an object x exemplifies α at a world w? That can only make sense if x's exemplifying α at w consists of the members of some set X of assertions being true at w (i.e., being members of w). It seems that the only way X could play this role is by there being a designator δ such that $(\alpha{:}\delta){\in}X$ and the other members of X somehow determine that δ designates x at w. How can a set of assertions being true at w determine that δ designates x at w? This is just the problem of transworld identity set against the background assumption that transworld identity must be determined by what assertions are true at a world.

I will call theories conforming to the latter assumption *qualitative theories of transworld identity*, because they attempt to reduce transworld identity to the qualities possessed by objects at different worlds. There are just two possible kinds of qualitative theories of transworld identity. Let us define:

(2.5) φ is a *singular assertion about* x iff φ is an assertion and there is some quality α such that $\square_{\alpha,x,\varphi}(\varphi$ is true iff x exemplifies $\alpha)$.

---

[3] Taking assertions to be propositions, I endorsed this move in Pollock [1976], although at that point I was unclear about what I meant by 'proposition'. Plantinga [1974] appears to endorse a similar move, but I doubt that he means by 'proposition' what I mean here by 'proposition'.

Singular assertions are those equivalent to assertions that are necessarily such that they are about certain fixed objects. An assertion about x that is not singular will be called *general*. For example, a general assertion about x might be about x by virtue of containing some definite description that x exemplifies only contingently. Assertions are about objects by virtue of containing designators designating those objects. Thus, in order for φ to be necessarily such that it is about a particular object x, φ must be equivalent to an assertion containing a designator that is necessarily such that it designates x. More precisely:

(2.6) δ is a *haecceity of x* iff $\Box_{\delta,x}$[if x exists then δ designates x, and if x does not exist then δ does not designate anything].

Then it seems that an assertion is singular by virtue of being equivalent to an assertion containing a haecceity of some object.[4]

Let us define:

(2.7) α is an *essence of x* iff $\Box_{\alpha,x}(\forall y)[y$ exemplifies α iff $y = x]$.

On the traditional assumption that all designators were definite descriptions, it followed that δ is a haecceity of x iff δ is a definite description of the form $\imath\alpha$ for some α that is an essence of x. However, we have already noted several examples of haecceities not related to essences in this manner. Personal designators are haecceities of persons, and if φ is a proposition then $\langle\varphi\rangle$ is a haecceity of φ, but neither of these kinds of haecceities is a definite description.

Now let us return to the problem of transworld identity. There are just two kinds of theories that make transworld identity a function of what assertions are true at a world—essentialism and nonessentialism. By 'essentialism' I mean the following:

Essentialism: x exemplifies α at w iff $(\exists\delta)[\delta$ is a haecceity of x and $(\alpha{:}\delta)$ is true at w]; and a designator δ^* designates

---

[4] A singular assertion need not itself contain a haecceity. For example, if $\imath\alpha$, is a haecceity of x then $(\exists y)[(\beta{:}y)$ & $(\alpha{:}y)]$ is a singular assertion about x. It is equivalent to but not identical with $(\beta{:}\imath\alpha)$.

x at w iff $(\exists\delta)[\delta$ is a haecceity of x and $(\delta^* \approx \delta)$ is true at $w]$.

Before considering the merits of essentialism, let us consider nonessentialist theories of transworld identity. As we are only considering qualitative theories, we are still operating with the assumption that what determines whether a designator δ designates x at w is the set of assertions containing δ that are true at w. According to nonessentialism, δ's designating x at w must at least sometimes result from a number of general assertions containing δ being true at w. These are assertions that are in fact about x, but that could be about something else. These assertions ascribe various qualities to the designatum of δ, and it is by virtue of the designatum exemplifying those qualities that it is x. By hypothesis, these qualities cannot be essences of x. Some of them may be necessary qualities of x (e.g., 'is not a number'), but most of them will be the contingent qualities we normally employ in talking and thinking about objects. A nonessentialist qualitative theory must claim that the fact that an object x in a world w and an object y in another world w^* exemplify certain sets of qualities is sufficient to guarantee that they are one and the same object. Various theories of this sort might be proposed. For example, it might be claimed that an object in one world is to be identified with that object in another world with which it is most similar.[5] For the present discussion, however, we need not settle upon any particular nonessentialist theory.

It will now be argued that no nonessentialist theory of transworld identity can be correct. Consider a possible world w consisting of just two billiard balls α and β, identical except for color. α is red and β is blue. It seems clear that it is possible for the roles of α and β to be interchanged, with α being blue instead of red and β being red instead of blue, but everything else unchanged.[6] Assuming that world books satisfy our

---

[5] There are a number of familiar difficulties for this simple theory. For example, it makes identity nontransitive. See also the discussion in Chisholm [1976].

[6] One theory that I will not explicitly discuss is Lewis's "counterpart

second desideratum for possible worlds, this means that there is a possible world w^* that is just like w except that α is blue and β is red. There is no qualitative difference between the configuration of billiard balls in w and w^*. It follows that the set of general (i.e., nonsingular) assertions true at w is the same as the set true at w^*. But the designator expressed by 'the red billiard ball' designates different balls at the different worlds. Accordingly, the identity of the object designated by this designator cannot be determined by the set of general assertions involving it that are true at a world. No nonessentialist qualitative theory of transworld identity can differentiate between these two worlds. Thus, all such theories must be false.[7]

The only way to avoid the preceding difficulty and salvage the construal of possible worlds as world books is to embrace an essentialist theory of transworld identity. The two configurations of billiard balls are qualitatively the same, so in order for there to be assertions true of the one configuration but false of the other, those assertions cannot simply describe the general qualitative structure of the two configurations. The difference between the two configurations lies exclusively in the identity of the billiard balls of different colors, so if there are to be assertions true of the one configuration and false of the other, they must be singular assertions. Therefore, the world-book construal of possible worlds can satisfy the second desideratum only if there are haecceities for our billiard balls.

Of the designators mentioned so far in this book, only personal designators, temporal designators, and logical designators are regularly haecceities, and none of these can be haecceities of billiard balls. Is there any reason at all to think that billiard balls have haecceities? It is noteworthy that the aforementioned haecceities are all *propositional* designators. It may seem that if we look instead to statemental designators, it is

---

theory'' (see Lewis [1968]). The reader interested in counterpart theory may notice, however, that the present example is a counterexample to counterpart theory. Counterpart theory implies that it is not possible for the roles of α and β to be interchanged.

[7] This is a familiar form of argument. See Max Black [1952] and R. M. Adams [1979].

quite easy to find haecceities. We have talked about directly referential statements, and we can analogously construct directly referential statemental designators. According to the denotation theory, these are the senses of proper names. A directly referential statemental designator can be characterized in terms of its diagram:

(2.8) ∂ is a *directly referential statemental designator for x* iff for any assignment of values to the dynamic parameters, the possible sent and acceptable received designators for ∂ are all propositional designators designating x.

Somewhat surprisingly, directly referential statemental designators are not haecceities. A statemental designator designates an object iff its sent and received designators do. Thus, a statemental designator can designate an object x at every possible world at which x exists only if at every such possible world there is some propositional designator designating x. That is precisely which what is in doubt in the world with the red and blue billiard balls. It appears that without propositional haecceities, there will not be statemental haecceities for the billiard balls either. Thus, an essentialist theory of transworld identity must proceed in terms of propositional haecceities.

It appears that if billiard balls have haecceities, they must be derived from essences; so do billiard balls have essences? It seems extraordinarily unlikely that any normal descriptive qualities can be essences of our billiard balls. However, Plantinga [1974] has made the ingenious suggestion that there are essences constructed out of "world-indexed qualities". The idea is that for each quality γ that an object x exemplifies at a world w, there is also the quality of *exemplifying γ at w*, which x exemplifies necessarily. The latter is a world-indexed quality. Thus, if we choose a quality γ that x alone exemplifies at w, *exemplifying γ at w* is an essence of x.

By employing world-indexed qualities, can we generate a haecceity of our billiard ball β that will enable us to identify it in w? In order to do so, we must find a world w^* and a property γ that only β exemplifies at w^*. Then the proposal is that *exemplifying γ at w^** is a haecceity of β. Unfortunately, there is a difficulty for this proposal. The quality we are calling 'the quality of exemplifying γ at w^*' must have the form

(2.9) $(\mathbf{Exemp}{:}x,\langle\gamma\rangle,\omega)$

where ω is some designator designating the world w^*. The difficulty is now in justifying the assumption that there is such a designator as ω. Notice that in order for (2.9) to be an essential quality of β, ω must designate w^* necessarily, i.e., ω must be a haecceity for w^*. Otherwise, it would be possible for ω to designate some other world at which β does not exemplify γ, and hence β would not exemplify (2.9) necessarily. Thus, we have "reduced" the problem of finding haecceities for physical objects to the problem of finding haecceities for world books. But the latter problem is, if anything, more intractable than the former. I think it must be concluded that the appeal to world-indexed qualities will not provide us with haecceities.

Plantinga has often talked about another kind of essence. For example, he talks about the property of *being Socrates*. This is supposed to be what is expressed by the predicate $\ulcorner x = \text{Socrates}\urcorner$. His remarks suggest that he takes this property to be directly referential. It involves Socrates "directly" rather than via some representation. I do not want to deny that there is such a property, but I do insist that it is neither a concept nor an attribute. Once we have a workable notion of a possible world, we will be able to define a broad notion of a property that includes properties like that of being Socrates. But such properties cannot be used in constructing world books, because they are not constituents of either propositions or statements. I will grant that these properties are constituents of proposition-like objects—what we might call 'truths' (and what Plantinga calls 'propositions'). But these are neither fine-grained objects of belief nor products of assertion.[8]

---

[8] It might be suggested that possible worlds be taken to be maximal consistent sets of "truths". That is, in effect, just the proposal explored in section three.

My conclusion is that the search for haecceities is in vain. Most objects do not have haecceities. It follows that there is no way for the world-book construal of possible worlds to satisfy the second desideratum for possible worlds. We cannot paraphrase attributions of *de re* necessity in terms of world books. A more sophisticated conception of possible worlds is required for that purpose.

3. Possible Worlds as Maximal States of Affairs

The world-book construal of possible worlds fails because there is no way to identify objects across worlds in terms of the qualities they have at worlds. If possible worlds are to satisfy our second desideratum, it must make sense to talk about an object x in the actual world exemplifying a quality in another world. As we have seen, this cannot make sense if we insist that objects be described in each world qualitatively. The alternative is to make the identity of the object part of the specification of the world. This is the "stipulative account" of transworld identity proposed by Kripke [1972]. What it amounts to is the identification of possible worlds with maximal possible states of affairs.

The simplest states of affairs consist of objects exemplifying qualitites or assertions being true, such as *Nixon's being president*, *there being little green men on the moon*, *5+7 being 12*, and *my not existing*. We normally express states of affairs in English by employing gerund clauses. Where α is a quality, let $[x|\alpha]$ be *x's being α*. More generally, if α is an *n*-place quality, let $[x_1,\ldots,x_n|\alpha]$ be *$x_1,\ldots,x_n$ being α*. Similarly, if φ is an assertion, let $[\varnothing|\varphi]$ be *φ's being true*.[9] We talk about states of affairs *obtaining* or *not obtaining* (*Nixon's being president* obtains iff Nixon is president). States of affairs can exist without obtaining. For example, there is such a state of affairs as *my not existing* even though I do exist.

In many ways, states of affairs resemble propositions. In

---

[9] The motivation for this notation is that we can think of assertions as zero-place qualities and the empty set as a zero-tuple.

particular, they are truth bearers of a sort. States of affairs are not literally true or false, but obtaining and not obtaining are truth-like properties. There is at least one respect, however, in which states of affairs differ importantly from propositions. States of affairs are directly referential in a strong sense in which propositions are not.[10] For example, if Mary is the girl in the red hat, then (on at least one construal of the definite description) *the girl in the red hat's looking lost* is the same state of affairs as *Mary's looking lost*.[11] States of affairs may involve objects directly rather than under a description. Precisely:

(3.1) If $x_1 = y_1$ and ... and $x_n = y_n$ then $[x_1,...,x_n|\alpha] = [y_1,...,y_n|\alpha]$.

It is this directly referential character that makes states of affairs suitable for the construction of possible worlds satisfying our second desideratum.

States of affairs are very much like directly referential propositions.[12] They are "about" objects but not in terms of some mode of representation. States of affairs, in some sense, contain objects as direct constituents. Whether we distinguish between directly referential propositions and states of affairs seems to me mainly a matter of convenience. The term 'directly referential proposition' is a philosophical term of art, and I doubt that there is any basis for saying that directly referential propositions objectively are or are not states of affairs.

It is generally (though not universally) acknowledged that distinct propositions can be logically equivalent. The question arises whether this is also true of states of affairs; i.e., can two distinct states of affairs be necessarily such that one obtains iff the other does? I do not see any basis in intuition for

[10] Recall that I argued in Chapter Two that propositions, as fine-grained objects of belief, are not directly referential.

[11] This point is slightly obscured by the fact that ⌜the β's being α⌝ is ambiguous. It can denote either $[\eta\beta|\alpha]$ or $[\varnothing|(\alpha:\eta\beta)]$. I am taking it in the former way here.

[12] Recall that directly referential propositions are not really propositions in my sense.

deciding this matter, so I am going to follow the simpler course and suppose that logically equivalent states of affairs are identical. In other words, I shall assume:

(3.2) If S and S^* are states of affairs, $S = S^*$ iff S and S^* are necessarily such that one obtains iff the other does.

This is a safe assumption even if there is another sense of 'state of affairs' in which equivalent states of affairs need not be identical, because we can always regard states of affairs in the present sense as being equivalence classes of the more finely individuated kind of states of affairs.

Contrary to what I have just maintained, there is a familiar argument, used by Donald Davidson [1970] and attributed by him to Frege, which purports to show that (3.2) is not a safe assumption. The argument appears at first to show that if we assume both (3.1) and (3.2), it follows that there are only two states of affairs—one that obtains and one that does not. The argument goes as follows. Let S and S^* be any two states of affairs that either both obtain or both fail to obtain. Necessarily, S obtains iff $\{0\} = \{x|\ x = 0\ \&\ S\ \text{obtains}\}$, so S is equivalent to

$$[\{0\},\{x|\ x = 0\ \&\ S\ \text{obtains}\} \mid y \approx z].$$

Similarly, S^* is equivalent to

$$[\{0\},\{x|\ x = 0\ \&\ S^*\ \text{obtains}\} \mid y \approx z].$$

But as S and S^* either both obtain or both fail to obtain,

$$\{x|\ x = 0\ \&\ S\ \text{obtains}\} = \{x|\ x = 0\ \&\ S^*\ \text{obtains}\}.$$

Hence by (3.1),

$$[\{0\},\{x|\ x = 0\ \&\ S\ \text{obtains}\} \mid y \approx z] = [\{0\},\{x|\ x = 0\ \&\ S^*\ \text{obtains}\} \mid y \approx z].$$

But then by (3.2), $S = S^*$. Fortunately, this argument is fallacious, turning upon a scope ambiguity in the definite description $\ulcorner[\{0\},\{x|\ x = 0\ \&\ S\ \text{obtains}\} \mid y \approx z]\urcorner$. The sentence

Necessarily, S obtains iff $[\{0\},\{x|\ x = 0\ \&\ S\ \text{obtains}\} \mid y \approx z]$ obtains

54

is ambiguous between

$\square(\exists Y)[(\forall x)(x \in Y \leftrightarrow (x = 0$ & S obtains)) & (S obtains iff $[\{0\},Y|\ y \approx z]$ obtains))]

and

$(\exists Y)[(\forall x)(x \in Y \leftrightarrow (x = 0$ & S obtains)) & $\square(S$ obtains iff $[\{0\},Y|\ y \approx z]$ obtains))].

The former is true and the latter false, but it is the latter that is required in order for us to infer from (3.2) that:

$S = [\{0\},\{x|\ x = 0$ & S obtains$\}\ |\ y \approx z]$.

This is because states of affairs are directly referential with respect to the objects listed left of the vertical bar. Thus, what it means for $[\{0\},\{x|\ x = 0$ & S obtains$\}\ |\ y \approx z]$ to obtain is that the object that is *actually* $\{x|\ x = 0$ & S obtains$\}$ is such that it is $\{0\}$. If S obtains, the object that is actually $\{x|\ x = 0$ & S obtains$\}$ is $\{0\}$, in which case $[\{0\},\{x|\ x = 0$ & S obtains$\}\ |\ y \approx z]$ is $[\{0\},\{0\}|\ y \approx z]$ and obtains necessarily. Similarly, if S fails to obtain, then the object that is actually $\{x|\ x = 0$ & S obtains$\}$ is $\varnothing$, in which case $[\{0\},\{x|\ x = 0$ & S obtains$\}\ |\ y \approx z]$ is $[\{0\},\varnothing|\ y \approx z]$ and is necessarily such that it fails to obtain. In neither case is $[\{0\},\{x|\ x = 0$ & S obtains$\}\ |\ y \approx z]$ equivalent to S (unless S happens to be either necessary or inconsistent). Consequently, Davidson's argument fails to establish that $S = S^*$.

States of affairs can be combined in various ways to form more complex states of affairs. For example, from the states of affairs *Mary's divorcing Charlie* and *Charlie's eloping with Ginger* we can construct the composite state of affairs *Mary, Charlie, and Ginger being such that the first divorced the second and the second eloped with the third*. In this manner, given two states of affairs S and S^*, there is another state of affairs $S\&S^*$ that is such that, necessarily, it obtains iff both S and S^* obtain. Given (3.1), it follows that $S\&S^*$ is unique. We can define $S\&S^*$ precisely as follows:

(3.3) $S\&S^*$ = its being the case that S and S^* both obtain.

We can similarly define negation, disjunction, and conditionals for states of affairs:

(3.4) $\sim S$ = its being the case that S does not obtain.

(3.5) $S \lor S^*$ = its being the case that either S or S^* (or both) obtain.

(3.6) $S \rightarrow S^* = \sim S \lor S^*$.

I will sometimes abbreviate $\ulcorner \sim S \urcorner$ as $\ulcorner \bar{S} \urcorner$. Obviously, it follows from these definitions that states of affairs satisfy the axioms for the propositional calculus, or what comes to the same thing, states of affairs form a Boolean algebra under the operations &, $\sim$, and $\lor$.

In introducing the notion of a proposition in Chapter Two, we encountered the distinction between transient and nontransient propositions. Transient propositions are true of a time and thus may be true at one time and false at another. Nontransient propositions are true or false *simpliciter*, and it is only the latter that I call 'propositions'. There is an analogous distinction between transient and nontransient states of affairs. *Nixon's running for president* is a state of affairs that obtains at some times and not at others. *Nixon's running for president sometime* or *Nixon's running for president in 1970* are nontransient states of affairs that, if they obtain at one time, obtain at all times. Both kinds of states of affairs are reasonable items for investigation, but only nontransient states of affairs enter into the construction of possible worlds. Let us define:

(3.7) S is a *nontransient state of affairs* iff S is a state of affairs that is necessarily such that if it obtains at one time then it obtains at all times.[13]

Even most nontransient states of affairs are not the sorts of things philosophers have wanted to call 'possible worlds'. A

---

[13] The distinction between nontransient and transient states of affairs is similar to the distinction in Chisholm [1976] between propositions and other states of affairs. As Chisholm uses the term, a proposition is simply a nontransient state of affairs. It is unclear, however, whether all of our states of affairs are states of affairs in Chisholm's sense. His distinction may be the same as the distinction between transient and nontransient propositions.

possible world must be a "maximal" state of affairs—one that combines descriptions of everything. In order to make this precise, let us begin by observing that there is a containment relation between states of affairs that can be defined as follows:

(3.8) $S \subseteq S^*$ iff S and S^* are necessarily such that if S^* obtains then S obtains.

Equivalently:

(3.9) $S \subseteq S^*$ iff ($S^* \to S$) is necessarily such that it is obtains.

A state of affairs is *possible* iff it is possible for it to obtain, and it is *necessary* iff it is necessarily such that it obtains. Then the conception of possible worlds as maximal states of affairs is made precise as:

(3.10) w is a *possible world* iff w is a nontransient possible state of affairs and for any nontransient state of affairs S, if it is possible that w and S both obtain then $S \subseteq w$.[14]

A possible world is *actual* iff it obtains.

Where w is a possible world, we can define:

(3.11) An assertion φ is *true at w* iff φ and w are necessarily such that if w obtained then φ would be true, i.e., $S \subseteq w$.

[14] This notion of a possible world is in the general tradition of Wittgenstein [1921], C. I. Lewis [1946], and Carnap [1947]. I may have been the first to construct this notion of a possible world, in Pollock [1967], and Plantinga [1974] endorsed this notion and made it popular. As far as I know, the restriction to nontransient states of affairs has been previously overlooked by everyone.

There is an alternative conception of possible worlds according to which there is something called 'the world', and possible worlds are ways *the* world could have been. I have difficulty with the notion that there is such a thing as "the world' that exists necessarily but can have different properties. But if it is granted that this makes sense then it seems to come to the same thing as the conception of possible worlds as maximal possible states of affairs. Possible worlds will not literally *be* maximal possible states of affairs, but presumably to describe a way the world could have been is just to say what states of affairs would have obtained had the world been that way.

(3.12) An object *x exemplifies* a quality α *at w* iff
[*x*|α] ⊂ *w*.

(3.13) A state of affairs *S obtains at w* iff *S* ⊂ *w*.

We have defined possible worlds to be maximal possible
states of affairs, but how do we know that there are any? Our
definition is a bit like observing that there are larger and larger
numbers and then defining infinity to be the largest number.
That does not work because there is no largest number. How
do we know that there are not just more and more compre-
hensive states of affairs without there being any maximal states
of affairs? This is a question that has rarely even been raised,
but it cannot be ignored. As far as I can see, the only way to
defend the existence of possible worlds is by acknowledging
the existence of infinite conjunctions of states of affairs. Although this sounds like a suspiciously strong assumption, I
think it is defensible. Given a set *X* of states of affairs, *X's
being such that every state of affairs in it obtains* is a perfectly
good state of affairs. Let ⋀*X* be this state of affairs. ⋀*X* can
be thought of as the (possibly infinite) conjunction of the
members of *X*.[15] Given these conjunctions, we can prove the
following:

(3.14) Necessarily, if *W* is the set of all nontransient states
of affairs that obtain then ⋀*W* is a possible world
that obtains.

Proof: Suppose *W* is the set of all states of affairs that
obtain. Then ⋀*W* obtains. Furthermore, for every state
of affairs *S*, either *S*∈*W* or *S̄*∈*W*, so either *S* ⊂ ⋀*W* or
S̄ ⊂ ⋀*W*. Suppose it is possible that *S* and ⋀*W* both obtain.
Then *S* is not necessarily such that it fails to obtain whenever ⋀*W* obtains, i.e., it is false that *S̄* ⊂ ⋀*W*. But then
S ⊂ ⋀*W*. Therefore, ⋀*W* is a possible world.

On the reasonable assumption that, necessarily, there is a set

[15] In terms of the Boolean algebra of states of affairs, ⋀*X* is the infimum
of *X*.

58

of all states of affairs that obtain, it follows that, necessarily, some possible world obtains.

Thus far I have left it intentionally vague whether our construction of states of affairs and possible worlds should proceed in terms of both concepts and attributes and both propositions and statements. For what it is worth, that appears to accord with common usage. But I will now argue that it makes no difference whether we include statements and attributes in the construction. Had we instead begun with just concepts and propositions, we would have arrived at the same possible worlds and states of affairs. Consider a state of affairs of the form $[\varnothing|\psi]$ where ψ is a statement. $[\varnothing|\psi]$ obtains iff ψ is true. In turn, ψ is true iff all of its possible sent and acceptable received propositions relative to the present values of the dynamic parameters are true. Dynamic parameters are properties of the world.[16] Thus, the values of the dynamic parameters at a world are fixed by the world itself. For any assignment π of possible values to the dynamic parameters, let $\bar{\pi}$ be the state of affairs consisting of those being the actual values of the dynamic parameters. π is the assignment of values to the dynamic parameters at a world w iff $\bar{\pi} \subset w$. Let $SR_\psi(\pi)$ be the set of all possible sent and acceptable received propositions for ψ relative to π. Then if π is the actual assignment of values to the dynamic parameters, ψ is true iff every member of $SR_\psi(\pi)$ is true. If X is any set of propositions, let $\bigwedge X$ be the state of affairs consisting of all of the members of X being true.[17] Then ψ is true (at the actual world) iff $\bigwedge SR_\psi(\pi)$ obtains. Next, let DP be the set of all possible assignments of values to the dynamic parameters, and consider all states of affairs of the form $[\bar{\pi} \rightarrow \bigwedge SR_\psi(\pi)]$ for $\pi \in DP$. At any world w, all such conditional states of affairs whose antecedents represent values of the dynamic parameters not actual in that world will obtain vacuously, and the one whose antecedent represents the actual values at that world will obtain iff ψ

---

[16] In this they are to be contrasted with pragmatic parameters, which are properties of utterances.

[17] That is, $\bigwedge\{[\varnothing|\psi]|\ \psi \in X\}$.

is true at that world. Thus, necessarily, $[\varnothing|\psi]$ obtains iff $\bigwedge\{[\bar{\pi} \to \bigwedge SR_\psi(\pi)] \mid \pi \in DP\}$ obtains. But then by (3.2):

(3.15) $[\varnothing|\psi] = \bigwedge\{[\bar{\pi} \to \bigvee SR_\psi(\pi)] \mid \pi \in DP\}$.

The right side of (3.15) is a state of affairs constructed entirely out of concepts, objects, and propositions. Thus, our construction of states of affairs will include $[\varnothing|\psi]$ even if we begin with just concepts and propositions and without including statements and attributes.

In the same way we can show that where α is an attribute, the state of affairs $[x_1,\ldots,x_n|\alpha]$ can be constructed without appealing to statements or attributes. Letting $SR_\alpha(\pi)$ be the set of all possible sent and acceptable received concepts for α relative to π, we have:

(3.16) $[x_1,\ldots,x_n|\alpha] =$
$\bigwedge\{[\bar{\pi} \to \bigwedge\{[x_1,\ldots,x_n|\alpha] \mid \alpha \in SR_\alpha(\pi)\}] \mid \pi \in DP\}$.

Consequently, it makes no difference to the states of affairs and possible worlds we arrive at whether we build them out of just concepts and propositions or include statements and attributes in the construction. In either case, we will be able to talk about the truth of statements at possible worlds.

Where α is a concept or φ is a proposition, let us call nontransient states of affairs of the form $[x_1,\ldots,x_n|\alpha]$ or $[\varnothing|\varphi]$ *elementary states of affairs*.[18] Not all nontransient states of affairs are elementary. Consider, for example, possible worlds. Possible worlds contain infinitely many elementary states of affairs. There is no way to combine all of those into a single state of affairs consisting of a finite sequence of objects exemplifying a quality. Thus, a possible world is not elementary. A possible world will contain many elementary states of affairs, but it will also contain many nonelementary states of

---

[18] To avoid trivializing the notion of an elementary state of affairs, we must restrict what kinds of objects $x_1,\ldots,x_n$ can be. Otherwise, every state of affairs would be elementary, because S is the same state of affairs as S's *obtaining*. We must require that $x_1,\ldots,x_n$ be, in some sense, "basic" objects. These are, roughly, concrete objects (construed so as to include shadows, rainbows, etc.).

4. Necessity and Possible Worlds

affairs. It is reasonable to assume, however, that a possible world can be characterized by the set of elementary states of affairs contained in it. Thus, I will assume:

(3.17) If w and w^* are possible worlds, $w = w^*$ iff w and w^* contain the same elementary states of affairs.

Corresponding to each state of affairs S is its *extension* $\|S\|$, which is the set of all possible worlds at which S obtains. The question arises whether every set of possible worlds is the extension of some state of affairs. That it is can be argued as follows. If X is a set of possible worlds, let S be the state of affairs *there being some member of X that obtains*, i.e., the disjunction $\bigvee X$ of all members of X.[19] Then $\|S\| = X$. For many purposes we could identify states of affairs with their extensions, taking states of affairs to be arbitrary sets of possible worlds.[20]

I believe that the conception of possible worlds as maximal states of affairs is adequate for three of our four desiderata for possible worlds. The process of establishing this becomes quite involved and will occupy the rest of the chapter. It will follow from section six that no conception of possible worlds can satisfy the third desideratum.

4. Necessity and Possible Worlds

The two principal desiderata for any concept of a possible world are:

(4.1) If φ is a proposition, φ is necessarily true iff φ is true at all possible worlds.

(4.2) If α is a concept, an object x is necessarily such that it exemplifies α iff x exemplifies α at every possible world.

It is quite easy to establish that the conception of possible

[19] $\bigvee X$ is just $\sim\bigwedge\{\sim S|\ S \in X\}$.
[20] But not for all purposes. We cannot identify a possible world with its extension. That would be to have the possible world a member of itself.

worlds as maximal possible states of affairs satisfies both of these desiderata.[21] The simplest way of establishing (4.1) and (4.2) is by appealing to a well-known theorem regarding Boolean algebras, but before we can do that we must prepare the ground a bit.

Thus far we have only talked about propositions and statements being necessary, but we can extend the notion of necessity to states of affairs in the obvious way:

(4.3) A state of affairs S is *necessary* iff S is necessarily such that it obtains.

Because logically equivalent states of affairs are identical, there is just one necessary state of affairs. Definition (4.3) has the immediate consequence that:

(4.4) A proposition φ is necessary iff $[\varnothing|\varphi]$ is necessary; φ is possible iff $[\varnothing|\varphi]$ is possible.

We defined entailment between propositions as follows:

If φ and θ are propositions, φ entails θ iff, necessarily, if φ is true then θ is true.

We can define entailment between states of affairs analogously:

(4.5) If S and S^* are states of affairs, S *entails* S^* iff, necessarily, if S obtains then S^* obtains.

Equivalently, S entails S^* iff $S^* \subset S$.

It was remarked in section three that states of affairs form a Boolean algebra with '$\subset$' as the Boolean 'less than' relation. Because equivalent states of affairs are identical, there is just one necessary state of affairs, which in Boolean terminology will be called '1', and there is one inconsistent state of affairs, called '0'. It follows from (4.3) and the identity of equivalent states of affairs that for any state of affairs S:

---

[21] In Pollock [1984] I maintained that this was difficult to show and required the use of a substantial amount of modal logic. Al Plantinga disabused me of that opinion and suggested an argument basically similar to the one I am giving here.

(4.6) S is necessary iff $S = 1$;

(4.7) S is possible iff $S \neq 0$.

In our Boolean algebra of states of affairs, a proper ultra-filter is a maximal consistent set of states of affairs closed under conjunction and entailment:

(4.8) Γ is a *proper ultrafilter* iff Γ is a set of states of affairs such that:
   (a) $\wedge\Gamma \neq 0$;
   (b) if $S,S^* \in \Gamma$ then $(S\&S^*) \in \Gamma$;
   (c) if $S \in \Gamma$ and $S^* \subset S$ then $S^* \in \Gamma$;
   (d) for every state of affairs S, either $S \in \Gamma$ or $\bar{S} \in \Gamma$.

Equivalently, a proper ultrafilter is the set of all states of affairs obtaining at some possible world. Thus:

(4.9) If Γ is a proper ultrafilter then $\wedge\Gamma$ is a possible world.

The following is a well-known theorem regarding Boolean algebras:

(4.10) Every nonzero element of a Boolean algebra is a member of some proper ultrafilter.[22]

From (4.7) and (4.10) we can conclude that if S is possible then S is a member of some proper ultrafilter Γ. If $S \in \Gamma$ then $S \subset \wedge\Gamma$. By (4.9), $\wedge\Gamma$ is a possible world. By definition, S obtains at a possible world iff S is contained in that possible world, so:

(4.11) If S is possible then S obtains at some possible world.

Conversely, possible worlds are possibly such that they obtain, so if S obtains at a possible world then S is possible. Consequently:

(4.12) For any state of affairs S, S is possible iff S obtains at some possible world.

Equivalently:

---

[22] See, for example, corollary (3.6) of Bell & Slomson [1969], 16.

(4.13) For any state of affairs S, S is necessary iff S obtains at every possible world.

Thus, from (4.4) we obtain (4.1):

For any proposition φ, φ is necessary iff φ is true at every possible world.

This is the first of our two desiderata. The second desideratum follows by observing that, necessarily, x exemplifies α iff $[x|\alpha]$ obtains, and hence x is necessarily such that it exemplifies α iff $[x|\alpha]$ is necessary. Consequently, we also have (4.2):

x is necessarily such that it exemplifies a concept α iff x exemplifies α at every possible world.

It is often claimed that the appeal to possible worlds provides us with an analysis of the concept of necessary truth. But we have had to use the concepts of necessity and possibility in defining the notion of a possible world—a possible world is a maximal *possible* nontransient state of affairs. We cannot, without circularity, define possible worlds in this way and then define necessity and possibility in terms of possible worlds. For this reason David Lewis [1973] takes possible worlds to be primitive and defines necessity (and a number of other philosophical concepts) in terms of them. Lewis's argument for this procedure is twofold: (1) We all believe that there are many ways things could have been besides the way they are. On the face of it, 'ways things could have been' are possible worlds, so barring a good argument to the contrary, it seems that we all understand the notion of a possible world and believe that there are such things. Thus, it is philosophically acceptable to take the concept of a possible world as primitive and analyze other concepts in terms of it. (2) We must take possible worlds as primitive in order to get a reasonable theory of necessity. Necessity can be defined in terms of possible worlds and in no other way. Any attempt to *construct* possible worlds must employ the notion of necessity, in which case possible worlds can no longer be used to explain necessity.

The best response to Lewis' argument is to observe that it can be turned on its head. It can be claimed with considerable justification that (1) we all understand the notion of necessity and (2) we must take necessity as basic in order to get a reasonable theory of possible worlds. In connection with the second point, observe that Lewis' first claim seems to be false. We do all believe that there are many ways things could have been besides the way they are, but among ways things could have been are such things as *my having arisen an hour later this morning*. In other words, ways things could have been are states of affairs and not just possible worlds. Lewis is right that we all have the concept of a state of affairs, but this is not sufficient to support his position. We must still say which states of affairs are possible worlds—namely, those that are maximal, nontransient, and *possible*—and to do that we need the notion of possibility (or necessity). Thus, even taking states of affairs as primitive (which we have done), we cannot give a noncircular account of necessity in terms of possible worlds.

Furthermore, I think it is a mistake to suppose that no reasonable theory of necessity can be propounded except in terms of possible worlds. In my opinion, the most promising approach is epistemological. In Pollock [1974], I proposed an analysis of *a priori* truth in epistemological terms.[23] Although I will not pursue the details here, it is plausible to suppose that necessary truths are those generated from *a priori* truths by certain closure conditions.

Having established that necessary truth for propositions coincides with truth at all possible worlds, the framework of possible worlds can be used to justify the choice of S5 as our modal logic.[24] For non-quantificational S5, the only principle that is normally considered problematic is the "characteristic axiom of S5": $\Diamond\varphi \to \Box\Diamond\varphi$. We might try to defend it as follows:

(1) Suppose $\Diamond\varphi$ is true.

---

[23] Chapter Ten.

[24] Several authors have given arguments of this sort. See, for example, Plantinga [1974], 51–54.

(2) Then φ is possible.

(3) So φ is true at some possible world w.

(4) If φ is true at w, then φ comprises part of the makeup of w and hence φ is necessarily such that it is true at w.

(5) Hence φ is necessarily such that there exists a possible world at which φ is true.

(6) So φ is necessarily such that it is possible.

(7) Therefore, $\Box\Diamond\varphi$ is true.

There is an assumption concealed in this argument. It is generally assumed that possible worlds have necessary existence. This assumption is not shared universally, however. Plantinga calls its denial "existentialism", and it is the topic of section eight. Suppose existentialism is true and possible worlds do not have necessary existence. Line (4) of the argument might then be deemed problematic, but even if we grant that (4) is true, (5) will not follow from (4). If possible worlds do not have necessary existence, then from the fact that φ is necessarily such that it is true at w, it does not follow that φ is necessarily such that there exists a possible world at which it is true.

In light of these considerations, it behooves us to be more careful. Let us begin by making explicit the assumption that possible worlds have necessary existence, that they are necessarily such that they are possible worlds, and that if a proposition φ is true at a possible world w then φ is part of the makeup of w and hence φ and w are necessarily such that φ is true at w. Symbolizing ⌜x exists⌝ as ⌜$E(x)$⌝, ⌜w is a possible world⌝ as ⌜$W(w)$⌝, and ⌜φ is true at w⌝ as ⌜$T_w\varphi$⌝, the assumption is:

(4.14) $\Box(\forall w)\{$if $[W(w)$ and $T_w\varphi]$ then $\Box_{w,\varphi}[E(w)$ and $W(w)$ and $T_w\varphi]\}$.

S5 can be axiomatized as follows:

(4.15) Axioms and rules for S5:

(A1) If p is truth-functionally valid then $\Box p$ is an axiom;

(A2) $\Box p \rightarrow p$;

(A3) $\Box(\Box p \rightarrow p)$;
(A4) $\Box[\Box(p \rightarrow q) \rightarrow (\Box p \rightarrow \Box q)]$;
(A5) $\Box[\Diamond p \rightarrow \Box \Diamond p]$;
(A6) $\Box p \rightarrow \Box \Box p$.
(R) *modus ponens*: If $\vdash p$ and $\vdash (p \rightarrow q)$ then $\vdash q$.[25]

Modus ponens is truth preserving, so if we can show that any proposition having the form of one of the axioms (A1)–(A6) is true, it will follow that any proposition having the form of a theorem of S5 is true. Let us consider the axiom schemes one at a time:

(A1) is trivial. Obviously, if a proposition φ is truth-functionally valid, it is true at every possible world, and so $\Box \varphi$ is true.

If a proposition φ is true at every possible world, then it is true at the actual world. Thus $(\Box \varphi \rightarrow \varphi)$ is true. This justifies (A2).

The justification of (A3) results from observing that in the justification of (A2) it makes no difference which world is the actual world. Consequently, $(\Box \varphi \rightarrow \varphi)$ is true at every possible world; i.e., $\Box(\Box \varphi \rightarrow \varphi)$ is true.

The justification of (A4) is analogous to that of (A3). If $(\varphi \rightarrow \theta)$ is true at every possible world and φ is true at every possible world, then θ is true at every possible world; i.e., $[\Box(\varphi \rightarrow \theta) \rightarrow (\Box \varphi \rightarrow \Box \theta)]$ is true. In establishing this, it makes no difference which world is the actual world, so it is true at every possible world; i.e., $\Box[\Box(\varphi \rightarrow \theta) \rightarrow (\Box \varphi \rightarrow \Box \theta)]$ is true.

The arguments in defense of (A5) and (A6) are somewhat

[25] This is a somewhat unusual axiomatization of S5. It is more common to see an axiomatization that does not contain (A3) or (A6), that does contain axioms like (A4) and (A5) but without the initial necessity operator, and that includes an additional rule of inference of *necessitation*: if $\vdash p$ then $\vdash \Box p$. This can be found, for example, in Hughes and Creswell [1968]. The reason I prefer the present axiomatization is that although the rule of necessitation may be ''validity preserving'', it is not truth preserving. It is more difficult to construct certain kinds of arguments if the rules are not truth preserving. By contrast, the only rule of inference in (4.15) is *modus ponens*, which is truth preserving. Necessitation becomes a derived rule for the logic axiomatized in (4.15).

more involved. We must begin by establishing three first-order modal principles:

(4.16) If $\Diamond(\exists x)Fx$ and $\Box(\forall x)(Fx \to Gx)$ then $\Diamond(\exists x)Gx$.

Proof: If $\Diamond(\exists x)Fx$ and $\Box(\forall x)(Fx \to Gx)$ then there is a possible world at which something is F, and at every possible world all F's are G's, so there is a possible world at which something is G, i.e., $\Diamond(\exists x)Gx$.

(4.17) If $(\exists x)[\Box_x E(x)$ and $\Box_x Fx]$ then $\Box(\exists x)Fx$.

Proof: Suppose there is some object x that has necessary existence and is necessarily such that it is F. Then x exists at every possible world and x is F at every possible world. But then at each possible world there exists an object (namely, x) that is F at that world.

(4.18) If $\Diamond(\exists x)[\Box_x E(x)$ and $\Box_x Fx]$ then $(\exists x)Fx$.

Proof: Suppose $\Diamond(\exists x)[\Box_x E(x)$ and $\Box_x Fx]$. Then there is a possible world at which $\ulcorner(\exists x)[\Box_x E(x)$ and $\Box_x Fx]\urcorner$ is true. By (4.17), $\ulcorner\Box(\exists x)Fx\urcorner$ is true at that world, i.e., $\ulcorner(\exists x)Fx\urcorner$ is true at every possible world. But then $\ulcorner(\exists x)Fx\urcorner$ is true at the actual world.

With the help of (4.14) and (4.17) we can establish (A5):

(4.19) For any proposition φ, $\Box[\Diamond\varphi \to \Box\Diamond\varphi]$ is true.

Proof:
(1) Suppose $\Diamond\varphi$ is true.
(2) Then $(\exists w)[W(w)$ and $T_w\varphi]$.
(3) Then by (4.14), $(\exists w)\{\Box_w E(w)$ and $\Box_{w,\varphi}[W(w)$ and $T_w\varphi]\}$.
(4) By (4.17), (3) implies that $\Box(\exists w)[W(w)$ and $T_w\varphi]$, i.e.,
(5) $\Box\Diamond\varphi$ is true. It follows that $(\Diamond\varphi \to \Box\Diamond\varphi)$ is true. In establishing this, it makes no difference which world is the actual world, so this proposition is true at every possible world, i.e., $\Box[\Diamond\varphi \to \Box\Diamond\varphi]$ is true.

We use (4.14), (4.16), and (4.18) to establish (A6):

(4.20) For any proposition φ, $(\Box\varphi \to \Box\Box\varphi)$ is true.

Proof:
(1) Suppose $\Box\varphi$ is true.
(2) Then $(\forall w)$[if $W(w)$ then $T_w\varphi$].
(3) Then by (4.14), $(\forall w)$[if $W(w)$ then $\Box_{w,\varphi}T_w\varphi$].
(4) Suppose $\Box\Box\varphi$ is false.
(5) Then $\sim\Box(\forall w)$[if $W(w)$ then $T_w\varphi$].
(6) So $\Diamond(\exists w)[W(w)$ and $\sim T_w\varphi]$, i.e.,
(7) $\Diamond(\exists w)[W(w)$ and $T_w\sim\varphi]$.
(8) Thus by (4.14) and (4.16), $\Diamond(\exists w)\{\Box_w E(w)$ and $\Box_{w,\varphi}[W(w)$ and $T_w\sim\varphi]\}$.
(9) Thus by (4.18), $(\exists w)[W(w)$ and $T_w\sim\varphi]$, i.e.,
(10) $(\exists w)[W(w)$ and $\sim T_w\varphi]$.
But (10) contradicts (3), so supposition (4) is incompatible with supposition (1).

It follows that every proposition having the form of any theorem of S5 is true. It must be emphasized, however, that in establishing this we have assumed (4.14) according to which (1) possible worlds have necessary existence and are necessarily such that they are possible worlds, and (2) if a proposition is true at a possible world then the proposition and world are necessarily such that the proposition is true at that world. In section eight, we will explore the possibility of relaxing this assumption. Until section eight, I will continue to assume (4.14) but will not generally note it explicitly.

Thus far we have confined our attention to propositions. Let us turn to statements and consider what connection there is between the necessary truth of a statement and its being true at all possible worlds. In the case of statements, we have two kinds of necessity: internal necessity and external necessity. A statement is externally necessary iff it is necessarily such that it is true. A statement is internally necessary iff it is necessarily such that its possible sent and acceptable received propositions are all necessary. Corresponding to each statement ψ is the state of affairs $[\varnothing|\psi]$, and ψ is externally necessary iff $[\varnothing|\psi]$ is necessary. Thus, an immediate consequence of (4.13) is:

(4.21) For any statement ψ, ψ is externally necessary iff ψ is true at every possible world.

Thus, we obtain one expected connection between necessity for statements and possible worlds. Notice that this can be used to justify some of the claims of Kripke [1972] and Putnam [1975]. They maintained that if it is true that water is H_2O, then there is no possible world at which water is not H_2O. I argued in Chapter Two that statements formulating physical necessities concerning nomic kinds (such as the statement that water is H_2O) are externally necessary. It now follows that they are true at all possible worlds, and thus Kripke and Putnam were right. It is interesting that the argument for this conclusion turns essentially on there being the distinction I have proposed between statements and propositions.

Internal necessity is a stricter modality than external necessity. Internally necessary statements are also externally necessary, but we have seen examples of externally necessary statements that are not internally necessary. It follows that internal necessity does *not* coincide with truth at all possible worlds. There are statements true at all possible worlds that are not internally necessary. This is of considerable importance when we consider *statemental modal logic*—the logic of modal statements. It was established in Chapter Two that if φ is a statement then $\Box\varphi$ is true iff φ is internally necessary. Furthermore, it was argued that there can be *no* modal operator $\boxplus$ such that $\boxplus\varphi$ is true iff φ is externally necessary. It follows that the truth of $\Box\varphi$ does not correspond to φ being true at all possible worlds. In other words, there is no way to base a statemental modal logic directly on possible worlds. This is a rather startling conclusion, so let us consider it more carefully. If it were to be possible to base statemental modal logic directly on possible worlds, the modal operator involved would have to correspond to external necessity. The reason there can be no such modal operator $\boxplus$ is that it must be possible to describe a statement in terms of its diagram, but there is no apparent way to construct a diagram for $\boxplus\varphi$ that would have the result that $\boxplus\varphi$ is true iff φ is externally necessary.

As we have seen, the only obvious way to construct a diagram for a modal statement makes the modal operator correspond to internal necessity instead.

Despite the fact that there is no direct connection between statemental modal operators and possible worlds, we can easily show that statemental modal operators satisfy S5. This follows from the fact that propositional modal operators satisfy S5. For example, consider statements of the form $\Box[\Diamond\psi \to \Box\Diamond\psi]$. A statement is true iff its possible sent and acceptable received propositions relative to the actual values of the dynamic parameters are all true. The possible sent and acceptable received propositions for a statement of the form $\Box[\Diamond\psi \to \Box\Diamond\psi]$ are propositions of the form $\Box[\Diamond\varphi \to \Box\Diamond\varphi]$. We have already established that all such propositions are true, so it follows that all statements of the form $\Box[\Diamond\psi \to \Box\Diamond\psi]$ are true. Analogously, any statement having the form of an axiom of S5 is true, and consequently any statement having the form of a theorem of S5 is true.

We generally think of logic as having to do with propositions and statements, but it is worth noting that we can also define a modal operator for states of affairs and consider what logical properties it has. Because of the directly referential character of states of affairs, we can define modal operators for states of affairs much more simply than we can for either propositions or statements:

(4.22) If S is a state of affairs, $\Box S = S$'s *being necessarily such that it obtains*.

It follows from (4.13) that $\Box S$ obtains iff S obtains at every possible world. Furthermore, we can establish that the modal logic of states of affairs is at least S5 by using an argument precisely analogous to that used above to establish that propositional modal operators satisfy S5.

5. Properties

The term 'property' is bandied about with great regularity in philosophical logic, but rarely with any careful explanation of what properties are supposed to be. We have already discussed two kinds of property-like entities—concepts and attributes—but for some purposes a broader notion is required. For example, Plantinga is fond of talking about the property of *being Socrates*. R. M. Adams [1979] calls such properties 'thisnesses'. The thisness of Socrates is supposed to be a kind of directly referential property involving Socrates "directly" rather than under a description or via some mode of representation.

It is fashionable to treat properties as functions on possible worlds. In modal and intensional logic it is popularly alleged that a property **P** can be identified with that function that assigns to each world w the extension of **P** at w. This function is defined precisely as follows:

(5.1) If w is a possible world and **P** is a one-place property then $\Sigma_\mathbf{P}(w) = \{x|\ x \text{ has } \mathbf{P} \text{ at } w\}$.

P is then identified with $\Sigma_\mathbf{P}$. n-place properties are treated analogously. It is generally added that every function from worlds to extensions is a property. Then properties can be defined as follows:

(5.2) **P** is an n-place property iff **P** is a function from possible worlds to sets of n-tuples of objects.

Montague [1969] attributes the germ of this analysis to Carnap in unpublished work and the final development of the idea to Kripke [1963].

Although one frequently encounters something like (5.2), it is subject to a serious problem. Consider the property of *being red*. That is to be identified with the function **R** that assigns to each world w the set $\mathbf{R}(w)$ of objects that are red at w. It is commonly believed that sets only exist insofar as their members exist, and an argument in support of this will be given in section seven. Consequently, the set $\mathbf{R}(w)$ is the set of all objects *from the actual world* that are red at w. No other objects exist, so there exists no broader set of objects red at w. But now let w^* be a different world containing different objects than those in the actual world. If w^* were actual then the set of objects that are red at w would be different than it is—it would be a set of objects existing at w^*. Thus the function $\mathbf{R}$ corresponding to the property of being red would be different than it actually is—it would have different values at different worlds and hence would be a different function. But the property of being red is the same property in w^* as it is in the actual world, so it cannot be identified with the function defined by (5.1).

Various contorted repairs might avoid this difficulty, but it seems to me that there is a better way to proceed. We have remarked that there are supposed to be directly referential properties, like that of *being Socrates*. In this respect, properties are much like states of affairs. Roughly, properties are to states of affairs as concepts are to propositions and as attributes are to statements. This suggests taking properties to be functions from objects to states of affairs. On this proposal, a property $\mathbf{P}$ is identified with that function that assigns to each object x the state of affairs consisting of x's having the property $\mathbf{P}$. For example, the property of being red is identified with the function that assigns x's *being red* to each object x. More generally, an n-place property is taken to be a function from n-tuples of objects to states of affairs.

A distinction must be made between *functions-in-extension* and *functions-in-intension*. Functions-in-extension are sets of ordered pairs. Functions-in-intension are intensional entities akin to concepts. More precisely, functions-in-intension can be taken to be "functional" concepts:

(5.3) f is a *function-in-intension* iff f is a two-place concept that is necessarily such that for any x,y,z, if $\langle x,y \rangle$ and $\langle x,z \rangle$ both exemplify f then $y = z$.

If $\langle x,y \rangle$ exemplifies f, we write $\ulcorner f(x) = y \urcorner$.

Properties cannot be identified with functions-in-extension. A function-in-extension, being a set of ordered pairs, must have the same domain at every world at which it exists. But the function-in-extension that assigns to each object the state of affairs consisting of the object's having a certain property will have different domains in different worlds and hence will be a different function. Therefore, at least as a first approximation, properties must be identified with functions-in-intension rather than with functions-in-extension. My initial proposal regarding properties is thus:

(5.4) An *n-place qualitative property* is any function-in-intension from *n*-tuples of objects to states of affairs. An *n*-tuple σ *has* the property **P** *at* a world *w* iff **P**$(\sigma) \subseteq w$.

Definition (5.4) defines 'qualitative property'. The reason for the qualification 'qualitative' is that in (5.4) we have still not managed to construct properties like that of *being Socrates*. Given a haecceity δ of Socrates, we could construct such a function quite easily. It would be the binary concept expressed by $\ulcorner y = [x|\alpha]\urcorner$ where α is the monadic concept expressed by $\ulcorner x = \delta\urcorner$. But we have seen that there is reason to doubt the existence of haecceities for most objects, and without a haecceity of Socrates there is no way to construct a function-in-intension **S** that assigns to an object *x* the state of affairs *x's being Socrates*. This is connected with a general feature of functions in intension. If f(x,y) is a binary function-in-intension and *b* is an object, there is generally no such function-in-intension as the monadic function f(x,b). Without a haecceity of *b*, you cannot fill an argument place in a function-in-intension and still have a function-in-intension. This is an undesirable constraint both on functions-in-intension and on properties. It is easily circumvented. Where *k* is a number, let us define a *k-ary assignment of degree n* to be a function-in-extension assigning objects to *k* of the integers between 0 and *n*+1. We can regard a *k*-ary assignment of degree *n* as telling us how to fill *k* of the argument places in an *n*-ary function-in-intension with objects. We can then define:

(5.5) *f* is a *generalized n-place function-in-intension* iff either *f* is an *n*-place function-in-intension or for some *m* > *n* and some *k* there is an *m*-ary function-in-intension *g* and a *k*-ary assignment σ of degree *m* such that *n* = *m*−*k* and *f* = $\langle g, \sigma \rangle$.

For example, if g is a binary function-in-intension and σ is the monadic assignment $\{\langle 2,b \rangle\}$ and $f = \langle g,\sigma \rangle$, then $f(x) = g(x,b)$. We can then define the general notion of a property as follows:

(5.6) An *n-place property* is any generalized n-place function-in-intension from n-tuples of objects to states of affairs. An n-tuple σ *has* the property **P** *at* a world w iff $\mathbf{P}(\sigma) \subset w$.

This definition will be refined further in section eight, but let us adopt it as it is for now. It follows that there is such a property as that of *being Socrates*, although it is not a qualitative property.

I can imagine it being protested that properties cannot literally be functions. At best they "correspond" to functions, in much the same way natural numbers "correspond" to sets. I am not inclined to regard this objection as telling. Philosophers have so extended the use of the term 'property' that it can no longer be claimed to mean what the ordinary man means by it. Most nonphilosophers would view with amusement the claim that there is such a property as that of *being Socrates*. In philosophy, 'property' has become a term of art. As such, we can have properties be anything we want them to be that work in roughly the way properties are supposed to work in philosophy. My claim is that the best way to do that is by taking properties to be functions.[26]

As we have defined 'property', concepts and attributes are not properties. But there is a property corresponding to each concept or attribute. If α is a concept or attribute, then the corresponding property is the function-in-intension $\mathbf{P}_\alpha$ that assigns to an object x the state of affairs $[x|\alpha]$. More generally, if α is an n-place concept or attribute, and $b_1,\ldots,b_k$ are objects, then corresponding to the "partially filled" concept or attribute $(\alpha:b_1,\ldots,b_k,x_{k+1},\ldots,x_n)$ is the nonqualitative property (i.e., generalized function-in-intension) $\mathbf{P}(b_1,\ldots,b_k,x_{k+1},\ldots,x_n)$. Note

---

[26] There remains a residual problem for the identification of properties with functions-in-intension when the latter are defined as in (5.4). This will be discussed in section eight.

that $(\alpha{:}b_1,\ldots,b_k,x_{k+1},\ldots,x_n)$ is not itself a concept or attribute. Concepts and attributes cannot have *objects* filling their argument places. Their argument places must be filled by designators. It thus becomes notationally convenient to simply identify $(\alpha{:}b_1,\ldots,b_k,x_{k+1},\ldots,x_n)$ with $(\mathbf{P}{:}b_1,\ldots,b_k,x_{k+1},\ldots,x_n)$.

We have defined what it is for an object to have a property. We can also define what it is for an object to have a property necessarily:

(5.7) *x* has **P** *necessarily* iff *x* has **P** at every possible world.

Properties that an object has necessarily are called *essential properties* of that object. We can then define an *essence* of an object to be a property that the object has at every possible world and that no other object has at any possible world. Defining 'essence' in this way, the thisness of Socrates may or may not be an essence of Socrates, depending upon just what property we take this to be. It is most natural to take the thisness of Socrates to be that function that assigns to each object *x* the state of affairs *x's being (numerically) identical to Socrates*. It is generally maintained, however, that 'Socrates = Socrates' is only true if Socrates exists. If we adopt that view of identity, then Socrates does not have the property of being Socrates at worlds in which he does not exist. It might be suggested that we should instead take the thisness of Socrates to be the property of *being such that if it exists then it is identical to Socrates*. But this is a property that objects other than Socrates have at worlds at which they do not exist. To avoid these difficulties, I suggest that we take the thisness of Socrates to be the property of *being possibly such that it is identical with Socrates*. It can be argued as follows that this is indeed an essence of Socrates. We have assumed (Chapter Two, principle (1.11)) that identities hold necessarily, i.e., that:

$$\square_{a,s}[a = s \rightarrow \square_{a,s}(E(a) \rightarrow a = s)].$$

By S5 this is equivalent to

$$\square_{a,s}[\Diamond_{a,s}(a = s) \rightarrow \Diamond_{a,s}\square_{a,s}(E(a) \rightarrow a = s)]$$

and hence to

$$\Box_{a,s}[\Diamond_{a,s}(a = s) \rightarrow \Box_{a,s}(E(a) \rightarrow a = s)],$$

which implies

$$\Box_{a,s}[\Diamond_{a,s}(a = s) \rightarrow (E(a) \rightarrow a = s)].$$

Consequently,

$$\Box_{a,s}[(E(a) \,\&\, a \neq s) \rightarrow {\sim}\Diamond_{a,s}(a = s)].$$

The latter tells us that nothing distinct from Socrates has the property of being possibly identical to Socrates at any possible world. Thus, taking the thisness of Socrates to be the property of being possibly identical to Socrates makes it an essence of Socrates. Note, however, that essences in the present sense are properties rather than concepts or attributes, and hence cannot be constituents of propositions or statements and cannot be used in the construction of possible worlds. Instead, they presuppose the notion of a statement.

Plantinga objects to the preceding definition of 'essence' and 'essential property'. Instead, he defines an essential property of an object to be a property the object has at every world *at which the object exists*, and he defines an essence to be an essential property never possessed by any other object. This has the somewhat surprising consequence that every object has the property of *existence* essentially. The definition I proposed above seems somewhat more natural, although it has the consequence that most essential properties of most objects are conditional properties whose antecedents require existence. For example, *being sentient* is not an essential property of Socrates, because Socrates lacks that property at worlds at which he does not exist. Instead, *being such that if he exists then he is sentient* is an essential property of Socrates.

The reason Plantinga defines 'essence' and 'essential property' as he does rather than as I have proposed is that he champions what he calls *serious actualism*. This is the view that an object cannot have a property at a world at which that object does not exist. Although Plantinga endorses this view, I regard it as problematic. In my opinion, serious actualism is either false or uninteresting, depending upon how it is interpreted. Here is a potential counterexample: Socrates has the property of not existing at every world at which he does not exist. Plantinga's response to this is that there is no such property as that of *not existing*. There is the property of *nonexistence*, but that is a property nothing can have because in order to have it an object would have to exist without existing. Why would anyone say this? There is a very seductive modal fallacy to which I have found myself succumbing on occasion, and I suspect that Plantinga is succumbing to it here. The fallacy consists of endorsing instances of the following modal principle:

(5.8) $\Box(\forall x)(Fx \rightarrow Gx) \rightarrow \Box(\forall x)\Box(Fx \rightarrow Gx)$.

To see that this principle is invalid, let F be a tautologous predicate and let G be 'exists'. Assuming that our quantifiers range only over existing objects (which can be regarded as a convention rather than an endorsement of actualism—see section six), the antecedent of (5.8) is true because it is necessary that everything exists; but the consequent is false because it says that everything has necessary existence.

Once one thinks about (5.8) in this way, it is apparent that it is invalid, and one's inclination is to question whether people really are seduced by it. Perhaps the simplest way to see that they are is to note that philosophers almost universally assume that logical analyses can be given the forms

(5.9) $\Box(\forall x)(Fx \leftrightarrow \varphi)$, $\Box(\forall x)(\forall y)(Rxy \leftrightarrow \theta)$, etc.

where φ, θ, etc., are open formulas. To see that this cannot be the proper form of logical analyses, suppose we take $\ulcorner x \equiv y \urcorner$ to abbreviate $\ulcorner \Diamond x = y \urcorner$. We have assumed the following modal principle:

(5.10) $\Box(\forall x)(\forall y)[x = y \rightarrow \Box(x \text{ exists} \rightarrow x = y)]$.

Given (5.10) and S5, the following is true:

(5.11) $\Box(\forall x)(\forall y)[x \equiv y \leftrightarrow x = y]$.

The reason (5.11) is true is that the quantifiers range only over existing objects, and at worlds in which x and y both exist, $x = y$ iff $x \equiv y$. But clearly $\ulcorner x = y \urcorner$ is not an adequate logical analysis of $\ulcorner x \equiv y \urcorner$. This is because there can be worlds at which the latter holds but the former fails—these are worlds at which x and y do not exist.[27] This amounts to the observation that although (5.11) is true, the following is not:

(5.12) $\Box(\forall x)(\forall y)\Box[x \equiv y \leftrightarrow x = y]$.

It is conditions like (5.12) that are required for logical analyses. In general, logical analyses must have the forms

(5.13) $\Box(\forall x)\Box(Fx \leftrightarrow \varphi)$, $\Box(\forall x)(\forall y)\Box(Rxy \leftrightarrow \theta)$, etc.[28]

The confusion of (5.9) with (5.13) is precisely the modal fallacy of endorsing (5.8).

Plantinga's endorsement of serious actualism is based upon the intuition that an object could not have a property if it did not exist. But the assertion that an object could not have a property if it did not exist is ambiguous between

(5.14a) $\Box(\forall x)(x$ has $\mathbf{P} \to x$ exists)

and

(5.14b) $\Box(\forall x)\Box(x$ has $\mathbf{P} \to x$ exists).

It seems to me that our intuition is only an intuition that (5.14a) is true, but serious actualism requires (5.14b). The conflation of (5.14a) and (5.14b) is precisely our modal fallacy.

Plantinga's response to this allegation is to admit that it is a fallacy to endorse (5.8), but to insist that (5.14b) is still

---

[27] I assume that identity is an existence entailing property, i.e., $x = y$ at a world only if x exists at that world. One might instead understand identity as $\ulcorner x \equiv y \urcorner$. In that case, we can simply define $\ulcorner x = y \urcorner$ as $\ulcorner x \equiv y$ & x exists$\urcorner$. A second example of this same sort consists of observing that $\Box(\forall x)[x$ exists $\leftrightarrow (x$ is red or $\sim x$ is red)], but an object satisfies $\ulcorner x$ is red or $\sim x$ is red$\urcorner$ even at worlds at which it does not exist.

[28] Many philosophers will find this particularly disturbing because it means that the statement of a logical analysis presupposes the concept of *de re* necessity.

true.[29] After all, invalid principles can have valid instances. Plantinga defends this move by observing that, for example, Socrates could not be snubnosed without existing. This is intended as a defense of

$$(\forall x)\square(x \text{ has } \mathbf{P} \rightarrow x \text{ exists})$$

and hence of (5.14b).

It seems to me that the appropriate response to Plantinga's rejoinder is to agree that (5.14b) is true of some properties, such as the property of *being snubnosed*, but false of others, for instance, the property of *not existing*. As we have seen, Plantinga rejects this move by insisting that there is no such property as that of *not existing*. If this is merely a partial stipulation regarding how he is going to use the term 'property', then we cannot object to it except on the grounds that it makes serious actualism trivial and uninteresting. But Plantinga intends it to be more than this. Suppose we give Plantinga his use of the term 'property', agreeing that (5.14b) and serious actualism are true by stipulation for properties. Then it is natural to want a more general term that would include both properties and things like *not existing*. I want to say that although objects cannot have properties at worlds in which they do not exist (by the definition of 'property'), they can *satisfy conditions* at worlds in which they do not exist, and one such condition is that of *not existing*. Another such condition is that of being such that *if one existed then one would be sentient*. Socrates satisfies the latter at worlds in which he does not exist.

Plantinga's response to all of this is to doubt that the notion of a condition makes sense. The simplest answer is to observe that in (5.6) we have defined a perfectly workable notion of a condition. That definition cannot be faulted on logical grounds. The only way to defend serious actualism against this move is to grant that there are conditions that are not "existence entailing" (i.e., such that an object can satisfy them at a world without existing at that world) and then go on to define prop-

---

[29] In conversation.

erties to be existence entailing conditions. The effect of this is to make serious actualism true by definition, but pointless. It seems to me that a more reasonable alternative is to call both conditions and properties 'properties' (as I have in (5.6)) and acknowledge that some properties are existence entailing while others are not. This has the effect of making serious actualism false, but not trivially false because it is of some interest that there are properties (or conditions) that are not existence entailing. The upshot of this is that serious actualism is either false or uninteresting, depending upon just how we choose to use the term 'property'. Henceforth, I will use it in the broad sense that includes conditions.

Predicates bear intimate relations to a variety of abstract entities. The sense of a predicate is an attribute, and this is what explains how the predicate functions in making statements. I have urged that synthetic predicates also "connote" nomic kinds, the latter playing a role in determining what attribute is expressed by a synthetic predicate. In addition, predicates are related in an important way to properties. Each attribute determines a property, viz.,

(5.15) If α is an attribute, *the property corresponding to α* is that function-in-intension that assigns to any object x the state of affairs *x's exemplifying α*.

Relative to any particular assignment of values to the pragmatic parameters, a predicate expresses an attribute. I will say that the predicate *designates* the property corresponding to that attribute. When a predicate F designates a property **P**, I will describe **P** as ⌜the property of being F⌝ (e.g., 'the property of being water').

Let us say that two predicates F and G are *nomically equivalent* iff it is physically necessary that something is an F iff it is a G. More accurately, two predicates are nomically equivalent (relative to a particular assignment of values to the pragmatic parameters) iff their senses are nomically equivalent. Kripke and Putnam have urged that nomically equivalent natural kind terms designate the same property. It is impossible to tell the extent to which what they mean by 'designate' and 'property' is the same as what I mean, but our present framework does enable us to make sense of their claim. Natural kind terms are synthetic predicates. Nomically equivalent synthetic predicates connote the same nomic kind and hence express the same attribute. It follows that nomically equivalent synthetic predicates designate the same property. This seems at least to be a reasonable reconstruction of what Kripke and Putnam were getting at.

In section four, it was shown that if (4.14) holds (according to which possible worlds have necessary existence and are necessarily possible worlds, and any proposition true at a possible world is necessarily such that it is true at that world), then *de dicto* modal operators satisfy S5. Now that we have introduced the concept of a property, we are in a position to consider *de re* modal operators and first-order modal logic. Kripke [1963] constructs a first-order version of S5, which I will call KS5. Let us define a *closure* of an open formula to be a closed formula resulting from appending to the beginning of the formula an alternating string of universal quantifiers and necessity operators, beginning with a necessity operator and ending with a universal quantifier. For example, $\ulcorner\Box(\forall x)\Box(\forall y)Fxy\urcorner$ is a closure of $\ulcorner Fxy\urcorner$. The single rule of inference for KS5 is *modus ponens* for the material conditional, and the axioms are closed formulas of the following forms and all closures of formulas of the following forms:

(A1) $\Box p$ where p is truth-functionally valid;

(A2) $\Box p \rightarrow p$;

(A3) $\Box(\Box p \rightarrow p)$;

(A4) $\Box[\Box(p \rightarrow q) \rightarrow (\Box p \rightarrow \Box q)]$;

(A5) $\Box[\Diamond p \rightarrow \Box\Diamond p]$;

(A6) $\Box p \rightarrow \Box\Box p$;

(A7) $\Box[p \rightarrow (\forall x)p]$ provided x does not occur free in p;

(A8) $\Box\{(\forall x)(p \rightarrow q) \rightarrow [(\forall x)p \rightarrow (\forall x)q]\}$;

(A9) $\Box(\forall y)[(\forall x)p \rightarrow Sb(y/x)p]$ where $Sb(y/x)p$ results from replacing all free occurrences of x in p by y, and y does not occur in p.[30]

---

[30] These axioms are not the same as Kripke's, but they are equivalent.

We can show quite easily that any proposition having the form of some theorem of KS5 is true, provided the following holds in addition to (4.14):

(5.16) $\Box(\forall w)(\forall \mathbf{P})(\forall x)$[if w is a possible world and $\mathbf{P}$ is a property and x has $\mathbf{P}$ at w then $\Box_w(w$ is a possible world and w exists) and $\Box_\mathbf{P}(\mathbf{P}$ is a property and $\mathbf{P}$ exists) and $\Box_{w,x,\mathbf{P}}x$ has $\mathbf{P}$ at w].

The argument is simple. Any closed formulas having the form of one of (A1)–(A9) will be true for the same reasons the axioms of S5 were all true. Now consider an open formula of one of these forms. For instance, consider (A3) (the other axioms being analogous). Suppose p contains a single free variable 'x'. Then $\ulcorner \Box(\Box p \to p) \urcorner$ is the form of a monadic concept. If α is such a concept, then $\Box(\forall x)(\alpha{:}x)$ is a proposition of the form $\ulcorner \Box(\forall x)\Box(\Box p \to p) \urcorner$. For the same reason every proposition of the form $\ulcorner \Box(\Box p \to p) \urcorner$ is true, every object exemplifies any concept of the form $\ulcorner \Box(\Box p \to p) \urcorner$. Thus every object exemplifies α, i.e., $(\forall x)(\alpha{:}x)$ is true. In arguing this it makes no difference which world is actual, so this is true at every possible world, i.e., $\Box(\forall x)(\alpha{:}x)$ is true.

Next suppose p contains two free variables 'x' and 'y'. Then $\ulcorner \Box(\Box p \to p) \urcorner$ is the form of a binary concept. Let α be such a concept. Then $\Box(\forall x)\Box(\forall y)(\alpha{:}x,y)$ is a proposition having the form of a closure of $\ulcorner \Box(\Box p \to p) \urcorner$. For any object b, there is such a monadic property as $(\alpha{:}b,y)$. Then by (5.16), there is necessarily such a monadic property as $(\alpha{:}b,y)$. Just as above, it is necessarily true that every object has that monadic property, i.e., $\Box(\forall y)(\alpha{:}b,y)$. This holds for any object b, so we have established that necessarily, for every x, the latter holds. That is, $\Box(\forall x)\Box(\forall y)(\alpha{:}x,y)$ is true.

Next suppose p contains three free variables 'x', 'y', and 'z', and α is a ternary concept having the form $\ulcorner \Box(\Box p \to p) \urcorner$. We want to establish the truth of $\Box(\forall x)\Box(\forall y)\Box(\forall z)(\alpha{:}x,y,z)$. As above, necessarily, for any object b there is such a binary property as $(\alpha{:}b,y,z)$. Then by (5.16), necessarily, for any object c there is such a monadic property as $(\alpha{:}b,c,z)$. Then as above, it is necessarily true that every object has this monadic

III. Possible Worlds

property. Consequently, $\Box(\forall x)\Box(\forall y)\Box(\forall z)(\alpha{:}x,y,z)$ is true.

Obviously, we can establish in an analogous fashion that any proposition having the form of an axiom of KS5 is true. Thus if (5.16) holds, *de re* modal operators for propositions satisfy KS5.

We have been talking about modal propositions. Next consider modal statements. We have noted that statemental modal operators are not related in any simple way to possible worlds. Nevertheless, it is easily established that any statement having the form of some theorem of KS5 will be true. If ψ is such a statement, then the possible sent and acceptable received propositions for ψ will be propositions having the form of that same theorem. All such propositions are true, so it follows that ψ is true. Consequently, given (5.16), KS5 holds for statemental modal operators as well as for propositional modal operators.

6. Actualism

Actualism is the view that there isn't anything that doesn't exist.[31] Actualism is apt to seem like the merest tautology, but there must be more to it than that, or people would not have thought it worth discussing. Consequently, the initial difficulty in assessing actualism is in deciding what it means. The exact way in which it is phrased is important. It cannot be rephrased as the view that there does not exist anything that does not exist, because that really is a tautology. No one would deny that. The content of actualism is intimately connected with the *sentence* 'There are things that don't exist'. If actualism is to be claiming something interesting, it must imply that there is no reasonable sense in which this sentence can be understood that makes it express a truth. This is really a claim about the interpretation of quantifiers and the meaning

---

[31] Unfortunately, the term 'actualism' has also been used for a number of other views. See Alan McMichael [1983], 49–53. I follow Plantinga [1976] in my use of the term.

Despite the similarity of the names, there is no close connection between actualism and serious actualism. Plantinga [1979] argued that serious actualism could be derived from actualism, but he has since given up that claim.

of 'there is'. The claim of the actualist is that there is no reasonable way to understand $\ulcorner(\exists x)\urcorner$ that allows it to range over merely possible objects. Let us call the denial of actualism 'possibilism'.[32]

Actualism seems to me to be false. Suppose we agree to interpret $\ulcorner(\exists x)\urcorner$ as the actualist wants it interpreted—"existentially". The question is then whether we can make sense of another quantifier that can be interpreted as "ranging over all possible objects". Given the existential quantifier together with other notions respectable to the modal logician, I believe that we can do just that. For this purpose we have the ordinary modal operators at our disposal. This immediately suggests defining a "possibilistic" quantifier $\ulcorner\langle\exists x\rangle\urcorner$ as $\ulcorner\Diamond(\exists x)\urcorner$. In a sense, this does give us a way of talking about merely possible objects, but it will not work as a possibilistic quantifier. If there is to be any way of defining a possibilistic quantifier $\ulcorner\langle\exists x\rangle\urcorner$, it must make possibilism true by making $\ulcorner\langle\exists x\rangle$ x does not exist$\urcorner$ true. But what $\ulcorner\Diamond(\exists x)$ x does not exist$\urcorner$ says is, roughly, that there are possible worlds at which it is true that there exist things that do not exist—and that is false. The difficulty with taking $\ulcorner\Diamond(\exists x)\urcorner$ as a possibilistic quantifier is that although it talks about possible objects, it does not talk about how they are at the actual world but rather how they are at other possible worlds. What we want $\ulcorner\langle\exists x\rangle Fx\urcorner$ to say is that there are possible objects that are *actually* F, i.e., that are F in the actual world. This cannot be expressed in ordinary quantified modal logic, but it can be expressed with the addition of another modal operator—the 'actually' operator '**A**'. For example, suppose we want to symbolize the true statement, 'It is possible for there to be something that doesn't actually exist'. This cannot be symbolized in standard first-order modal logic, but using the 'actually' operator, it can be symbolized as '$\Diamond(\exists x)\mathbf{A}$ x does not exist'. Although 'actually'

---

[32] The version of possibilism I will be discussing here is that allowing quantification over possible objects. Plantinga points out (in conversation) that there are stronger versions of possibilism involving quantification over impossible objects as well (round squares and the like), but I do not propose to defend them here.

can be understood without appealing to possible worlds (after all, ordinary people understand it), possible worlds do provide a vehicle for its analysis. At least in many contexts, $\ulcorner(...\mathbf{A}P...)\urcorner$ can be analyzed as $\ulcorner(\exists w)[w$ is a world & w obtains & $(...$it is true at w that $P...)]\urcorner$. 'Actually' works like a wide-scope occurrence of 'at the actual world'. Applying this to possibilistic quantifiers, $\ulcorner\langle\exists x\rangle Fx\urcorner$ is supposed to say that there are possible objects that are actually F. I propose that the most reasonable way of understanding this is as saying that it is possible for there to be objects that are actually F, i.e., as $\ulcorner\Diamond(\exists x)\mathbf{A}Fx\urcorner$. Thus, my preliminary proposal for the *particular possibilistic quantifier* is that $\ulcorner\langle\exists x\rangle\urcorner$ be defined as $\ulcorner\Diamond(\exists x)\mathbf{A}\urcorner$. The *universal possibilistic quantifier* $\ulcorner\langle\forall x\rangle\urcorner$ can be defined as $\ulcorner\sim\langle\exists x\rangle\sim\urcorner$, or equivalently as $\ulcorner\Box(\forall x)\mathbf{A}\urcorner$. For reasons I will explain shortly, this definition must be refined somewhat for use in modal contexts, but it is entirely adequate for a possibilistic quantifier of use in nonmodal contexts. This quantifier has the effect of ranging over possible objects (i.e., objects that exist in other possible worlds) and saying how they are at the actual world. And it does so in a metaphysically innocuous way. Furthermore, it makes the possibilistic thesis $\ulcorner\langle\exists x\rangle$ x does not exist$\urcorner$ true. I would stop short of claiming that $\ulcorner\langle\exists x\rangle\urcorner$ is one meaning of the English 'there is'. I don't know whether that is true or not, but that does not seem to me where the important question lies anyway. All I want to claim is that $\ulcorner\langle\exists x\rangle\urcorner$ is one reasonable thing a philosopher might mean by 'there is' in possibilistic contexts, and that is enough to make possibilism true and actualism false.

In order to explain the need for a further refinement in the definition of possibilistic quantifiers, let us first consider the logic of 'actually'. I have explained 'actually' as involving a wide-scope occurrence of 'at the actual world'. The requirement that the occurrence always be wide scope has the consequence that the logic of 'actually' behaves rather peculiarly in certain respects.[33] For example, $\ulcorner P \rightarrow \Box\mathbf{A}P\urcorner$ is valid. This

---

[33] The logic of 'actually' has been investigated independently by Crossley and Humberstone [1977] and Kaplan [1976].

can be seen by noting that $\ulcorner P \rightarrow \Box AP \urcorner$ expands to

$(\exists w)[w$ is the actual world &
$(P \rightarrow \Box($it is true at w that $P))]$.

This is true because if a proposition is true at a world then it is necessarily such that it is true at that world. Thus, for example, because

(6.1) Grass is green

is true,

(6.2) Necessarily, grass is actually green

is also true. This is because according to the proposal we are considering, (6.2) means:

(6.3) $(\exists w)(w$ is the actual world & $\Box($grass is green at $w))$.

But it is counterintuitive that (6.2) should be true. There is a strong tendency to read (6.2) as meaning

(6.4) $\Box(\exists w)(w$ is the actual world & grass is green at $w)$.

(6.4) is false. The difference between (6.3) and (6.4) is one of scope. Realistically, I think it must be admitted that the English sentence (6.2) is ambiguous between (6.3) and (6.4), with (6.4) being the preferred reading.

The explanation of 'actually' as involving a wide-scope occurrence of 'at the actual world' makes it work the way logicians have taken it to work, but for the reasons just given, that strikes me as an oversimplification. 'Actually' often works like a wide-scope occurrence of 'at the actual world', but not invariably. We could obtain a more accurate representation of 'actually' as it functions in English by describing it as short for 'at the actual world' where the scope of the latter is ambiguous (just as it is for most definite descriptions). Accordingly, (6.2) can be used to mean either (6.3) or (6.4). Differences in the scope of 'actually' only make a difference insofar as they include or exclude different modal operators. When the scope of 'actually' occurs within the scope of several modal operators, it is the modal operator of narrowest scope that controls the behavior of 'actually'. For example, in $\ulcorner \Box AP \urcorner$ the scope of '**A**' can either include or be included in the scope of '$\Box$', yielding the two readings:

(6.5) $(\exists w)[w$ is the actual world & $\Box$(it is true at w that $P)]$;

(6.6) $\Box (\exists w)(w$ is the actual world & it is true at w that $P)$.

Formally, we can resolve the ambiguity by indexing modal operators and 'actually' operators with numerical subscripts when necessary (the ordering of the subscripts having no significance). In general, if '**A**' occurs without a subscript or if $\ulcorner A_i \urcorner$ does not occur within the scope of a modal operator having the same subscript, its use is analyzed as above as involving wide-scope. But if $\ulcorner A_i \urcorner$ does occur within the scope of a modal operator having the same subscript, $\ulcorner (...\Box_i(...A_i\psi...)...) \urcorner$ is analyzed as $\ulcorner (...\Box(\exists w)(w$ is the actual world & $(...\psi$ is true at $w...))...) \urcorner$. This allows us to distinguish between (6.5) and (6.6) by writing $\ulcorner \Box AP \urcorner$ (or $\ulcorner \Box_1 A_0 P \urcorner$) and $\ulcorner \Box_1 A_1 P \urcorner$, respectively. With this convention, $\ulcorner P \rightarrow \Box AP \urcorner$ is valid, but $\ulcorner P \rightarrow \Box_1 A_1 P \urcorner$ is not.

Now let us apply these refinements in the analysis of 'actually' to the definition of possibilistic quantifiers. That definition must be refined to make possibilistic quantifiers work properly in modal contexts. Suppose, for example, that we think there is a "maximally populated" world at which all possible objects exist. We would like to express that hypothesis as:

(6.7) $\Diamond \langle \forall x \rangle$ x exists.

But (6.7) does not say what we want it to say. Expanding (6.7) in terms of our definition of the possibilistic quantifiers, we obtain

(6.8) $\Diamond \sim \Diamond (\exists x) A \sim x$ exists,

which means:

(6.9) $(\exists w)[w$ is the actual world & $\Diamond \sim \Diamond (\exists x) \sim x$ exists at $w]$.

Assuming S5, (6.9) is equivalent to:

(6.10) $(\exists w)[w$ is the actual world & $\Box(\forall x)$ x exists at $w]$.

But (6.10) says that the *actual world* is maximally populated, whereas all we wanted (6.7) to say was that *there is* a maximally populated world, i.e.,

(6.11) $\Diamond(\exists w)[w$ is a world &
w is actual & $\sim\Diamond(\exists x)\sim$ x exists at $w]$.

The difference between (6.9) and (6.11) is a difference between the relative scopes of '**A**' and the initial occurrence of '$\Diamond$'. In (6.9) the initial occurrence of '$\Diamond$' is contained within the scope of '**A**', whereas in (6.11) the scope of '**A**' is contained within the scope of the initial occurrence of '$\Diamond$'. This example illustrates that in a formula of the form $\ulcorner(...\langle\exists x\rangle\varphi...)\urcorner$, we want the scope of '**A**' to be φ. Thus, if the possibilistic quantifier does not occur within the scope of a modal operator, $\ulcorner(...\langle\exists x\rangle\varphi...)\urcorner$ should be defined to mean $\ulcorner(...\Diamond(\exists x)\mathbf{A}\varphi...)\urcorner$. On the other hand, if the possibilistic quantifier does occur within the scope of a modal operator, so that the formula has the form $\ulcorner(...\Box...\langle\exists x\rangle\varphi...)\urcorner$ with the indicated modal operator being the innermost modal operator containing the possibilistic quantifier within its scope, then $\ulcorner(...\Box...\langle\exists x\rangle\varphi...)\urcorner$ should be defined to mean $\ulcorner(...\Box_1...\Diamond(\exists x)\mathbf{A}_1\varphi...)\urcorner$. With this refined convention, (6.7) becomes equivalent to (6.11) rather than to the undesirable (6.10). This implies that, completely in general, $\ulcorner(...\langle\exists x\rangle\varphi...)\urcorner$ is equivalent to $\ulcorner(...(\exists w)[w$ is a world & w is actual & $\Diamond(\exists x)(\varphi$ is true at $w)]...)\urcorner$.

Some of the logical properties of possibilistic quantifiers are of considerable interest. It has frequently been observed that classical first-order logic is in certain respects unreasonable. It has often been felt that first-order logic should be modified to accommodate nondenoting singular terms and empty domains, the resulting logic being a "free logic".[34] In this connection, it is significant that the nonmodal fragments of most first-order modal logics are not the same as classical first-order

---

[34] See section five of Chapter Six for further discussion of this.

logic. Suppose, however, that we begin with such a first-order modal logic and then define our possibilistic quantifiers as above. Assuming the validity of S5 modal principles, it turns out that the logic of $\ulcorner \langle \exists x \rangle \urcorner$ is classical first-order logic. Suppose we also define $\ulcorner E(x) \urcorner$ as $\ulcorner (\exists y) \; y = x \urcorner$ and $\ulcorner x \equiv y \urcorner$ as $\ulcorner \Diamond \; x = y \urcorner$ (or equivalently as $\ulcorner \Box(E(x) \rightarrow x = y) \urcorner$. Assuming the validity of principle (5.10) (the necessity of identity), the logic of $\ulcorner \langle \exists x \rangle \urcorner$ and $\ulcorner \equiv \urcorner$ includes all of classical first-order logic with identity. It includes more, however. Presumably, it is necessarily possible that there are two different objects, that there are three different objects, and so on, so the following principles should be valid:

$$\langle \exists x \rangle \langle \exists y \rangle \; x \neq y$$
$$\langle \exists x \rangle \langle \exists y \rangle \langle \exists z \rangle [x \neq y \; \& \; x \neq y \; \& \; y \neq z].$$

But these are not theorems of classical first-order logic.

It is worth noting that if we take $\ulcorner \langle \exists x \rangle \urcorner$, $\ulcorner E(x) \urcorner$, and $\ulcorner \equiv \urcorner$ as primitive, we can define our ordinary operators in terms of them:

$$\ulcorner (\exists x) P \urcorner = \ulcorner \langle \exists x \rangle (E(x) \; \& \; P) \urcorner$$
$$\ulcorner x = y \urcorner = \ulcorner E(x) \; \& \; x \equiv y \urcorner.$$

Possibilistic quantifiers and "reference" to possible objects can proceed just like existential quantifiers and reference to actual objects. If we know that $\ulcorner \langle \exists x \rangle \langle \forall y \rangle (Fy \leftrightarrow y \equiv x) \urcorner$ is true, then we know that "there is exactly one possible object that is F", and we can use this to introduce a singular term "denoting" that possible object. For example, we could contextually introduce sharp-bracket definite descriptions $\ulcorner \langle \iota x \rangle Fx \urcorner$ a la Russell using possibilistic quantifiers. An example of this is due to Gary Rosenkrantz, who considers a factory in which objects are manufactured out of parts. We might have tables manufactured out of table tops and pedestals. Consider a particular table top X and pedestal Y that are never actually joined to form a table (each becomes part of a different table). Nevertheless, it seems that at every possible world in which they are joined, the same table results. Thus, there is a unique possible table resulting from their being joined, and we could refer to it by using the term $\ulcorner \langle \imath t \rangle$ t results from joining X and $Y \urcorner$. Of course, it could reasonably be objected that this is not actually reference or denotation because a term cannot denote something that does not exist, but that strikes me as a verbal quibble. We can call it '⟨denoting⟩' if that makes people feel better.

In sum, I think it must be concluded that actualism, taken as the claim that no sense can be made of quantification over possible objects, is false.

7. Possibilistic Set Theory

The legitimacy of quantification over possible objects is interesting. What is of even more interest is that possibilistic quantifiers allow us to talk about *sets* of nonexistent but possible objects. In this connection, let us begin by noting that there is a fairly compelling argument purporting to show that a set cannot exist if its members do not exist.[35] Let X be a set of actual objects and suppose $x \in X$. Let w be a world at which x does not exist. Suppose X exists at w. Then

$$(\forall y)(y \in X \leftrightarrow y \in (X - \{x\}))$$

is true at w. We would like to conclude from this, by the axiom of extensionality, that $\ulcorner X = X - \{x\} \urcorner$ is true at w. For this purpose we must formulate the axiom of extensionality as:

(7.1) $\square(\forall X)(\forall Y)\{(Set(X) \ \& \ Set(Y)) \rightarrow [X = Y \leftrightarrow (\forall z)(z \in X \leftrightarrow z \in Y)]\}$.

Using (7.1), we cannot yet conclude that $\ulcorner X = X - \{x\} \urcorner$ is true at w unless we know not only that X exists at w, but also that X is a set at w. This follows from the apparently true assumption:

(7.2) $\square(\forall X)[Set(X) \rightarrow \square(E(X) \rightarrow Set(X))]$.

Given (7.1) and (7.2), we can conclude that $\ulcorner X = X - \{x\} \urcorner$ is true at w. But then by (5.10) (the necessity of identity), we

---

[35] This argument is based upon an argument given by Plantinga [1976].

obtain the conclusion that $\ulcorner X = X - \{x\} \urcorner$ is true at the actual world. Consequently, the assumption that X exists at w is false. What we have proven is:

(7.3) $\Box(\forall X)(\forall x)[(Set(X) \ \& \ x \in X) \rightarrow \Box(E(X) \rightarrow E(x))]$.

It follows from (7.3) that we cannot literally have sets of non-existent objects. But we can achieve the *effect* of sets of non-existent objects using possibilistic quantifiers. Sets of *possible objects* can be regarded as *possible sets* of objects, i.e., sets that actually exist at other worlds (worlds at which their members exist). For this purpose, let us define:

(7.4) $\ulcorner \langle Set \rangle (X) \urcorner = \ulcorner \Box(E(X) \rightarrow Set(X)) \urcorner$

(7.5) $\ulcorner x \langle \in \rangle X \urcorner = \ulcorner \Box(E(X) \rightarrow x \in X) \urcorner$.

Then through the use of possibilistic quantifiers we can achieve the effect of talk about sets of possible objects. For example, 'There is a set consisting of two possible unicorns' is translated as

(7.6) $\langle \exists X \rangle (\langle Set \rangle (X) \ \& \ \langle \exists y \rangle \langle \exists z \rangle [y \ne z \ \& \ \Diamond U(y) \ \& \ \Diamond U(z) \ \& \ \langle \forall w \rangle (w \langle \in \rangle X \leftrightarrow (w \equiv y \Diamond w \equiv z))])$,

which is presumably true.

It is of interest to ask what principles are true of possible sets. Let us begin by assuming that Zermelo-Fraenkel set theory holds for actual sets. More accurately, consider the following standard set-theoretic axioms:

(7.7) *Extensionality*: $(\forall X)(\forall Y)\{(Set(X) \ \& \ Set(Y)) \rightarrow [X = Y \leftrightarrow (\forall z)(z \in X \leftrightarrow z \in Y)]\}$.

(7.8) *Union*: $(\forall X)(Set(X) \rightarrow (\exists Y)(\forall z)[z \in Y \leftrightarrow (\exists W)(z \in W \ \& \ W \in X)])$.

(7.9) *Power Set*: $(\forall X)[Set(X) \rightarrow (\exists Y)(\forall z)(z \in Y \leftrightarrow z \subseteq X)$.

(7.10) *Pair*: $(\forall x)(\forall y)(\exists Z)(\forall w)[w \in Z \leftrightarrow (w = x \lor w = y)]$.

(7.11) *Infinity*: $(\exists X)[\emptyset \in X \ \& \ (\forall Y)(Y \in X \rightarrow Y \cup \{Y\} \in X)]$.

(7.12) *Regularity*: $(\forall X)((\exists y)y \in X \rightarrow (\exists y)[y \in X \ \& \ X \cap y = \emptyset])$.

(7.13) *Set*: $(\forall X)[(\exists y)y \in X \rightarrow Set(X)]$.

(7.14) *Separation*: If Fy is a formula in which y occurs free but X and Y do not, then the following is an axiom: $(\forall X)(\exists Y)[Set(Y) \ \& \ (\forall x)(z \in Y \leftrightarrow (z \in X \ \& \ Fy))]$.

(7.15) *Replacement*: If Fxy is a formula in which x and y occur free but X and Y do not, then the following is an axiom: $(\forall X)(\text{if } (\forall x)(x \in X \rightarrow (\exists! y)Fxy)$ then $(\exists Y)[Set(Y) \ \& \ (\forall y)(y \in Y \leftrightarrow (\exists x)(x \in X \ \& \ Fxy))])$.[36]

I assume that (7.7)–(7.15) are necessarily true. (7.7)–(7.14) constitute a version of Zermelo set theory. (7.7)–(7.9), (7.11)–(7.13), and (7.15) constitute a version of Zermelo-Fraenkel set theory, which includes all of Zermelo set theory.

We can transcribe the preceding axioms into axioms regarding possible sets. Assuming (7.1), (7.2), and (7.8)–(7.15), the following can be established without further assumptions:

(7.16) *Extensionality*: $\langle\forall X\rangle\langle\forall Y\rangle\{(\langle Set\rangle(X) \ \& \ \langle Set\rangle(Y)) \rightarrow [X \equiv Y \leftrightarrow \langle\forall z\rangle(z\langle\in\rangle X \leftrightarrow z\langle\in\rangle Y)]\}$.

(7.17) *Union*: $\langle\forall X\rangle(\langle Set\rangle(X) \rightarrow \langle\exists Y\rangle\langle\forall z\rangle[z\langle\in\rangle Y \leftrightarrow \langle\exists W\rangle(z\langle\in\rangle W \ \& \ W\langle\in\rangle X)])$.

(7.18) *Power Set*: $\langle\forall X\rangle(\langle Set\rangle(X) \rightarrow \langle\exists Y\rangle\langle\forall z\rangle[z\langle\in\rangle Y \leftrightarrow \langle\forall w\rangle(w\langle\in\rangle z \rightarrow w\langle\in\rangle X)])$.

(7.19) *Infinity*: $\langle\exists X\rangle[\varnothing\langle\in\rangle X \ \& \ \langle\forall Y\rangle(Y\langle\in\rangle X \rightarrow Y_\cup\{Y\}\langle\in\rangle X)]$

(7.20) *Set*: $\langle\forall X\rangle[\langle\exists y\rangle y\langle\in\rangle X \rightarrow \langle Set\rangle(X)]$.

The formula $\ulcorner Fy \urcorner$ in the axiom scheme of separation (principle (7.14)) is required to be a formula of first-order set theory. The analogue of (7.14) for possible sets will allow $\ulcorner Fy \urcorner$ to contain possibilistic quantifiers, modal operators, and so forth. Accordingly, we cannot derive that analogue from our present assumptions. However, (7.14) presumably holds only because a stronger (essentially second-order) principle holds:

---

[36] $\ulcorner(\exists! y)Fxy\urcorner$ means $\ulcorner$there is a unique y such that $Fxy\urcorner$.

(7.21) *Strong Separation*: If α is any monadic concept then the following is necessarily true: $(\forall X)(\exists Y)[Set(Y)$ & $(\forall z)(z \in Y \leftrightarrow (z \in X$ & z exemplifies $\alpha))]$.

Given (7.21) we can immediately establish:

(7.22) *Strong Separation*: If α is any monadic concept then the following is necessarily true: $\langle\forall X\rangle\langle\exists Y\rangle[\langle Set\rangle(Y)$ & $\langle\forall z\rangle(z\langle\in\rangle Y \leftrightarrow (z\langle\in\rangle X$ & z exemplifies $\alpha))]$.

The only axioms remaining to be established are the pair axiom and the axiom scheme of replacement. The pair axiom is as follows:

(7.23) *Pair*: $\langle\forall x\rangle\langle\forall y\rangle\langle\exists Z\rangle\langle\forall u\rangle[u\langle\in\rangle Z \leftrightarrow (u \equiv x \lor u \equiv y)]$.

Given our other assumptions, (7.23) is equivalent to the assumption that if a possible object x exists at a world w, and another possible object y exists at a world w^*, then there is a world at which both x and y exist. Given the latter assumption, it follows from (7.10) that there is such a possible set as $\{x,y\}$. Conversely, given (7.23), there must be a world at which $\{x,y\}$ exists, and that must be a world at which x and y both exist. This seems like a safe assumption, so I conclude that (7.23) is true.

As in the case of separation, if we are to derive the axiom scheme of replacement for possible sets from our assumptions about actual sets, we must replace (7.15) with a stronger second-order principle:

(7.24) *Strong Replacement*: If α is any binary concept then the following is necessarily true: $(\forall X)($if $(\forall x)(x \in X$ $\rightarrow (\exists! y)\langle x,y\rangle$ exemplifies $\alpha)$ then $(\exists Y)[Set(Y)$ & $(\forall y)(y \in Y \leftrightarrow (\exists x)(x \in X$ & $\langle x,y\rangle$ exemplifies $\alpha))])$.

The possibilistic analogue of (7.24) is:

(7.25) *Strong Replacement*: If α is any binary concept then the following is necessarily true: $\langle\forall X\rangle($if $\langle\forall x\rangle(x\langle\in\rangle X$ $\rightarrow \langle\exists! y\rangle\langle x,y\rangle$ exemplifies $\alpha)$ then $\langle\exists Y\rangle[\langle Set\rangle(Y)$ & $\langle\forall y\rangle(y\langle\in\rangle Y \leftrightarrow \langle\exists x\rangle(x\langle\in\rangle X$ & $\langle x,y\rangle$ exemplifies $\alpha))])$.

Somewhat surprisingly, given two apparently innocuous assumptions, (7.25) is equivalent to the following very strong assumption about possible worlds:

(7.26) Given any set W of possible worlds, there is a possible world w such that anything existing at any of the members of W exists at w.[37]

To derive (7.25) from (7.26) we need the assumption that for any possible object x, there exists the set of all possible worlds at which x exists. Given this assumption, we can reason as follows. Suppose X is a possible set satisfying the antecedent of (7.25). Let w be a world at which X exists. Then at w we have:

$(\forall x)[x \in X \rightarrow (\exists! Y)(\exists y)(\langle x, y \rangle$ exemplifies α & Y is the set of all possible worlds at which y exists].

In other words, α restricted to X is a function, and Y is the set of all possible worlds at which $\alpha(x)$ exists. For each x in X, let $\beta(x)$ be this unique Y. Then by (7.24), $\{\beta(x) | x \in X\}$ exists at w. If $W = \{x\} \cup \cup\{\beta(x) | x \in X\}$, then W is a set of possible worlds such that for each x in X, $\alpha(x)$ exists in some member of W. By (7.26), there is a world w^* in which anything existing in any of the members of w exists. Thus for each x in X, both x and $\alpha(x)$ exist in w^*. It follows from (7.24) that $\{y | \langle \exists x \rangle(\langle x, y \rangle$ exemplifies α and $x \langle \in \rangle X)\}$ exists in w^* and hence is a possible set in the actual world. This establishes (7.25).

Conversely, in order to derive (7.26) from (7.25), we require a rather complicated assumption. The assumption has two parts. First, I assume that there is a kind of "basic" object (roughly, "concrete objects") such that if all the basic objects existing in a world w also exist in another world w^*, then every object existing in w exists in w^*. For example, if all the basic objects of w exist in w^*, then all sets of basic objects existing in w also exist in w^*. The second part of the as-

---

[37] Of course, the quantification in this principle is to be understood as possibilistic quantification.

sumption is that for each possible world w, there is a possible set $D(w)$ (the *domain* of w) whose members are all the possible basic objects existing in w. We can then reason as follows. Let W be a set of possible worlds. We are assuming that possible worlds exist necessarily, so W exists at the actual world. We have $(\forall w)(w \in W \rightarrow \langle \exists! D \rangle$ D is the domain of w), so by (7.25) there is a possible set Y whose members are just the domains of the members of W. By (7.17), there is such a possible set as $\cup Y$, which is a possible set consisting of every basic object existing in any member of W. To say that $\cup Y$ is a possible set is to say that there is a world w at which it is an actual set, i.e., at which all of its members exist. w is then a world such that every basic object existing in any of the members of W exists in w. But then it follows from our assumption that everything existing in any of the members of W exists in w.

Having seen that (7.25) is equivalent to (7.26), what can we conclude about the truth of (7.25)? (7.25) must be regarded as problematic, because (7.26) is problematic. (7.26) implies that if there is a set of all possible worlds then there is a world at which all possible objects exist. It is normally assumed that there is a set of all possible worlds, but the conclusion that there is a world at which all possible objects exist is extremely implausible. To the contrary, I would suppose that the following is a necessary truth:

$$\Diamond (\exists x) \sim \mathbf{A} \ x \text{ exists.}$$

Thus, we must either reject (7.25) and (7.26) or reject the assumption that there is a set of all possible worlds. I feel some temptation to reject the latter assumption on the grounds that a set of all possible worlds would be a "very large" set of the sort we know to cause trouble in connection with the set-theoretic antinomies.[38] But the situation is far from clear. Without further argument, we cannot assume (7.25), and hence

---

[38] Fortunately, this assumption is not needed for most of the purposes of philosophical semantics.

we do not have all of Zermelo-Fraenkel set theory for possible sets. We can, however, safely assume that we have all of Zermelo set theory.

Within axiomatic set theory, the failure of the axiom scheme of replacement would be a disaster. It plays an essential role in the development of ordinal number theory, which in turn is fundamental to most of the interesting parts of set theory. But this is not a problem for possibilistic set theory. Presumably, sets of ordinal numbers have necessary existence. That would seem to hold for all sets built exclusively from objects themselves having necessary existence.[39] We can actually prove this from our set-theoretic axioms if we assume the following principle:

(7.27) $\Box(\forall X)\{[Set(X)$ & $(\forall y)(y \in X \rightarrow y$ exists at $w)] \rightarrow X$ exists at $w\}$.

This implies that sets of necessarily existing objects exist necessarily:

(7.28) $\Box(\forall X)([Set(X)$ & $(\forall y)(y \in X \rightarrow \Box E(y))] \rightarrow \Box E(X))$.

Given (7.28), it follows by transfinite induction on the rank of a set that all sets built exclusively from necessarily existing objects have necessary existence. Thus, all of "pure" set theory is going to hold in every possible world. It is only when we turn to sets built in part from contingently existing objects that the axiom scheme of replacement will fail for possibilistic set theory, and that will be a very minor failing. When we apply set theory to sets of concrete objects, we rarely use very powerful principles. We can get along quite nicely without applying the axiom scheme of replacement to contingently existing sets.

My conclusion is that there are no serious obstacles to talking about sets of possible objects and manipulating them in familiar set-theoretic ways. At least in all mundane respects, they work exactly like sets of actual objects.

---

[39] More accurately, it would seem to hold for all sets whose transitive closures contain only objects having necessary existence.

8. Existentialism

I have assumed in a number of places that states of affairs and possible worlds exist necessarily. That might reasonably be doubted, however. If we consider a state of affairs like *Keith's winking at a pretty girl*, it might seem that this state of affairs would not exist if Keith did not exist. It would follow that a possible world does not exist if any of the objects in it fail to exist. Plantinga calls this thesis *existentialism*, and rejects it.[40] We can formulate existentialism precisely as follows:

(8.1) *Existentialism*: For any state of affairs S, if $[x_1,\ldots,x_n|\alpha] \subset S$ then, necessarily, S does not exist if any of $x_1,\ldots,x_n$ fail to exist.

At one time, I was convinced that existentialism was true, but I have recently become convinced that Plantinga is right and existentialism is false.[41]

States of affairs "involve" objects in them. For example, *Socrates' being snubnosed* involves Socrates in a special way. Advocates of existentialism feel that Socrates is a "constituent" of this state of affairs in much the same way that members of a set are constituents of the set, and accordingly they feel that the state of affairs cannot exist without Socrates existing. More generally, any state of affairs containing *Socrates' being snubnosed* will fail to exist if Socrates does not exist. Ultimately, the defense of existentialism comes down to this intuition.[42] Plantinga's response is to object that the notion of a constituent is too vague and unclear to be of much use here. It must be admitted that there is a certain amount of justice to this charge. But it must also be admitted that the

[40] See Plantinga [1979] and [1983].

[41] My conversion has been a slow one. Originally, I thought that existentialism was true. Then in Pollock [1984] I maintained that the question was a peculiar one not admitting of a determinate 'yes' or 'no' answer. Now I think it is false.

[42] See, for example, R. M. Adams [1981] and Alan McMichael [1983]. In interpreting the latter, note that he conflates what are here called 'actualism' and 'existentialism'.

existentialist intuition is a fairly compelling one. The issue has proven to be a very difficult one to resolve.[43]

I now feel, however, that a precise argument can be given establishing that the existentialist intuition is subtly incoherent and existentialism is inconsistent. The argument turns upon the observation that if existentialism is correct then there is a distinction between a possible world's obtaining and its being actual. The distinction arises as follows. Possible worlds are states of affairs. Thus, if existentialism is correct and states of affairs do not exist when their constituent objects do not exist, then neither do possible worlds. Consider a possible world w containing *Socrates' not existing*. Socrates is a constituent of w, so if w obtains then w does not exist. For this reason, if w obtained then w would not be the actual world. In fact, w would not be a world at all, i.e.,

$\Box$[if w obtains then $\sim(\exists w^*)(w^*$ is a possible world and $w^* = w)$].

We established principle (3.14) according to which it is necessarily true that there is a possible world that is actual, i.e.,

$\Box(\exists w^*)(w^*$ is a possible world and w^* obtains).

Consequently, if w obtained then there would be a state of affairs w^* distinct from w that would then be a possible world and would obtain and hence be the actual world. If w^* contained either *Socrates' existing* or *Socrates' not existing*, then contrary to supposition, it would not exist if w obtained. It follows that w^* is not a maximal state of affairs relative to the set of all states of affairs now existing, and hence w^* is not now a possible world. On the other hand, if w^* obtained then w^* would be maximal because *Socrates' not existing* would not exist. Most possible worlds (i.e., most things that are possible worlds at the actual world) either require that some currently existing objects do not exist or that some additional ob-

[43] Plantinga [1983] gives an argument intended to refute existentialism, but I have responded to it in Pollock [1984], maintaining that it begs the question.

III. Possible Worlds

jects do exist, in which case it follows from existentialism that if they obtained, they would not be possible worlds and hence would not be actual.

Existentialism is thus committed to there being a distinction between a world obtaining and its being actual. But as I will now show, that distinction leads to an inconsistency. Let S be *Socrates' not existing*. As S is possible, it follows by (3.14) that there is a world w at which S obtains, i.e., $S \subset w$. If w obtained then Socrates would not exist and hence, according to existentialism, neither w nor S would exist. It is a necessary truth that there is an actual world (by (3.14) it is the infinite conjunction of all (existing) states of affairs that actually obtain), so if w obtained then there *would be* a world w^* (which is not now a world) that would exist and obtain. w^* would be the actual world if w obtained. As w^* would exist if w obtained, it must not be the case that $S \subset w^*$. As w^* would be a possible world, it would be maximal with respect to the states of affairs then existing, but as we have seen, that does not require w^* to contain either S or $\sim S$ because neither of these states of affairs would exist. However, because it would be maximal, w^* would have to contain an "enumerative" state of affairs **E** listing all of the contingent objects existing at w^*. **E** would be a state of affairs of the form ⌜*X's being the set of all contingent objects*⌝. As Socrates is not among the contingent objects existing at w^*, **E**, and hence also w^*, is necessarily such that if it obtains then Socrates does not exist. But that means, by definition, that $S \subset w^*$. Thus, existentialism requires that S both is and is not contained in w^*. Therefore, existentialism is inconsistent.

What the preceding argument actually shows is that the existentialist intuition is incoherent. We cannot simultaneously allow that states of affairs contain objects in some literal sense that makes their existence dependent upon the existence of those objects, and also agree that a necessary and sufficient condition for $x's$ *being F* to obtain is that x is F. The latter requires that if F is such that an object is automatically F if it does not exist, then $x's$ *being F* is contained in worlds at which x does not exist, and that in turn requires those worlds

100

both to exist and not exist. Thus I take existentialism to be definitively refuted.

The failure of existentialism does not by itself imply that states of affairs and possible worlds have necessary existence. As formulated in (8.1), existentialism only concerns one way in which states of affairs and possible worlds might fail to exist, namely, by containing as constituents objects that fail to exist. But I take it this is the only plausible way in which states of affairs and possible worlds might have only contingent existence. Consequently, I will assume henceforth that states of affairs and possible worlds do have necessary existence. Among other things, it follows that the defense of S5 given in section four is unproblematic.

Having argued *that* states of affairs have necessary existence, we might still wonder *why* that is the case. Why should states of affairs that are in some sense built out of contingent objects, nevertheless have necessary existence? Some light can be thrown on this by considering some much more general questions. Philosophers have been perennially divided on their view of the status of abstract entities. In one camp we have the nominalists who eschew talk of abstract entities on the grounds that we do not perceive numbers, sets, etc., and hence have no way of knowing anything about them. The nominalist concludes that talk about abstract entities must be nonsensical. In the other camp we have the Platonists who insist that we all know many truths about abstract entities (e.g., we know that there is a number between 1 and 3), and hence we must have some way of "perceiving" facts about abstract entities.[44] If forced to classify myself, I would call myself a "nominalistic Platonist". It seems to me that both the nominalists and the Platonists have things partly right. The Platonist is surely right that we have knowledge about abstract entities. It cannot reasonably be denied, for example, that we know that there is a number between 1 and 3. This has led some Platonists to talk about a mystical "perception' of universals, but the nominalist is surely right that we do not *per-*

---

[44] No doubt this oversimplifies the actual dispute, but so be it.

ceive abstract entities. As we do have knowledge of abstract entities and it is not derived from perception of abstract entities, it must be derived from knowledge we have that is not of abstract entities. Accordingly, there must be logical connections between propositions about abstract entities and other propositions enabling knowledge of the former to be based upon knowledge of the latter. The search for such logical connections is apt to seem hopeless until it is realized that among our knowledge of nonabstract entities is modal knowledge. For example, I know not only that all bachelors are unmarried but also that it is necessary that all bachelors are unmarried. The latter *can* be construed as knowledge about a proposition, but surely it can also be construed as knowledge about bachelors. One can learn that it is necessary that all bachelors are unmarried before one learns anything about propositions.[45] Such modal knowledge provides the grounds upon which we come to have knowledge of abstract entities. For example, we come to know that there is a number between 1 and 3 by learning modal truths of the form ⌜It is possible for it to be the case that there is more than one *F* but there are less than three *F*'s⌝, where the latter is a proposition of the form

$$\Diamond[(\exists x)(\exists y)(Fx \ \& \ Fy \ \& \ x \neq y) \ \& \ \sim(\exists x)(\exists y)(\exists z)(Fx \ \& \ Fy \ \& \ Fz \ \& \ x \neq y \ \& \ x \neq z \ \& \ y \neq z)].$$

Such logical connections do not "tell us what numbers are" (it is unclear what could possibly count as doing that), but they do tell us what it is for there *to be* numbers of various sorts.

I am convinced on the basis of epistemological considerations of the preceding sort that all talk of abstract entities must be analyzable in terms of (possibly modal) talk of nonabstract entities.[46] Given such analyses, some philosophers will want to conclude that we have shown that there really are no ab-

[45] For an epistemological investigation of such knowledge, see Chapter Ten of Pollock [1974].

[46] Such analyses might not be truth-condition analyses. They might instead proceed in terms of justification conditions, as in Pollock [1974].

stract entities—we will have "analyzed them away". This will be accompanied by grandiose talk of Occam's Razor and the Principle of Parsimony. But such a conclusion is ridiculous. The analyses will tell us what it means to say that there are numbers and other kinds of abstract entities, and so rather than showing that there are none, the analyses will explain why it is true that there are. It is just *true* that there are numbers (e.g., there is a number between 1 and 3), and no amount of logical analysis is going to make that fact go away. All the analyses can do is explain why the fact is a fact.

My thesis is then that given rather liberal resources for analysis, all talk of abstract entities must be analyzable in terms of talk of nonabstract entities. This is a highly programmatic thesis and as such should be viewed with considerable suspicion. One case in which the program can be carried out with relative ease, however, is the case of states of affairs and possible worlds,[47] and the nature of the analysis throws considerable light on why states of affairs have necessary existence.

Recall that elementary states of affairs are those of the form $[x_1,\ldots,x_n|\alpha]$ where $x_1,\ldots,x_n$ are objects and α is a concept, and also those of the form $[\varnothing|\varphi]$ where φ is a proposition. Corresponding to $[x_1,\ldots,x_n|\alpha]$ is the ordered pair $\langle\langle x_1,\ldots,x_n\rangle,\alpha\rangle$, and corresponding to $[\varnothing|\varphi]$ is the ordered pair $\langle\varnothing,\varphi\rangle$. In general, taking a zero-tuple to be the empty set, a zero-place relation to be a proposition, and a nontransient concept to be one that if ever exemplified by an object is always exemplified by that object, let us define a *proto-state* to be an ordered pair $\langle\sigma,\alpha\rangle$ where for some $n \leq 0$, σ is an n-tuple and α is an n-place nontransient concept. It should be emphasized that I am not suggesting that $[\sigma|\alpha]$ is the same thing as $\langle\sigma,\alpha\rangle$. All I am doing is constructing set-theoretic entities corresponding to elementary states of affairs. Let us say that $\langle\sigma,\alpha\rangle$ *obtains* iff σ exemplifies α (or if $\sigma = \varnothing$, iff the proposition α is true).

Proto-states correspond to elementary states of affairs, but

---

[47] This will not analyze talk of states of affairs all the way down to talk of nonabstract entities. It proceeds in terms of properties and propositions, the assumption being that some further analysis is possible for the latter.

nonelementary states of affairs can be constructed by forming (possibly infinite) disjunctions, conjunctions, negations, etc. of elementary states of affairs. Set-theoretic surrogates for these complex states of affairs can be constructed by proceeding as follows. We first define:

(8.2) If $\langle\sigma,\alpha\rangle$ is a proto-state then $\sim\langle\sigma,\alpha\rangle = \langle\sigma,\sim\alpha\rangle$.

Then we let sets of proto-states represent conjunctions of proto-states, and we call such sets 'meso-states':

(8.3) S is a *meso-state* iff S is a set of proto-states. *S obtains* iff all of its members obtain.

Finally, we let sets of meso-states represent disjunctions of meso-states, and we call these 'ur-states':

(8.4) S is an *ur-state* iff S is a set of meso-states. *S obtains* iff at least one of its members obtains.

This construction guarantees the existence of conjunctions, disjunctions, and negations of ur-states. If S and S^* are ur-states, $S \vee S^*$ is $S \cup S^*$. More generally, if X is a set of ur-states then $\vee X = \cup X$. Negations are defined as follows. Where X is a meso-state, let $\text{Neg}(X) = \{\sim s \mid s \in X\}$. Then if S is an ur-state:

(8.5) $\sim S = \{\text{Neg}(X) \mid X$ is a set consisting of one element of each member of $S\}$.

The rationale for this definition is that if X is a set of sets of states of affairs, then:

$\sim\vee\{\wedge Y \mid Y \in X\} = \vee\{\text{Neg}(Y) \mid Y$ is a set consisting of one element of each member of $X\}$.

For example:

$\sim\vee\{\wedge\{S_1,S_2\},\vee\{S_3,S_4\}\}$
$= \sim[(S_1 \And S_2) \vee (S_3 \And S_4)]$
$= (\sim S_1 \vee \sim S_2) \And (\sim S_3 \vee \sim S_4)$
$= (\sim S_1 \And \sim S_3) \vee (\sim S_1 \And \sim S_4) \vee (\sim S_2 \And \sim S_3) \vee (\sim S_2 \And \sim S_4)$.

We then obtain other truth functions in the normal way: for example $S\&S^* = \sim(\sim S_\vee \sim S^*)$. More generally, if X is a set of ur-states then $\bigwedge X = \sim\bigvee\{\sim S|\ S\in X\}$.

We define the containment relation between proto-, meso-, or ur-states in the expected way:

(8.6) $S < S^*$ iff S and S^* are necessarily such that if S^* obtains then S obtains.

Two ur-states are *equivalent* iff each contains the other. I will use '$\Longleftrightarrow$' to symbolize equivalence between ur-states.

We can also talk about an ur-state being equivalent to a proto-state or meso-state as follows:

(8.7) If S is a proto-state, meso-state, or ur-state, and S^* is a proto-state, meso-state, or ur-state, then S is *equivalent to* S^* iff S and S^* are necessarily such that one obtains iff the other obtains.

This has the result, for example, that if S is a proto-state then both $\{S\}$ and $\{\{S\}\}$ are equivalent to S. This correspondence between proto-states, meso-states, and ur-states is not unique, however. S is also equivalent to $\{\{S,S^*\},\{S,\sim S^*\}\}$.

We can define meso-worlds and ur-worlds on strict analogy to our earlier definition of 'possible world':

(8.8) w is a meso-world (or ur-world) iff w is a meso-state (or ur-state) that is possibly such that it obtains and for every meso-state (or ur-state) S, if $(w\&S)$ is possibly such that it obtains then $S < w$.

This has the result that if w is a meso-world then $\{w\}$ is an equivalent ur-world. Not every ur-world is a unit set of a meso-world, but it is true that every ur-world is equivalent to a meso-world.[48] We can also define:

(8.9) If S is an ur-state and w is an ur-world, S *obtains at w* iff $S < w$.

---

[48] This construction of ur-states and ur-worlds improves upon the construction given in Pollock [1984].

Ur-states and ur-worlds can be regarded as set-theoretic surrogates for states of affairs and possible worlds, in the following sense:

(8.10) If S is a state of affairs and s is an ur-state, s is a *surrogate of S* iff S and s are necessarily such that one obtains iff the other obtains.

My suggestion is now that we can analyze talk of states of affairs and possible worlds in terms of ur-states and ur-worlds. The simplest proposal for such an analysis would be one that translates directly from talk of states of affairs to talk of ur-states, replacing quantification over states of affairs by quantification over ur-states, replacing talk of states of affairs obtaining by talk of their surrogates obtaining, and so on. Because a state of affairs can have more than one surrogate, identity between states of affairs must be translated by the equivalence relation '$\Longleftrightarrow$' rather than by identity between ur-states. It should be emphasized that this analysis does not identify states of affairs with ur-states. Rather, it proposes to analyze talk of the former in terms of talk of the latter. The analysis would not (and would not be intended to) tell us "what states of affairs are". That strikes me as a nonsensical enterprise. Rather, this would be an analysis of talk of states of affairs in the same sense as the analysis of number theory in terms of higher-order logic is an analysis of talk about numbers. The analysis would tell us what it is for there to be states of affairs of certain sorts, but not what states of affairs are.

In Pollock [1984] this simple analysis that translates talk of states of affairs directly into talk of ur-states was called the *existentialist analysis* because I thought it made existentialism true. It appears to make existentialism true because ur-states really do contain objects as literal constituents in a set-theoretic sense and hence do not exist when those objects fail to exist. But the analysis does not live up to its initial promise. It leads us directly into problems associated with the above proof that existentialism is inconsistent. Let **S** be the ur-state *Socrates' not existing*, and let w be an ur-world containing **S**. If the existentialist analysis really made existentialism true, it would follow that if *w* obtained it would not exist, so there would exist an ur-world *w** (which is not now an ur-world) that would both exist and obtain. Our earlier argument shows that **S** would obtain at *w**. But this implies that **S** is contained in *w**. Consequently, existentialism would require that *w** not exist if *w* obtained. That is where the contradiction arises. The proposed "existentialist analysis" does not actually have the consequence that *w** would not exist, so it does not make existentialism true. Of course, it *could not* have this consequence, because if it did it would be inconsistent.

The upshot of this is that the existentialist analysis is not a satisfactory analysis on any count. It cannot be possible to give an analysis of talk of states of affairs in terms of ur-states in such a way as to make existentialism true, because existentialism is inconsistent. But the existentialist analysis is not satisfactory as a nonexistentialist analysis either, because it endows states of affairs with highly contingent existence. Although it is not defensible in its own right, the existentialist analysis suggests an alternative analysis having the result that states of affairs and possible worlds exist necessarily. This analysis differs from the existentialist analysis primarily by translating existential quantifiers over states of affairs in terms of possibilistic quantifiers over ur-states. Like the existentialist analysis, it translates '=' as '$\Longleftrightarrow$'. According to this analysis, to say that there is a state of affairs satisfying a certain condition is just to say that it is possible for there to be an ur-state that actually satisfies the corresponding condition (the corresponding condition being what we get when we translate the condition regarding states of affairs into talk of ur-states). This has the effect that all existential claims about states of affairs are either necessarily true or necessarily false, and hence states of affairs do not have contingent existence. For example, $\ulcorner$*x's being* α *exists*$\urcorner$ is transcribed as $\ulcorner(\exists S)S = [x|\alpha]\urcorner$ and then analyzed as $\ulcorner\langle\exists S\rangle\ S \Longleftrightarrow \{x|\alpha\}\urcorner$. The latter is, by definition:

(8.11) $\Diamond(\exists S)\mathbf{A}\ S \Longleftrightarrow \{x|\alpha\}$.

(8.11) can be proven as follows. $\{x|\alpha\}$ exists, so:

(8.12) $\Diamond(\{x|\alpha\}$ exists).

III. Possible Worlds

Then by S5

(8.13) $\Box\Diamond(\{x|\alpha\}$ exists).

The following is a necessary truth:

(8.14) $\{x|\alpha\}$ obtains iff $\{x|\alpha\}$ obtains,

so it follows from S5 that it is necessarily necessary:

(8.15) $\Box\Box(\{x|\alpha\}$ obtains iff $\{x|\alpha\}$ obtains),

i.e.,

(8.16) $\Box(\{x|\alpha\} \Longleftrightarrow \{x|\alpha\})$.

Consequently:

(8.17) $\Box_1\mathbf{A}_1(\{x|\alpha\} \Longleftrightarrow \{x|\alpha\})$.

Thus, by S5, (8.13) is equivalent to:

(8.18) $\Box_1\Diamond[\{x|\alpha\}$ exists & $\mathbf{A}_1(\{x|\alpha\} \Longleftrightarrow \{x|\alpha\})]$.

This entails:

(8.19) $\Box_1\Diamond(\exists S)\mathbf{A}_1\ S \Longleftrightarrow \{x|\alpha\}$.

In other words, (8.11) is a necessary truth, so $[x|\alpha]$ exists necessarily. Similar reasoning leads us to the general principle that states of affairs have necessary existence:

(8.20) $\Box(\forall S)\Box[S$ is a state of affairs $\rightarrow \Box(\exists S^*)\ S^* = S]$.

The point of this lengthy digression on the analysis of talk about states of affairs has been to explain why states of affairs and possible worlds have necessary existence. This cannot be regarded as a *proof* that they do, only an explanation for *why* they do, because in order to show that the analysis yields the result that states of affairs have necessary existence, we have had to assume S5. Our earlier defense of S5, however, turned upon states of affairs having necessary existence.

There is a further point to our digression. Our defense of *quantified* S5 (i.e., KS5) made the additional assumption that properties have necessary existence. That is demonstrably false given the construction of properties in section five. Nonqual-

108

itative properties were defined to be ordered pairs $\langle \mathbf{P}, \sigma \rangle$ where $\mathbf{P}$ is a qualitative property and σ is an assignment of objects to some of the argument places of $\mathbf{P}$. Such an ordered pair will fail to exist if any of the objects in the assignment fail to exist. At this point, it could reasonably be protested, however, that properties are not really identical to such ordered pairs; rather, the ordered pairs are set-theoretic surrogates for the properties in much the same sense as ur-states are surrogates for states of affairs. The analysis of talk of states of affairs in terms of talk of ur-states makes this plausible, because a similar analysis can be given for talk of properties. Suppose we call the ordered pairs $\langle \mathbf{P}, \sigma \rangle$ 'property surrogates'. Then the analysis will translate existential quantification over properties into possibilistic quantification over property surrogates. Just as for states of affairs, the result will be that properties have necessary existence. Furthermore, insofar as the analysis is plausible (and I think it is), this constitutes an argument *that* properties have necessary existence and not just an explanation for *why they might*. This is because we need only S5—not KS5—to show that this analysis endows properties with necessary existence, and the justification of S5 does not presuppose that properties have necessary existence. On this basis, I will henceforth assume that properties do have necessary existence and that the principles of KS5 are valid.

IV
Counterfactuals

If we confine our attention to modal logic, possible worlds do not live up to their initial promise. They do not provide a vehicle for the analysis of necessity, because a workable notion of a possible world presupposes logical necessity. Thus, despite the high esteem in which they are held, one might begin to wonder whether possible worlds are good for anything in philosophical logic. I think that they are of importance, but their primary importance lies outside modal logic. The three areas in which I have found them to be of most use are the analysis of counterfactual conditionals, the analysis of causation, and the theory of probability. The last area is beyond the scope of the present book, but the usefulness of possible worlds can be amply illustrated by looking to counterfactuals and causation. Counterfactuals will be investigated in this chapter, and causation in the next.

The original idea of analyzing counterfactuals in terms of possible worlds is attributable to Robert Stalnaker [1968]. The idea was developed further by David Lewis ([1973] and [1979]), and his theory is unquestionably the most popular contemporary theory of counterfactuals. The analysis I will defend here differs importantly from both of those theories.

1. Preliminaries

There are several different kinds of conditionals expressible in English that can be regarded as "subjunctive".[1] The conditional normally studied in investigations of counterfactuals

---

[1] For a general discussion of these conditionals, see Pollock [1975], and Chapter Two of Pollock [1976].

is what I have called *the simple subjunctive conditional*.[2] This will be symbolized as $\ulcorner P > Q \urcorner$. This conditional has the characteristic that it can be true for either of two reasons. First, $(P > Q)$ can be true because there is a connection between P and Q such that P's being true in some sense "requires" Q to be true. Second, $(P > Q)$ can be true because Q is already true and P's being true would not interfere with this. Many objections to the existing theories of counterfactuals turn upon confusing the simple subjunctive conditional with the *necessitation conditional* $(P >> Q)$, which is true just in case P's being true "requires" Q to be true. In many ways, the necessitation conditional is of more interest to philosophers than the simple subjunctive. But in logical investigations there is a good reason for focusing our attention on the simple subjunctive rather than the necessitation conditional, namely, the simple subjunctive has nice logical properties, while the necessitation conditional satisfies virtually no logical laws. For example, even such an elementary law as

if $P >> Q$ is true and Q entails R then $P >> R$ is true

fails for necessitation conditionals. To illustrate, it may be that pushing the button necessitates that the doorbell rings. That the doorbell rings entails that the doorbell exists. But it is false that pushing the doorbell necessitates that the doorbell exists; i.e., pushing the button in no way "requires" that the doorbell exist. So if we set about investigating the logic of necessitation conditionals, we will find that there isn't much of one.[3] Furthermore, I argued in Pollock [1976] that the necessitation conditional can be defined in terms of the simple subjunctive. $\ulcorner P >> Q \urcorner$ is definable as

$(P > Q) \ \& \ [(\sim P \ \& \sim Q) > (P > Q)].$

Consequently, a theory of simple subjunctives will automat-

---

[2] In particular, this is the conditional studied in Stalnaker [1968], Lewis [1973], and Pollock [1976].
[3] For more on this, see Pollock [1976], 33–38.

ically give us a theory of necessitation conditionals, and hence nothing is lost by focusing on simple subjunctives.

Two other conditionals of note are the 'might be' conditional and the 'even if' conditional. I follow Lewis [1973] in taking (at least some uses of) ⌜It might be true that Q if it were true that P⌝ to be expressible as ⌜$\sim(P > \sim Q)$⌝.[4] For example, suppose we have two lights A and B, both off, and these are controlled by switches A and B respectively. Then it is true that light A might be on if at least one of the switches were closed, because it is false that if at least one of the switches were closed then light A would be off. One of the lights would be on, but it is indeterminate which, so each *might* be on.

I argued in Pollock [1976] that ⌜Q would (still) be true even if P were true⌝ can be expressed as ⌜Q & $(P > Q)$⌝. For example, light A would still be off even if switch B were closed, because light A is off and would be off if switch B were closed.[5] Given the logic SS of simple subjunctive conditionals (which will be defended below), it follows that the simple subjunctive is a disjunction of 'even if' and necessitation conditionals, i.e., ⌜$P > Q$⌝ is equivalent to ⌜$(P >> Q) \lor [Q \,\&\, (P > Q)]$⌝.[6] This is in accordance with the intuitive explanation of simple subjunctives I gave in the beginning of this section.

'>' is normally regarded as an operator that when applied to propositions yields a conditional proposition and when applied to statements yields a conditional statement. It is convenient, however, to regard it more generally as an operator on states of affairs. If P and Q are states of affairs, $(P > Q)$ will be that state of affairs that obtains iff Q would obtain if P were to obtain. Given an account of '>' for states of affairs, we can generate an account of the truth conditions for simple subjunctive propositions and statements as follows:

If P and Q are either both propositions or both statements, then $(P > Q)$ is true iff $([\varnothing|P] > [\varnothing|Q])$ obtains.

---

[4] For a dissenting opinion, see Stalnaker [1981].

[5] For a dissenting opinion, see Bennett [1983].

[6] This is proven in Pollock [1976], 42.

If $(P > Q)$ obtains at a world w, I will say that Q is a *counterfactual consequence* of P at w. When w is the actual world, I will drop the reference to w.

Entailment is ordinarily understood to be a relation between propositions or statements, but one can also take it to be a relation between states of affairs. To say that one state of affairs P entails another Q is just to say that, necessarily, if P obtained then Q would obtain, i.e., $P \subset Q$. To say that a *set* X of states of affairs entails Q is just to say that $\bigwedge X$ entails Q.

For the purpose of writing logical principles regarding states of affairs, we must write things like

If $(P\&Q)$ obtains then P obtains.

We can streamline our notation by systematically abbreviating $\ulcorner P$ obtains$\urcorner$ as $\ulcorner P \urcorner$. This enables us to write the preceding principle more simply as

$(P\&Q) \rightarrow P$.

I will adopt this abbreviation throughout.

Given these preliminaries, I will present my analysis of counterfactuals in section two, and I will contrast it with David Lewis's familiar analysis in section three.

2. A Possible Worlds Analysis

A simple justification can be given for the general "possible worlds approach" to the analysis of counterfactuals. This turns upon the *generalized consequence principle* (GCP) according to which anything entailed by the set of counterfactual consequences of P is itself a counterfactual consequence of P:

(2.1) If X if a set of states of affairs each member of which would obtain if P obtained, and X entails Q, then $(P > Q)$ obtains.

I take GCP to be an intuitively obvious fact about counterfactuals. Now let us define:

(2.2) $\mathbf{M}_w(P) = \{w^* |\ w^*$ is a world at which all of the counterfactual consequences of P at w obtain$\}$.

Given GCP, the members of $\mathbf{M}_w(P)$ are the worlds that (from the point of view of w) might be actual if P were to obtain:

(2.3) $w^* \in \mathbf{M}_w(P)$ iff $\sim(P > \sim w^*)$ obtains at w.

Proof: If $\sim(P > \sim w^*)$ does not obtain at w, then $(P > \sim w^*)$ does obtain at w. Thus, $\sim w^*$ is a counterfactual consequence of P at w, but of course $\sim w^*$ does not obtain at w^*, so $w^* \notin \mathbf{M}_w(P)$. Conversely, suppose $w^* \notin \mathbf{M}_w(P)$. Then there is some Q such that $(P > Q)$ obtains at w but Q does not obtain at w^*. If Q does not obtain at w^*, then w^* entails $\sim Q$, and hence Q entails $\sim w^*$. As $(P > Q)$ obtains at w and Q entails $\sim w^*$, it follows from GCP that $(P > \sim w^*)$ obtains at w, and hence $\sim(P > \sim w^*)$ does not obtain at w.

We will refer to the members of $\mathbf{M}_w(P)$ more briefly as 'the nearest P-worlds'. Recalling that $\|Q\|$ is the set of all Q-worlds, i.e., the set of all possible worlds at which Q obtains, the following theorem is easily proven:

(2.4) If GCP holds, then for any world w, $(P > Q)$ obtains at w iff Q is true at every nearest P-world to w, i.e., iff $\mathbf{M}_w(P) \subseteq \|Q\|$.[7]

Proof: Suppose $(P > Q)$ obtains at w. Then by the definition of $\mathbf{M}$, if $w^* \in \mathbf{M}_w(P)$ then Q obtains at w. Conversely, suppose $(P > Q)$ does not obtain at w. Then by GCP, Q is not entailed by the counterfactual consequences of P at w, so there is a world w^* at which Q does not obtain but at which all of the counterfactual consequences of P at w do obtain. The latter means that $w^* \in \mathbf{M}_w(P)$, so $\mathbf{M}_w(P) \nsubseteq \|Q\|$.

By virtue of this theorem, if we can provide an alternative definition of $\mathbf{M}$ that does not proceed in terms of counterfac-

[7] This theorem was first proven in Pollock [1976a].

tuals, it will provide us with an analysis of counterfactuals. Such will be the strategy of the present investigation.

Most recent theories of counterfactuals are based upon a common idea, which Stalnaker attributes indirectly to Frank Ramsey.[8] This is that the nearest P-worlds are worlds resulting from minimally altering the actual world in order to accommodate P's being true. The novelty in a particular theory lies in how it makes precise this notion of minimal alteration. Stalnaker [1968] and Lewis [1973] attempted to analyze it in terms of comparative similarity, while I tried (in Pollock [1976]) to do it in terms of minimal changes. I will say something in the next section about the difference between these approaches. The present analysis also proceeds in terms of minimal changes, but in a somewhat different fashion than in Pollock [1976].

Let us begin by constructing a precise way of talking about changes. Where X and Y are sets, two kinds of changes are involved in going from X to Y: we must add to X all objects in $(Y\text{-}X)$, and we must remove from X all objects in $(X\text{-}Y)$. We can represent this change by the *indexed difference*:

(2.5) $Y \Delta X = [(Y\text{-}X) \times \{1\}] \cup [(X\text{-}Y) \times \{0\}]$.

The change in going from X to Y is represented in $Y \Delta X$ by pairing the objects that must be added with the index 1 and pairing the objects that must be deleted with the index 0. Representing changes in this way, one change is included in another just in case the first is a subset of the second.

Changes are changes *to* something. The most natural construal of talk of the change involved in going from one world to another is that the change is a change in the set of states of affairs obtaining at the first world. In other words, letting [w] be the set of all states of affairs obtaining at a world w, the change in going from w to w^* is $[w^*]\Delta[w]$. However, this natural construal of change is inadequate for our present purposes, because it leads directly to the conclusion that the (non-empty) change in going from w to one world w^* can never be properly contained in the change in going from w to another world w^{**}. To see this, suppose $[w^*]\Delta[w] \subset [w^{**}]\Delta[w]$. Then

[8] See Stalnaker [1968], 101.

there is a state of affairs P obtaining at w that does not obtain at w^*, and by virtue of the inclusion of changes, P does not obtain at w^{**} either. As the inclusion is proper, there is also a Q obtaining at both w and w^* that does not obtain at w^{**}. But then the biconditional $(P \leftrightarrow Q)$ obtains at w and w^{**} but not at w^*, which contradicts the assumption that $[w^*]\Delta[w] \subseteq [w^{**}]\Delta[w]$.

It is clear intuitively what has gone wrong in the preceding example. In talking about the inclusion of changes, we should not look at logical compounds like $(P \leftrightarrow Q)$. We should just look at states of affairs that are logically simple. To make sense of this we must take the notion of logical structure seriously, agreeing that some concepts literally *are* conjunctions, disjunctions, etc., as opposed to merely being equivalent to conjunctions, disjunctions, etc. Those that are not logical compounds will be called 'simple'. A state of affairs whose obtaining consists of an object (or n-tuple of objects) exemplifying a simple nontransient concept or the negation of a simple nontransient concept will be called a *simple state of affairs*. This is to be understood in such a way that a simple state of affairs cannot obtain at a world unless the objects involved in it exist at that world. If α is a simple nontransient concept, the *internal negation* of $[x|\alpha]$ is $[x|\sim\alpha]$, and the internal negation of $[x|\sim\alpha]$ is $[x|\alpha]$. Thus, the internal negations of simple states of affairs are themselves simple states of affairs. If P is a simple state of affairs, let $-P$ be its internal negation. The difference between the internal negation $-P$ and the ordinary negation $\sim P$ is a matter of "existential import". Let $\langle w \rangle$ be the set of all simple states of affairs obtaining at w. I assume that the set of simple states of affairs obtaining at a world uniquely determines what other nonsubjunctive states of affairs obtain at that world. My proposal is that Ramsey's basic idea is to be explicated in terms of making minimal changes to $\langle w \rangle$ subject to two constraints that I will now discuss.

2.1 *Legal Conservatism*

The first constraint is that physical laws must be kept the same insofar as possible. Let us say that P is *counterlegal* at

w iff P cannot obtain at any world having the same laws as w. The constraint is then that if P is not counterlegal at w then the nearest P-worlds to w must have the same laws as w, and if P is counterlegal at w then the laws in the nearest P-worlds must be changed as little as possible from the laws in w. I think that most philosophers will accept this ''legal conservatism'', although David Lewis is a notable exception.[9] Despite Lewis's dissension, I am inclined to regard it as obviously true that this constraint must be satisfied in the construction of nearest P-worlds. It is generally supposed that one of the most important features of laws is that they ''support their counterfactuals''. The most obvious construal of this is the *instantiation principle*: whenever P is not counterlegal and $(P > Q)$ results from direct instantiation in a law, then it is true. This requires that the nearest P-worlds contain no violations of the laws of w. The only simple way to ensure this result semantically is to suppose that the nearest P-worlds to w retain the same laws as w.

David Lewis ([1973] and [1979]) has argued against the instantiation principle, and so derivatively against legal conservatism. His contention in Lewis [1979] is, basically, that the instantiation principle fails for ''backwards-directed conditionals''—counterfactuals to the effect that if something had been the case at a certain time, then something else that was not true would have been true at an earlier time. Lewis thinks that, standardly interpreted, such conditionals are always false.[10] I cannot concur with this claim. Lewis is certainly correct that it is hard to find true backwards-directed conditionals, but one case in which such conditionals seem clearly true is when they result directly from instantiation in physical laws. Consider, for example, a match that was struck and then lit. We cannot conclude that if it had not lit it would not have been struck. If it had not lit, something else might have gone wrong besides its being struck. But suppose C comprises a complete list of conditions under which, according to true physical laws, a struck

---

[9] See particularly Lewis [1979].

[10] Except for those dealing with a short ''transition period''.

match lights. There is no obstacle at all to our concluding that if the match had not lit, then either it would not have been struck or else conditions C would not have obtained. This conditional is as clearly true as counterfactuals ever get. It is precisely because it results directly from instantiation in a law that it is so clearly true. I know of no other plausible argument against legal conservatism, and there appear to be strong intuitions in its favor, so I embrace it in the analysis.

To formulate the constraint of legal conservatism precisely, we must say more about physical laws. Physical laws are assumed to be *subjunctive generalizations*. The reader is referred to Pollock [1976] for an account of this notion. Most of the details are not relevant to the present account. In order to deal with counterlegal conditionals I do assume, however, that there is a distinction between *basic* subjunctive generalizations, which are projectible in the sense of being directly confirmable by their instances, and others that are only confirmable by being entailed by basic subjunctive generalizations.[11] Let L_w be the set of basic subjunctive generalizations holding at w. Where X is a set of states of affairs and Q is a state of affairs, let us say that X *nomically implies* Q *at* w (symbolized: $\ulcorner X \underset{w}{\Rightarrow} Q \urcorner$) iff $X \cup L_w$ entails Q.

Legal conservatism is now the requirement that in constructing nearest P-worlds we make minimal changes to the laws in order to accommodate P's being true. Let $\mathbf{M}_w^L(P)$ be the set of worlds whose laws are thus minimally changed:

(2.6) $\mathbf{M}_w^L(P) = \{w^* \mid w^* \in \|P\|$ and there is no w^{**} in $\|P\|$ such that $L_{w^{**}} \Delta L_w \subset L_{w^*} \Delta L_w]\}$.

Legal conservatism requires:

(2.7) $\mathbf{M}_w(P) \subseteq \mathbf{M}_w^L(P)$.

2.2 *Undercutting*

Legal conservatism is not particularly novel, having been endorsed at least implicitly by most authors. The principal

---

[11] The details of this notion are spelled out in Pollock [1976], Chapter Three.

novelty of the present analysis concerns the logical phenomenon of "undercutting".[12] Consider a concrete case consisting of an open switch and a light wired in series with a battery. Let us suppose it is a law that in such a circuit if the switch is closed (S) and the circuit is intact (I) then shortly thereafter the light will come on (L): $(S\&I) \underset{w}{\Rightarrow} L$. We want to say that if the switch were closed then the light would come on: $S > L$. Legal conservatism requires that ($\sim I \vee L$) be true at all nearest S-worlds, and the requirement that we minimally change $\langle w \rangle$ in order to accommodate S requires that in any nearest S-world, either $\sim I$ is true and L is false or L is true and $\sim I$ is false. What justifies us in rejecting the former alternative and concluding $S > L$ rather than $S > \sim I$? This might reasonably be called "the central problem" in the analysis of counterfactuals. The solution to this problem, which I proposed in Pollock [1976] and to which I still adhere, is this. At least in deterministic worlds, both I and $-L$ have "historical antecedents"—sets of simple states of affairs that obtain earlier and that nomically imply them. The historical antecedents of I describe the way the circuit came to have the structure it does. These historical antecedents (we can suppose) have nothing in particular to do with the switch's being open. The historical antecedents of $-L$ are those earlier states of affairs that have brought it about that the light is not on. These historical antecedents must include either the switch's not being closed or else some earlier states of affairs that are themselves historical antecedents of the switch's not being closed. Consequently, S nomically implies the falsity of the historical antecedents of $-L$. This is what is meant by saying that S *undercuts* $-L$. On the other hand, S does not undercut I. My contention is that it is this asymmetry that is responsible for our affirming $S > L$ and not $S > \sim L$.

This basic idea is the same as that of Pollock [1976], although the way it will now be developed is quite different. First, we must construct a precise definition of undercutting.

---

[12] This also provided the intuitive rationale for the analysis of Pollock [1976], although there I attempted to capture it differently.

IV. Counterfactuals

We begin by noting that simple states of affairs are dated—they ascribe nontransient concepts to objects, which is to say that they ascribe concepts to objects *at specific times*. We must be careful just what we assume about temporal relations. Whether a counterfactual obtains cannot be relative to a frame of reference. This is an absolute matter independent of frames of reference. Accordingly, the temporal relations involved in the analysis of counterfactuals must also be absolute temporal relations and not relative to frames of reference. I will symbolize ⌜P is absolutely earlier than Q⌝ as ⌜$P < Q$⌝, and ⌜P is absolutely simultaneous with Q⌝ as ⌜$P \approx Q$⌝. I will leave open how these notions are to be defined. In special relativity, ⌜$P < Q$⌝ might be taken to require (in part) that there is a path of light from P to Q, and ⌜$P \approx Q$⌝ would then require that P and Q occur at the same location. We must make some minimal assumptions about the logical properties of these temporal relations. It would be assumed classically that '$<$' simple orders the states of affairs in its field, but that is incompatible with special relativity. I will assume only the following:

(2.8) If $P < Q$ and $Q < R$, then $P < R$.

(2.9) If $P \approx Q$ and $Q < R$, then $P < R$.

(2.10) If $P < Q$ and $Q \approx R$, then $P < R$.

Additional assumptions might be defensible, but we will not need them.

We have taken '$<$' to symbolize the "earlier than" relation between simple states of affairs. It is also convenient to define the following, where X is a set of simple states of affairs and Q is an individual simple state of affairs:

(2.11) $X < Q$ iff every member of X is earlier than Q.

We can define the notion of an historical antecedent as follows:

(2.12) X **HA**$_w$ P iff X is a set of simple states of affairs obtaining at w and $X < P$ and $X \underset{w}{\Rightarrow} P$.

We normally suppose that historical antecedents of states of affairs have their own historical antecedents, and so on. By tracing out this sequence of historical antecedents as far as we can, stopping only if we come to a state of affairs without historical antecedents, we construct a "causal history" for the state of affairs. In cases of causal overdetermination, a state of affairs will have several merging causal histories. To say that P undercuts Q is to say, roughly, that P nomically implies the falsity of every causal history of Q. The elements of a causal history of Q constitute what I will call a 'nomic pyramid':

(2.13) Λ is a *nomic pyramid* of w iff Λ is a set of simple states of affairs obtaining at w and:

(1) for each P in Λ, if P has historical antecedents in w then $(\exists X)[X \subseteq \Lambda$ and $X \mathbf{HA}_w P]$;

(2) if σ is an ω-sequence of elements of Λ such that $(\forall n \in \omega)(\exists X)[X \subseteq \Lambda$ and $\sigma_{n+1} \in X$ and $X \mathbf{HA}_w \sigma_n$ and $\sim((X - \{\sigma_{n+1}\}) \mathbf{HA}_w \sigma_n)]$ and $(\exists X)(\forall n \in \omega) X \mathbf{HA}_w \sigma_n$, then $(\exists X)[X \subseteq \Lambda$ and $(\forall n \in \omega) X \mathbf{HA}_w \sigma_n]$.

A nomic pyramid is supposed to contain an entire causal history of each of its members. Condition (1) requires that in tracing out causal histories we do not stop unless we reach a state of affairs without a causal history. Condition (2) is included to avoid a complex way in which nomic pyramids might otherwise fail to contain complete causal histories. We might have a causal chain of states of affairs, each causing all of the later ones, where the chain is temporally dense in the sense that between any two members of the chain is another member of the chain. For example, think of a ball rolling down an inclined plane. A causal history of any of these states of affairs must include all of the earlier ones in the chain. But now let us select an arbitrary member of this chain, and let Λ be the set of all subsequent members of the chain. Then every member of Λ has an historical antecedent in Λ, i.e., condition (1) is satisfied. But Λ does not contain a complete causal history. To ensure that a nomic pyramid does contain a complete causal history, we must require that given any temporally descending sequence of states of affairs in the pyramid, if each member

IV. Counterfactuals

of the sequence is part of the historical antecedents of the temporally later members of the sequence and there is something that is an historical antecedent of all of the members of the sequence, then some such historical antecedent is included in the nomic pyramid. This is what condition (2) requires.

The simplest way in which P can undercut Q is by being nomically incompatible with every nomic pyramid containing Q. This led me in Pollock [1981] to define:

P undercuts Q at w iff $Q \in \langle w \rangle$ and $(\forall \Lambda)$(if Λ is a nomic pyramid of w and $Q \in \Lambda$ then $\Lambda \underset{w}{\Rightarrow} \sim P$).

But this definition of undercutting must be broadened. For example, suppose P is nomically incompatible with the conjunction $(Q\&R\&S)$ of simple states of affairs, and incompatible with the combined historical antecedents of Q and R without being incompatible with the historical antecedents of either Q or R by themselves. Under these circumstances, we would judge that S would still obtain even if P obtained, but either Q or R might fail to obtain. To illustrate, consider a system of three lights A, B, and C. Light C is perpetually on. Lights A and B are controlled by switches A and B, both of which are actually closed. Clearly, if switches A and B were not both closed, light C would still be on, but either of lights A and B might be off. To accommodate the latter we must define undercutting in terms of minimal sets of states of affairs whose joint historical antecedents are nomically incompatible with P:

(2.14) *P undercuts Q* iff $(\exists \Gamma)[Q \in \Gamma$ and Γ is a minimal set of simple states of affairs such that $(\forall \Lambda)$(if Λ is a nomic pyramid of w and $\Gamma \subseteq \Lambda$ then $P \underset{w}{\Rightarrow} \sim \wedge \Lambda)]$.

Let $\mathbf{U}_w(P)$ be the set of simple states of affairs undercut by P at w together with the internal negations of those states of affairs.

Now consider how undercutting imposes a constraint on the construction of nearest P-worlds. Our original observation was that when $P \underset{w}{\Rightarrow} \sim(Q\&R)$ where Q and R both obtain at w, and

122

P undercuts Q but not R, then we conclude that $P > R$ obtains at w. In other words, if in minimally altering $\langle w \rangle$ to accommodate the obtaining of P we must give up one of Q or R, we give precedence to the one that is not undercut, preserving it in preference to the other. In making minimal changes we are not allowed to delete a state of affairs that is not undercut in order to preserve one that is undercut. Similarly, we are not allowed to add a state of affairs not in $\mathbf{U}_w(P)$ in order to preserve an undercut state of affairs. Simply put, members of $\langle w \rangle - \mathbf{U}_w(P)$ take precedence over undercut states of affairs in deciding what to preserve in making minimal changes. Let us define:

(2.15) $\mathbf{M}_w^U(P) = \{w^* | \ \mathbf{M}_w^L(P)$ and there is no w^{**} in $\mathbf{M}_w^L(P)$ such that $(\langle w^{**} \rangle - \mathbf{U}_w(P))\Delta(\langle w \rangle - \mathbf{U}_w(P)) \subset (\langle w^* \rangle - \mathbf{U}_w(P))\Delta(\langle w \rangle - \mathbf{U}_w(P))]\}$.

$\mathbf{M}_w^U(P)$ consists of those members of $\mathbf{M}_w^L(P)$ that satisfy our undercutting constraint, i.e., that result from making minimal changes to the non-undercut states of affairs. Thus, that constraint can be formulated precisely as the requirement that:

(2.16) $\mathbf{M}_w(P) \subseteq \mathbf{M}_w^U(P)$.

Note that this formulation includes the constraint of legal conservatism.

The question arises as to whether there should be a stronger constraint related to undercutting. In most ordinary cases in which P undercuts Q, we conclude that $P > \sim Q$. For example, suppose a button is pushed and the doorbell rings. The button's not being pushed undercuts the ringing of the doorbell, and so we conclude that if the button had not been pushed, the doorbell would not have rung. It is not true completely in general that if P undercuts Q then $P > \sim Q$ obtains, because P can both undercut Q and reinstate it in various ways. One way P could reinstate Q is by providing new historical antecedents for it. Or P might undercut both Q and R but entail that at least one of Q and R obtains. However, leaving the notion of reinstatement a bit vague, it does seem to be true in all ordinary cases that if P undercuts Q and does not reinstate it, then $P > {\sim}Q$ obtains. Should we add a constraint on the construction of nearest P-worlds that will guarantee that this is the case? The matter is complicated and I am not sure of the answer, but we can throw some light on it by noting that this constraint follows from (2.16) for the case of deterministic worlds. Let us say that a simple state of affairs is *grounded* just in case it has arbitrarily early historical antecedents:

(2.17) Q is *grounded in* w iff $Q \in \langle w \rangle$ and $(\forall P)$(if $P \in \langle w \rangle$ then $(\exists X)[X < P$ and X **HA**$_w Q])$.

Then let us say that a world is *weakly deterministic* just in case every simple state of affairs obtaining in it is grounded. A world could be weakly deterministic "by accident". That is, it could happen that all simple states of affairs in w have arbitrarily early historical antecedents but that the laws of w do not require that to be the case. Accordingly, let us define:

(2.18) w is *deterministic* iff every world with the same laws as w is weakly deterministic.

Now suppose that P undercuts Q at w, and w is deterministic. Then in order to accommodate the obtaining of P, we must delete all of the causal histories of Q. But then in order to preserve the laws of w, if we are to preserve Q we must add a new causal history for Q. Such an addition, however, would violate constraint (2.16) unless P also reinstates Q in some way. Thus (2.16) leads automatically to the deletion of Q as long as w is deterministic. Hence in the case of deterministic worlds, the proposed new constraint is a consequence of (2.16). This suggests that (2.16) is the only constraint required for deterministic worlds, and hence that:

(2.19) If w is deterministic then $\mathbf{M}_w(P) = \mathbf{M}_w^U(P)$.

This gives us an analysis of counterfactuals in deterministic worlds.

I am reasonably confident of (2.19), but when we turn to nondeterministic worlds I find that my intuitions grow less clear. Still, some arguments can be given suggesting an analysis of counterfactuals applicable both to deterministic and nondeterministic worlds. First, consider whether undercut states of affairs must automatically be deleted in nondeterministic worlds unless they are reinstated. Suppose that although Q has historical antecedents in w, w is nondeterministic with respect to Q in the sense that there are worlds with the same laws as w in which Q obtains without having historical antecedents. In this case, if P undercuts Q and does not reinstate Q, should it follow that $P > {\sim}Q$ obtains? It appears not. If Q can obtain without historical antecedents, then removing what historical antecedents it has should not require it to not obtain. For example, suppose there are some circumstances C under which a proton can emit a photon spontaneously, but under which it can also be forced to emit a photon by subjecting it to a strong magnetic field. Suppose that in the actual world the proton is forced to emit a photon by being subjected to a magnetic field under circumstances C. It seems to me that if the proton is not being subjected to a magnetic field, it might still have emitted a photon. Thus, we are not automatically required to delete undercut states of affairs in nondeterministic worlds.

In the preceding example, it also seems to me that if the proton had not been subjected to a magnetic field, then it might not have emitted a photon. In other words, although we are not automatically required to delete undercut states of affairs, we are *allowed* to do so (unless they are reinstated). If P undercuts and does not reinstate Q, then Q might or might not obtain if P obtained. If this is correct, what it means is that in constructing nearest P-worlds we are not required to minimize changes to undercut states of affairs. This suggests that, in general, the nearest P-worlds are those that result from making minimal changes first to the basic laws and then to the nonundercut states of affairs. In other words, for all worlds w,

$$(2.20)\ \mathbf{M}_w(P) = \mathbf{M}_w^U(P).$$

(2.20) is the analysis I proposed in Pollock [1981], but Donald Nute [1981] and Pavel Tichý [1984] quickly presented me with counterexamples to it. Their counterexamples both have the same structure. Nute observes that in the preceding example, if our proton is in circumstances C but is not being subjected to a strong magnetic field and is not emitting a photon, we will still want to affirm that if the proton were subjected to a strong magnetic field then it would emit a photon. But that is not forthcoming from (2.20). The proton's being subjected to a strong magnetic field undercuts neither its being in circumstances C nor its not emitting a photon, and so according to (2.20) there are nearest P-worlds in which it is in circumstances C and emits a photon, and there are other nearest P-worlds in which it is not in circumstances C and does not emit a photon.

It has since occurred to me that there are much simpler non-deterministic counterexamples to (2.20). Suppose, as seems likely, that the laws governing the lighting of a match when it is struck are only probabilistic, and consider a match struck under appropriate circumstances C (i.e., while dry, in the presence of oxygen, and so on) and lit. We would normally judge that the match would still have been in circumstances C had it not been struck, but it would not have lit if it had not been struck. Intuitively, the fact that the laws involved are only probabilistic makes no difference to this example. The match's not being struck still undercuts its lighting, because its being struck played a (nondeterministic) role in the match's actually lighting. In order to handle this kind of case, we must liberalize our notion of an historical antecedent. The match's being struck in circumstances C "probabilistically disposes" it to light even if it does not nomically necessitate its lighting. Leaving aside for the moment the question of how to define the notion of probabilistic disposing, let us symbolize the latter as $\ulcorner P \Rrightarrow Q \urcorner$ and then revise the definition of 'historical antecedent' as follows:

(2.21) $X \mathbf{HA}_w P$ iff X is a set of simple states of affairs obtaining at w and $X < P$ and $X \underset{w}{\Rrightarrow} P$.

With this revision, the match's not being struck undercuts its lighting, and so the example of the nondeterministic match is handled properly by the newly interpreted (2.20). In order to

126

handle more complicated nondeterministic cases, we must also replace '$\underset{w}{\Rightarrow}$' by '$\underset{w}{\Rrightarrow}$' in the definition of undercutting (2.14).

Now let us consider how to define the relation of probabilistic disposing. A necessary condition for P to probabilistically dispose Q to obtain is for P to be positively relevant to Q, i.e., $\text{prob}(Q/P) > \text{prob}(Q/\sim P)$. But that is not sufficient, because there might be other features of the current circumstances that offset this positive relevance. That is, there might be another simple state of affairs R that obtains and is such that $\text{prob}(Q/R\&P) \leq \text{prob}(Q/R\&\sim P)$. This suggests the following definition:

(2.22) $P \underset{w}{\Rrightarrow} Q$ iff P and Q are simple states of affairs obtaining at w and and $\text{prob}(Q/P) > \text{prob}(Q/\sim P)$ and $(\forall R)$(if R is a simple state of affairs obtaining at w and $R < Q$ and $(R\&\sim P)$ is physically possible, then $\text{prob}(Q/R\&P) > \text{prob}(Q/R\&\sim P)$.[13]

Thus, probabilistic disposing becomes a kind of ''strong positive relevance''. With this understanding of probabilistic disposing, (2.20) also handles the Nute-Tichý counterexample. In that case, the proton's not being in a strong magnetic field is strongly positively relevant to its not emitting a photon, so the latter is undercut by the proton's being in a strong magnetic field. The proton's being in the appropriate circumstances for emitting a photon while in a strong magnetic field is not undercut, so we conclude that if the proton were in a strong magnetic field, it would have emitted a photon.

I propose that with these modifications (2.20) provides a correct analysis of counterfactuals both in deterministic and nondeterministic worlds. Informally, the nearest P-worlds are those that result from, first, making minimal changes to the laws to accommodate P's obtaining and, second, making minimal changes to the nonundercut states of affairs to accommodate P's obtaining along with the revised set of laws.

[13] We must consider what kind of probability is symbolized by 'prob' here. I propose that it is the objective definite probability symbolized by 'prob' in Pollock [1983].

The analysis (2.20) validates all of the theorems of the logic SS, which can be axiomatized as follows:

(A0) All tautologies;
(A1) $[(P > Q)$ & $(P > R)] \to [P > (Q\&R)]$;
(A2) $[(P > R)$ & $(Q > R)] \to [(P \lor Q) > R]$;
(A3) $[(P > Q)$ & $(P > R)] \to [(P\&Q) > R]$;
(A4) $(P\&Q) \to (P > Q)$;
(A5) $(P > Q) \to (P \to Q)$
(R1) If $\vdash P$ and $\vdash (P \to Q)$ then $\vdash Q$.
(R2) If $\vdash (P \leftrightarrow Q)$ then $\vdash (P > R) \leftrightarrow (Q > R)$.
(R3) If $\vdash (Q \to R)$ then $\vdash (P > Q) \to (P > R)$.
(R4) If $\vdash (P \to Q)$ then $\vdash (P > Q)$.[14]

For many purposes, it is more convenient to formulate the logic of counterfactuals somewhat differently, adding '>' to propositional modal logic. If we do that, we get *Modal SS*, which results from adding the following axioms to the axioms and rules of S5:

(A1) $[(P > Q)$ & $(P > R)] \to [P > (Q\&R)]$;
(A2) $[(P > R)$ & $(Q > R)] \to [(P \lor Q) > R]$;
(A3) $[(P > Q)$ & $(P > R)] \to [(P\&Q) > R]$;
(A4) $(P\&Q) \to (P > Q)$;
(A5) $(P > Q) \to (P \to Q)$;
(A6) $\Box(P \leftrightarrow Q) \to [(P > R) \leftrightarrow (Q > R)]$;
(A7) $[(P > Q)$ & $\Box(Q \to R)] \to (P > R)$;
(A8) $\Box(P \to Q) \to (P > Q)$.

Modal SS holds regardless of whether the variables are taken to range over propositions, statements, or states of affairs.

3. Minimal Change vs. Maximal Similarity

The best-known analysis of counterfactuals is unquestionably that of David Lewis [1973], which proceeds in terms of

---

[14] SS was first described in Pollock [1975]. The variables in these axioms and rules can be interpreted either as ranging over propositions, statements, or states of affairs. The logic holds in each case.

comparative similarity. Minimal change and maximal similarity sound like two sides of the same coin, so it may be suspected that there is little difference between the two analyses. Both analyses are motivated by the same basic idea due to Ramsey, and my analysis was strongly influenced by Lewis's analysis. Furthermore, the analyses can even be formulated in a parallel fashion, as follows. Suppose that for each possible world w, $\leq_w$ is a transitive and symmetric binary relation (i.e., a partial ordering) on possible worlds. We will read $\ulcorner w^* \leq_w w^{**} \urcorner$ neutrally as $\ulcorner w^*$ is at least as near to w as w^{**} is$\urcorner$. Let us define $\ulcorner w^*$ is nearer to w than w^{**} is$\urcorner$ as:

(3.1) $w^* <_w w^{**}$ iff $w^* \leq_w w^{**}$ but not $w^{**} \leq_w w^*$.

Let us also define:

(3.2) '$>$' is *strictly based upon* $\leq$ iff for each possible world w, $(P > Q)$ obtains at w iff $(\forall w^*)$(if P obtains at w^* and there is no w^{**} such that P obtains at w^{**} and $w^{**} <_w w^*$, then Q obtains at w^*).

'$>$' is strictly based upon $\leq$ iff $\mathbf{M}_w(P)$ is the set of nearest P-worlds to w according to the ordering $\leq_w$. My analysis is equivalent to asserting that '$>$' is strictly based upon the relation:

(3.3) $\mathbf{L}_{w^*}\Delta\mathbf{L}_w \subset \mathbf{L}_{w^{**}}\Delta\mathbf{L}_w$ or $[\mathbf{L}_{w^*}\Delta\mathbf{L}_w = \mathbf{L}_{w^{**}}\Delta\mathbf{L}_w$ and $(\langle w^*\rangle - \mathbf{U}_w(P))\Delta(\langle w\rangle - \mathbf{U}_w(P)) \subset (\langle w^{**}\rangle - \mathbf{U}_w(P))\Delta(\langle w\rangle - \mathbf{U}_w(P))]$.

Lewis's analysis also takes the simple subjunctive to be based upon an ordering of worlds, but he gives a different truth condition. Let us define:

(3.4) '$>$' is *weakly based upon* $\leq$ iff for each possible world w, $(P > Q)$ obtains at w iff $(\forall w^*)$(if P obtains at w^* then there is a w^{**} such that P obtains at w^{**} and $w^{**} \leq_w w^*$ and for every w^{***} at least as close to w as w^{**} is, if P obtains at w^{***} then Q obtains at w^{***}).

The rationale for this truth condition is that there may be no closest P-worlds to w, so what $(P > Q)$ requires is that Q

becomes true and remains true once we approach w sufficiently closely. Lewis's analysis alleges that '$>$' is weakly based upon the relation of comparative similarity between worlds.

My analysis differs from Lewis's in three respects: (1) he and I take counterfactuals to be based upon different ordering relations; (2) I take counterfactuals to be strongly based upon the appropriate ordering relation, whereas Lewis takes them to be only weakly based upon the appropriate ordering relation; and (3) Lewis assumes that $\leq_w$ is connected, i.e., that we can always compare worlds with respect to their nearness to a given world. The second and third differences are motivated by the first difference, but it is illuminating to explore them separately.

Consider the following five principles:

(SB) '$>$' is strictly based upon $\leq$.

(WB) '$>$' is weakly based upon $\leq$.

(LA) *The limit assumption*: $(\forall w^*)$(if P obtains at w^* then there is a w^{**} such that P obtains at w^{**} and $w^{**} \leq_w w^*$ and there is no w^{***} such that P obtains at w^{***} and $w^{***} <_w w^{**}$).

(GCP) *The generalized consequence principle*.

(NV) *Non-vacuity*: If $(\sim P > P)$ is possible then P is necessary.

There are numerous interconnections between these principles, some of the most important being the following:

(3.5) SB $\rightarrow$ GCP.

(3.6) [(SB $\vee$ WB) & NV] $\rightarrow$ (GCP $\leftrightarrow$ LA).

(3.7) LA $\rightarrow$ (SB $\leftrightarrow$ WB).

(3.8) (GCP & $\sim$LA) $\rightarrow$ $\sim$WB.

I take GCP to be intuitively correct. By (3.5), my analysis has no difficulty validating GCP, but Lewis's analysis does not validate it. Lewis rejects the limit assumption, so by (3.8), GCP fails on his analysis. In Pollock [1976] I assumed NV and affirmed GCP, so in light of (3.6), our difference seemed to revolve around the limit assumption. Lewis interpreted our difference in that way in Lewis [1981]. However, that is to mislocate it. I agree with Lewis that the limit assumption is false, and have done so all along. In Pollock [1976] I began the analysis of counterfactuals by giving an analysis according to which they were strongly based upon an ordering of worlds, but then because I assumed NV and GCP and agreed that the limit assumption failed, I rejected SB in accordance with (3.6) and proposed a much more complicated analysis according to which counterfactuals were not based upon an ordering at all. That analysis was logically messy, and I have since come to realize that it does not work anyway.[15] My present inclination is to endorse SB but reject NV for the reasons discussed below. I still endorse GCP and reject the limit assumption.

Where does this leave us with respect to the limit assumption? Lewis and I agree that it fails, but we differ about *when* it fails and about how to handle the cases in which it fails. Let us say that the limit assumption fails for P at w provided:

There is a w^* such that P obtains at w^* and for every w^{**}, if P obtains at w^{**} and $w^{**} \leq_w w^*$ then there is a w^{***} such that P obtains at w^{***} and $w^{***} <_w w^{**}$.

In other words, there are P-worlds that get closer and closer to w without limit. Lewis is of the opinion that the limit assumption fails frequently, while I believe it fails only in unusual cases. We differ on this because of our different choices for $\leq$. Assuming his comparative similarity analysis, Lewis gave the following counterexample to the limit assumption:

---

[15] I won't bore the reader by giving the analysis of Pollock [1976], but for anyone who wishes to pursue the matter, here is a counterexample to it. Suppose there are infinitely many F's in w, and let us symbolize the proposition that there are infinitely many F's as $\ulcorner(\exists_\infty x)Fx\urcorner$ and the proposition that there are at least n F's as $\ulcorner(\exists_n x)Fx\urcorner$. The latter is equivalent to $\ulcorner(\exists_\infty x)Fx \vee (\exists_\infty x)(Fx \ \& \ Gx)\urcorner$, which is the limit (in the sense of Pollock [1976]) of the sequence of propositions of the form $\ulcorner(\exists_\infty x)Fx \vee (\exists_n x)(Fx \ \& \ Gx)\urcorner$. Thus, it follows from the analysis of Pollock [1976] that if there were infinitely many F's then for any G, there might be infinitely many things that are both F and G. Such a conclusion seems clearly incorrect.

IV. Counterfactuals

Suppose we entertain the counterfactual supposition that at this point there appears a line more than an inch long.... There are worlds with a line 2'' long; worlds presumably closer to ours with a line 1 1/2'' long; worlds presumably still closer to ours with a line 1 1/4'' long; worlds presumably still closer .... But how long is the line in the *closest* worlds with a line more than an inch long? If it is $1+x$'' for any x however small, why are there not other worlds still closer to ours in which it is $1+x/2$'', a length still closer to its actual length? The shorter we make the line (above 1''), the closer we come to the actual length; so the closer we come, presumably, to our actual world. Just as there is no shortest possible length above 1'', so there is no closest world to ours among the worlds with lines more than an inch long.[16]

On the minimal change analysis, however, this is not a counterexample to the limit assumption. There is no undercutting involved in this example, so for any small value of x,[17] there will be worlds minimally changed from the actual world to make the line $1+x$ inches long. These will be nearest worlds in which the line is more than one inch long. Nevertheless, there are some cases in which the limit assumption fails on both analyses. To take an example that will figure prominently in the next section, suppose we have an infinite set X of white billiard balls. Suppose further that the colors of the members of X are entirely independent of one another, so that if we changed the colors of the members of any subset of X the rest would still be white. Let P be the counterfactual hypothesis 'Infinitely many of the members of X are black'. There are no nearest P-worlds to the actual world, because for any world w in which infinitely many members of X are black, there is a P-world w^* in which one fewer member of X is black, and w^* is both more similar to the actual world than w is and results from making a smaller change to the actual world than

[16] Lewis [1973], 20–21.
[17] There may be laws precluding the length of the line's being greater than some upper bound.

w does.[18] Thus, the limit assumption fails for both minimal change and comparative similarity.

It is no criticism of one analysis that it makes the limit assumption fail in more cases than another analysis does, provided the first analysis can handle those cases in a reasonable way. Lewis's analysis handles them differently than my analysis does, and the difference is precisely the difference between SB and WB. Lewis implicitly assumes that the only way to get SB is to adopt the limit assumption, and this makes SB appear unrespectable. But Lewis is wrong about that. It has been insufficiently appreciated that SB and WB are just two different ways of handling failures of the limit assumption. SB and WB agree in all cases in which the limit assumption holds, but handle failures of the limit assumption differently. Neither seems initially to handle such failures satisfactorily. If there are no nearest P-worlds to w, then SB makes all counterfactuals of the form $(P > Q)$ vacuously true at w. This seems intuitively incorrect. We do not want to affirm, for example, that Ghengis Khan would have conquered the world had there been infinitely many stars. But WB also seems to work incorrectly. For example, in Lewis's example of the line, WB leads to the result that for each x greater than zero, if the line were more than one inch long then it would not have been $1+x$ inches long. On the contrary, at least for small values of x, it seems that had the line been more than one inch long then it might have been $1+x$ inches long. For example, it might have been 1 1/4 inches long, and it might have been 1 1/2 inches long. Similarly, in the billiard ball case, if b is any member of X, WB leads to the result that if infinitely many members of X were black then b would not be black. But that also seems clearly wrong. It seems that if infinitely many members of X were black, then any member of X might be black.

Thus, although WB and SB handle failures of the limit assumption differently, neither handles them in ways congenial

---

[18] It was on the strength of this sort of example that I gave up SB in Pollock [1976]. Lewis [1981] has recently discussed examples of this sort.

to intuition. What conclusions should we draw from this? First, note that in Lewis's example of the line, a minimal change analysis endorses what are intuitively the right conditionals. Because there are minimal changes making the line 1 1/4 inches long, 1 1/2 inches long, and so on, it follows that the line might be any of these lengths if it were more than one inch long. In these cases in which the limit assumption fails for comparative similarity but not for minimal change, the minimal change analysis seems preferable. Second, although neither analysis seems initially to work properly in those cases in which the limit assumption fails on both analyses, I will argue in the next section that such cases can be explained away and do not constitute counterexamples to either SB or WB. Finally, GCP still seems to me to be intuitively correct, and by (3.8), given GCP and the failure of the limit assumption, WB must be false. This is at least weak confirmation of SB.

Next, let us turn to the issue of connectedness. Lewis asserts, and in this I think he is correct, that the 'at least as similar to' relation is a total pre-ordering, i.e., it is transitive, reflexive, and connected. The "containment of change" relation formulated by (3.3), on the other hand, is clearly not connected. There can be two changes neither of which is contained in the other. This makes an important difference to the logic of counterfactuals, regardless of whether we adopt SB or WB. Lewis's analysis validates the logic VC that results from adding the following axiom to SS:

(3.9) $[(P > Q) \& \sim(P > \sim R)] \rightarrow [(P\&R) > Q]$.

The validation of (3.9) makes essential use of connectedness. In Pollock [1976] I proposed a counterexample to (3.9). Barry Loewer [1979] has suggested that the counterexample was suspect because it involved English counterfactual sentences with disjunctive antecedents, and it is well known that those are problematic. Lewis [1981] endorses this objection. However, the appeal to counterfactual sentences with disjunctive antecedents is inessential to the counterexample. We can give an example with an essentially similar structure that does not involve any such sentences. Consider a circuit consisting of a power source, three switches, and two lights. Light L_1 can be turned on in either of two ways: by closing switch A, or by closing switches B and C together. Light L_2 can also be turned on in either of two ways: by closing switch A, or by closing switch B. Switch C is not connected with L_2 in any way. Suppose that all three switches are open and both lights are off. As there is no connection between L_2 and C, C would still be open even if L_2 were on and the circuit intact (symbolized: '$(L_2 \& I) > {\sim}C$'). If L_2 were on (and the circuit intact) this might be because A was closed, and it might also be because B was closed. If L_2 were on because A was closed, then L_1 would also be on. Thus, L_1 might be on if L_2 were on and the circuit intact, i.e., we have ${\sim}((L_2 \& I) > {\sim}L_1)$. If L_1 and L_2 were both on and the circuit intact, this might also be because B and C were both closed; i.e., we have ${\sim}[(L_1 \& L_2 \& I) > {\sim}(B \& C)]$. As we have $(L_2 \& I) > {\sim}C$, we also have $(L_2 \& I) > {\sim}(B \& C)$. But the triple

$(L_2 \& I) > {\sim}(B \& C)$
${\sim}((L_2 \& I) > {\sim}L_1)$
${\sim}[(L_1 \& L_2 \& I) > {\sim}(B \& C)]$

is a counterexample to (3.9). Thus eschewing disjunctive antecedents will not help.[19]

Lewis [1981] admits that regardless of whether the preceding counterexamples are deemed persuasive, there may well be examples in which there are apparent failures of connectedness. He writes:

Ordinary counterfactuals usually require only the comparison of worlds with a great deal in common, from the standpoint of worlds of the sort we think we might inhabit. An ordering frame that satisfies Comparability [i.e., connectedness] would be cluttered up with comparisons that matter to the evaluations of counterfactuals only in peculiar

---

[19] In the original formulation of this counterexample in Pollock [1981], I omitted 'I' throughout. Nute [1981] pointed out that the first member of the triple is then false.

IV. Counterfactuals

cases that will never arise. Whatever system of general principles we use to make the wanted comparisons will doubt-
less go on willy nilly to make some of the unwanted comparisons as well, but it seems not likely that it will settle
them all (not given that it makes the wanted comparisons
in a way that fits our counterfactual judgments). An ordering frame that satisfies Comparability would be a cumber-
some thing to keep in mind, or to establish by our linguistic
practice. Why should we have one? How could we? Most
likely we don't.

This argument is persuasive, and I know of no one who
would dispute it. However, it is not exactly an argument
against Comparability. Rather, it is an argument against the
combination of Comparability with full determinacy in the
ordering frame. We need no partial orderings if we are prepared to admit that we have not bothered to decide quite
which total orderings (weak or simple, as the case may be)
are the right ones. The advocates of Comparability certainly
are prepared to admit that the ordering frame is left under-
determined by linguistic practice and context.... So where
Pollock sees a determinate partial ordering that leaves two
worlds incomparable, Stalnaker and Lewis see a multiplicity of total orderings that disagree in their comparisons of
the two worlds, with nothing in practice and context to select one of these orderings over the rest. Practice and context determine a class of frames each satisfying Comparability, not a single frame that fails to satisfy Comparability.

Lewis then observes that to suppose '>' to be based upon a
partial ordering is equivalent to supposing that we evaluate
counterfactuals as true iff they are true with respect to each
of the multiplicity of total orderings that are in partial agreement with one another.[20] This is being proposed as a strategy
for saving the comparative similarity analysis of counterfactuals in the face of apparent nonconnectedness, but it does not
seem to me that it can succeed. To suppose that we have con-

[20] For a precise statement of this theorem, see Lewis [1981].

136

nectedness only because we haven't settled certain comparisons implies that we could settle them and hence restore connectedness in any particular case. But could we? Consider the example of the electrical circuit given above. It turns essentially on the fact that closing A and closing B are each minimal changes resulting in L_2's being on, while closing A and closing B and C together are each minimal changes resulting in L_1's being on. This is incompatible with connectedness, because that would require regarding the closing of both B and C as a bigger change than the closing of A in one case, but as a change of equal magnitude in another case. If this uncertainty were just a matter of our not having settled our comparisons, we could settle those comparisons in one way or the other. But that would have the effect of either making it false that if L_2 were on that might be because A was closed, or making it false that if L_1 were on that might be because B and C were both closed. Surely, that must be wrong. Both of these 'might be' propositions are objectively true. Their truth is not just a matter of our not having settled certain comparisons we could settle any time we like. Thus, it does not seem to me that this way of basing counterfactuals on comparative similarity can be successful. There seem to be clear counterexamples to connectedness that cannot be handled by appealing to comparative similarity.

Thus far I have been concentrating on the formal differences between the comparative similarity analysis and the minimal change analysis. But the ultimate test has to be which analysis gives the intuitively correct truth values for the counterfactuals in actual cases. We have seen that the minimal change analysis seems to give the correct result in cases like Lewis's example of the line and in the circuit example, and the comparative similarity analysis does not. But there are much simpler examples that have been proposed as counterexamples to the comparative similarity analysis. The best known is probably that of Nixon and his button.[21] Suppose Nixon had pushed the

---

[21] This was proposed by Fine [1975]. Basically similar examples have been proposed by a number of other authors. See Bowie [1979].

button that would cause a nuclear holocaust. We all agree that had he done so there would have been a nuclear holocaust. But now consider a world in which he pushed the button but a minor miracle occurred preventing current from flowing through the wire and hence preventing the holocaust. That world is more like the real world than a world in which the holocaust occurred, so the comparative similarity analysis leads to the incorrect conclusion that had Nixon pushed the button there would have been no holocaust. The minimal change analysis, on the other hand, leads to the correct result. By legal conservatism, a world minimally changed from ours to accommodate Nixon's pushing the button must be one in which either no current flows, or all the rockets fail to fly, or ..., or there is a nuclear holocaust. Only the negation of the last is undercut by Nixon's pushing the button, so it follows from the analysis that there would be a nuclear holocaust.

To meet this sort of difficulty, Lewis [1979] has come to admit that counterfactuals are not to be evaluated in terms of our ordinary construal of comparative similarity. Lewis proposes instead that we employ a special comparative similarity relation that satisfies the following constraints:

(1) It is of the first importance to avoid big, widespread, diverse violations of law.
(2) It is of the second importance to maximize the spatio-temporal region throughout which perfect match of particular fact prevails.
(3) It is of the third importance to avoid even small, localized, simple violations of law.
(4) It is of little or no importance to secure approximate similarity of particular fact, even in matters that concern us greatly.

At the same time, this is an attempt to handle the temporal asymmetry of counterfactuals. Let us say that a counterfactual is *backwards-directed* if it is to the effect that if something had happened at one time, then something else that did not happen would have happened at an earlier time; and it is *forwards-directed* if it is to the effect that if something had happened at one time, then something else that did not happen would have happened at a later time. The temporal asymmetry of counterfactuals lies in the fact that it is much harder to find true backwards-directed counterfactuals than forwards-directed counterfactuals. Lewis actually goes so far as to assert that there are no true backwards-directed counterfactuals,[22] but we have seen that that is false.

A number of comments are in order here. First, it is worth observing how much clauses (2) and (4) sound like a minimal change analysis. Talk of maximizing the spatiotemporal region throughout which perfect match of particular fact prevails sounds very much like an attempt to get at the notion of minimizing change to simple states of affairs. The principal difference other than precision of formulation may be that Lewis is still supposing that we have a similarity measure that smears together the effects of different changes and allows us to compare them even when one is not strictly contained in the other. If this is a correct assessment, we can no longer object to Lewis's analysis in terms of a difference between comparative similarity and minimal change. The only objection we can raise to the appeal to comparative similarity is the one we have already raised concerning connectedness.

However, the analysis proposed in section two does not proceed just in terms of minimal change, but in terms of minimal change constrained by legal conservatism and undercutting. We can raise objections to Lewis's analysis insofar as it diverges from those constraints. Clause (1) of Lewis's list of constraints sounds like legal conservatism, but in light of clause (3), his analysis does not satisfy legal conservatism and that seems to me to be a serious defect. Lewis's analysis would almost invariably have us construct nearest P-worlds by incorporating "minor miracles" into them, i.e., "small, localized, simple, violations of law". For example, consider the conditional 'Had I struck this match it would have lit'. Among

---

[22] More accurately, Lewis allows that there may be true backwards-directed counterfactuals regarding the immediate past, but none regarding the more distant past.

the nearest worlds in which I struck the match, Lewis would have us include a world in which "a few extra neurons fire in a corner of my brain" in violation of (what he supposes are) deterministic laws of physics.[23] But assuming that my brain now works in accordance with the laws of physics, surely it is true that my brain would still have worked in accordance with the laws of physics even if I had struck this match. At least in normal circumstances, my striking the match can have no effect on whether my brain works in accordance with the laws of physics. But Lewis's analysis would make this conditional false.

Lewis is led to his peculiar treatment of laws by his attempt to explain the temporal asymmetry of counterfactuals. We must agree with Lewis that there is some kind of temporal asymmetry in counterfactuals, but we need not agree that it is so great as he supposes, and what asymmetry there is is easily explicable within the analysis of section two.[24] It is a reflection of the role of undercutting in the operation of counterfactuals. If $(P > Q)$ is a forwards-directed counterfactual, it can be made true by virtue of P undercutting $-Q$, and P can undercut $-Q$ simply by being the denial of an essential part of Q's historical antecedents. But if $(P > Q)$ is a backwards-directed counterfactual, $(P > Q)$ will only be true if either P nomically implies Q or P nomically implies the falsity of some essential part of the historical antecedents of $-Q$. Such nomic implications are hard to come by. For example, consider a match that is struck and then lights. Its being struck is an essential part of the historical antecedents of its lighting, so it is true that if it had not been struck it would not have lit. It is not the case, however, that if it had not lit it would not have been struck. Its not lighting does not nomically imply that it was not struck because something else might have gone wrong, nor does it nomically imply the falsity of any historical antecedent of its being struck. Thus the backwards-directed

---

[23] This is adapted from Lewis's [1979] discussion of Nixon and his button.

[24] In fact, for deterministic worlds, which are the only ones Lewis considers, it was already explicable within the analysis of Pollock [1976].

counterfactual is just false. The only way to get a true backwards-directed counterfactual in this case is by direct instantiation in a law. If it is a law that any match struck under circumstances C will light, then we can correctly conclude that if the match had not lit, either it would not have been struck or else conditions C would not have obtained. Thus, the temporal asymmetry of counterfactuals is an automatic consequence of the analysis in terms of undercutting, and no special maneuvering is required to accommodate it.

Lewis's clause (3) appears to be an attempt to do what appeal to undercutting is supposed to do in my analysis, but as we have seen, it does not seem to be successful. The modified analysis of Lewis [1979] comes much closer to my analysis (that of Pollock [1976] and the present one) than did his earlier analysis. But it differs in all the respects enumerated here, and insofar as it does so it still seems to be wrong. Thus despite similarities in our analyses, there are important differences, and these differences seem to me to favor the present analysis.

4. Minimal Change and a Counterfactual Antinomy

The ultimate purpose of this section is to defend my use of SB for evaluating counterfactuals in cases in which the limit assumption fails. The intuitive difficulty with SB in such cases is that it makes all such counterfactuals vacuously true. That seems intuitively wrong, but as we have seen, WB fares no better intuitively. My strategy will be to present a counterfactual antinomy and propose a solution to it. That solution will at least make SB more plausible than it seems now.

Counterfactual conditionals tell us what would have been the case if something else had been the case. They are about "counterfactual situations" or states of affairs in a sense that requires that logically equivalent propositions describe the same situation. As such, the principle of logical interchange is undeniable:

(4.1) $\Box(P \leftrightarrow Q) \rightarrow [(P > R) \leftrightarrow (Q > R)]$.

Logical interchange is central to any attempt to analyze counterfactuals in terms of the nearest possible worlds in which their antecedents are true. Without logical interchange we would have to discriminate between antecedents more finely than can be done in terms of the possible worlds at which they are true.

Let us symbolize ⌜There are infinitely many F's⌝ as ⌜$(\exists_\infty x)Fx$⌝. Suppose we have an infinite set X of white billiard balls, and let b be any member of X. Suppose further that the colors of the members of X are entirely independent of one another, so that if we changed the colors of the members of any subset of X the rest would still be white. Thus, b would still be white and hence not black, even if infinitely many of the other billiard balls in X were black:

(4.2) $(\exists_\infty x)(x \in X \ \& \ x \neq b \ \& \ Bx) > \sim Bb$.

In fact, b would still be white even if *all* the other billiard balls were black.

If infinitely many of the balls in X were black, then any one of them might be black. In particular, b might be black:

(4.3) $\sim[(\exists_\infty x)(x \in X \ \& \ Bx) > \sim Bb]$.

If there is any temptation to deny (4.3), note that if it is possible for infinitely many of the balls in X to be black, then surely some of them must be such that they might be black if infinitely many of the balls in X were black. That is all we need for the present argument, because we can just choose b to be one of those balls. As there are no relevant differences between the different balls, however, it seems that it must also be true that any of them might be black.

(4.2) and (4.3) seem unexceptionable until we note that the antecedents of their conditionals are logically equivalent:

(4.4) $\Box[(\exists_\infty x)(x \in X \ \& \ Bx) \leftrightarrow (\exists_\infty x)(x \in X \ \& \ x \neq b \ \& \ Bx)]$.

Clearly, the right side of (4.4) entails the left side. Conversely, if only finitely many of the balls other than b are black, then even if b is black too there are only finitely many black balls in X. Hence by virtue of logical interchange, (4.2) and (4.3) are contradictories of each other. And yet they are both true! We have a paradox.

The simplest resolution of the paradox would be to take (4.2), (4.3), and (4.4) as a counterexample to logical interchange and conclude that the latter is false. Such a resolution is both implausible and unpalatable. It is unpalatable because it would destroy all of the recent work on counterfactuals that has proceeded in terms of possible worlds. It is implausible because it seems intuitively that counterfactuals are really about counterfactual situations or states of affairs in a sense that makes logical interchange valid. Furthermore, it seems that if logical interchange were the culprit here, then we should be able to construct counterexamples not involving appeal to infinity, and that does not seem to be possible.

(4.4) is unassailable. Can we then deny either (4.2) or (4.3)? I do not see how we can deny (4.2). Our supposition about the independence of the billiard balls can be made more precise as follows:

(4.5) $(\forall Y)\{$if $Y \subseteq X$ and $b \notin Y$ then
$\quad [(\forall x)(x \in Y \rightarrow Bx) > \sim Bb]\}$.

(4.5) is surely possible, and it certainly seems that it entails (4.2). But even if (4.5) does not entail (4.2), why can't we just assume (4.2)? (4.2) could be true even if (4.5) were false.

It seems that the culprit must be (4.3). But it seems that if infinitely many of the balls in X were black, and there are no relevant differences between the balls, then any infinite subset of X might consist of black balls, and hence any one of the balls might be black. At the very least, there must be some infinite subset of the balls in X such that its members might all be black if infinitely many of the balls in X were black, and for the sake of the argument all we have to do is pick b from the members of that subset. Thus it seems impossible to deny (4.3). We still have a paradox.

We can construct other examples of similar sorts that also appear to be counterexamples to logical interchange. But I am still inclined to affirm that the very nature of counterfactuals is such as to ensure that logical interchange must hold. Counterfactuals are not about particular propositions, but rather about the situations described by the propositions. Logically equivalent propositions describe the same situations, so logical interchange must hold.

It is noteworthy that antinomies of the preceding sort only seem to arise in contexts mixing counterfactuals with infinity. I think that the solution lies there. Consider an English sentence of the form ⌜If infinitely many of the members of X were black, then it would be the case that P⌝. Let us abbreviate this sentence as ⌜$X_\infty B > P$⌝. We have taken this sentence to express the counterfactual conditional $(\exists_\infty x)(x \in X \ \& \ Bx) > P$. Our difficulty is that the propositions expressed by ⌜$X_\infty B > P$⌝ and ⌜$(X-\{b\})_\infty B \setminus > P$⌝ seem to have different truth conditions, and yet $(\exists_\infty x)(x \in X \ \& \ Bx)$ is logically equivalent to $(\exists_\infty x)(x \in (X-\{b\}) \ \& \ Bx)$. It seems quite easy to describe the truth conditions of ⌜$X_\infty B > P$⌝. If infinitely many of the members of X were black, then the members of any infinite subset of X might all be black. Thus, in evaluating the proposition expressed by ⌜$X_\infty B > P$⌝, we must consider each infinite subset of X and ask whether P would be true if all the members of that subset were black. In other words, the proposition expressed by ⌜$X_\infty B > P$⌝ is true iff:

(4.6) $(\forall Y)$[if $Y \subseteq X$ and Y is infinite then
$\quad ((\forall x)(x \in Y \rightarrow Bx) > P)$].

This intuitive description of the truth conditions seems to capture exactly the reasoning that led us to conclude that ⌜$(X-\{b\})_\infty B > \sim Bb$⌝ is true but ⌜$X_\infty B > \sim Bb$⌝ is false. It seems that these truth conditions make logical interchange objectively invalid.

But perhaps things are not as they seem. Suppose Z is a finite set of white billiard balls, and let ⌜$Z_{1/2} B > P$⌝ be the English conditional ⌜If more than half of the members of Z were black then it would be the case that P⌝. There is a strong intuitive inclination to say in connection with this sentence that if more than half of the members of Z were black, then *any* subset containing more than half of the members of Z might consist of black balls. In other words, the following describes the truth conditions for $\ulcorner Z_{1/2}B > P\urcorner$:

(4.7) $(\forall Y)$[if $Y \subseteq Z$ and Y contains more than half of the members of Z then $((\forall x)(x \in Y \rightarrow Bx) > P)$].

This makes the truth conditions for $\ulcorner Z_{1/2}B > P\urcorner$ parallel to the truth conditions for $\ulcorner X_\infty B > P\urcorner$. It has the consequence that it is false that if more than half the members of Z were black, they would not all be black.

But there is also a strong intuitive argument for the conclusion that (4.7) cannot describe the appropriate truth conditions for the propositions expressed by $\ulcorner Z_{1/2}B > P\urcorner$. Suppose Z has five members. Then more than half the members of Z are black iff at least three of them are black. We are supposing that the colors of the different members of Z are independent, so supposing a certain number of them to be black has no effect on the colors of the rest of them. The rest would still be white. Thus, even if more than half the members of Z were black, they still would not all be black. In evaluating the counterfactual we consider worlds resulting from minimally changing the actual world to accommodate its being true that more than half the members of Z are black, but to suppose all the members of Z to be black is a gratuitously large change. We have conflicting intuitions here.

It is a commonplace that the English expression $\ulcorner$If either P or Q then it would be true that $R\urcorner$ is ambiguous, having what I will call the *literal reading* $\ulcorner(P \vee Q) > R\urcorner$ and the *distributive reading* $\ulcorner(P > R)\ \&\ (Q > R)\urcorner$. These are not equivalent. The latter implies the former, but not conversely.[25] I suggest similarly that $\ulcorner$If more than half of the members of Z were black then it would be the case that $P\urcorner$ has both a literal reading and a distributive reading. On the literal reading we take the antecedent of the conditional to be $\ulcorner$More than half

---

[25] Donald Nute has explored the possibility of adopting

$$[(P \vee Q) > R] \rightarrow [(P > R)\ \&\ (Q > R)]$$

as an axiom in the logic art of counterfactuals. If we add it to a theory containing logical interchange, we obtain the absurd theorem $\ulcorner(P > Q) \rightarrow [(P\&R) > Q]\urcorner$. See Nute [1984] for his most recent discussion of this.

the members of Z are black⌝ and consider whether P would be true in all worlds resulting from minimal changes to the actual world that accommodate the truth of that antecedent. Thus, on the literal reading it is true that if more than half the members of Z were black, they still would not all be black. On the distributive reading we take the English sentence to mean that given any set of more than half the members of X, if its members were all black then it would be true that P. Thus, on the distributive reading it is false that if more than half the members of Z were black, they would not all be black. Only on the literal reading does ⌜$Z_{1/2}B > P$⌝ express a simple subjunctive conditional. On the distributive reading it expresses the complex quantified proposition symbolized by (4.7).

What is it about the English sentences in the two preceding examples that leads us to say that they are alike in having both literal and distributive readings? Roughly, they are sentences having natural paraphrases of the form

(4.8) If any member of the set G of states of affairs were to obtain then it would be the case that P.

⌜If either P or Q then R⌝ can be roughly paraphrased as

If any member of the set $\{P,Q\}$ were true then it would be the case that R.

And ⌜If more than half the members of Z were black then it would true that P⌝ can be paraphrased as

If any member of the set of all states of affairs of the form ⌜$(\forall x)(x \in Y \rightarrow Bx)$⌝ where Y is a subset of Z containing more than half of the members of Z were to obtain, then it would be true that P.

But for ⌜$X_\infty B > P$⌝ there is a new twist. There are no minimal changes to accommodate the truth of ⌜Infinitely many members of X are black⌝. Thus, on the literal reading a counterfactual of the form ⌜If infinitely many members of X were black then it would be the case that P⌝ is vacuously true. Consequently, although there is theoretically such a literal reading, it is useless and hence the English conditional will only be understood in the distributive sense. The English conditional is most likely univocal, having truth conditions correctly described by (4.6).

Applying the preceding considerations to the antinomy, what they show is that $\ulcorner X_\infty B > P \urcorner$ does not express a simple subjunctive conditional. In particular, $\ulcorner (X-\{b\})_\infty B > \sim Bb \urcorner$ does not express (4.2), and $\ulcorner X_\infty B > \sim Bb \urcorner$ does not express what (4.3) denies. The intuitions that led us to conclude that the English sentences express true and false propositions respectively were correct, but we were mistaken in concluding from them that (4.2) and (4.3) are true. Instead, the propositions expressed by the English sentences are rather complicated quantificational propositions of the form of (4.6) and its negation. Thus, there is no conflict with the principle of logical interchange.

This resolution of the antinomy removes the sting of implausibility from SB. The purported counterexamples to SB all involve sentences that should be read distributively rather than literally. This does not prove, of course, that their literal readings are vacuously true, but it makes it plausible that they are. Basically, what this response amounts to is to make SB immune from the test of intuition in those cases in which SB and WB diverge. But of course this also makes WB immune, so it might also be taken to be a vindication of WB.[26] The upshot of this is that intuition cannot adjudicate the difference between SB and WB. Perhaps the most reasonable stance to take here is that because we do not use counterfactuals in which the limit assumption fails (they are not expressed by English sentences), there is no fact of the matter regarding which of WB and SB is correct. We can define two kinds of counterfactuals, one working in terms of SB and the other in terms of WB, and there is nothing to determine which is "really" expressed by English sentences. Perhaps the only way to choose between them is on the ground of simplicity, but there SB is the clear winner.

---

[26] Note, however, that this is not a defense of WB as used by Lewis in his original comparative similarity analysis, because there the limit assumption also fails for cases unrelated to the antinomy.

V
Causation

1. Counterfactual Analyses of Causation

Recent advances in the understanding of subjunctive conditionals have suggested that they may be of use in the analysis of causation. I will suggest here that although causation cannot actually be analyzed in terms of counterfactuals, the same framework of possible worlds and minimal change used in the analysis of counterfactuals can also be used to analyze causation.

David Lewis [1973] was the first to propose a counterfactual analysis of causation, and he was followed by Pollock [1976] and Swain [1978]. Lewis's proposal is very simple. Where P and Q report the occurrence of events, he defines:

(1.1) Q *depends causally on* P iff (P & Q & ($\sim P > \sim Q$)) is true.[1]

Lewis then maintains that if Q depends causally on P, then P causes Q. He found himself unable to identify causation with causal dependence because causation is transitive and causal dependence is not, so he proposed instead that causation should be identified with the ancestral of causal dependence:

(1.2) P causes Q iff there is a finite sequence $R_0,\ldots,R_n$ of propositions reporting the occurrence of events such that $R_0 = P$ and $R_n = Q$ and for each i $<$ n, R_{i+1} depends causally on R_i.

---

[1] This is not quite Lewis's definition, but it leads to the same result when incorporated into his analysis of causation.

Swain's analysis is similar, but generalizes the way of obtaining causation from causal dependence.

There are numerous counterexamples demonstrating that this analysis is too simple. Specifically, causal dependence does not entail causation. Jaegwon Kim [1973] presented several interesting counterexamples, although not everyone agrees that they are counterexamples. A pair of counterexamples that turn more directly on the logic of counterfactuals, and that seem to me to be decisive, are as follows. First, it follows from modal SS that if Q entails P then $(\sim P > \sim Q)$ obtains. But it clearly does not follow that P causes Q. For example, the doorbell's ringing entails that it exists, so it would follow on Lewis's account that the doorbell's existing caused it to ring. But that is absurd. Second, if $(\sim P > \sim Q)$ obtains and R is suitably independent of P and Q then $[(\sim P \ \& \ \sim R) > \sim Q]$ also obtains. That is equivalent to saying that $[\sim(P \lor R) > \sim Q]$ obtains. But then it follows that Q depends causally on $(P \lor R)$. Hence it follows from Lewis's account that because the light's being on was caused by the switch's being closed (due to causal dependence), the light's being on was also caused by its being the case that either the switch was closed or Caesar crossed the Rubicon. But that is again absurd.[2]

I take these difficulties to illustrate the need for a stronger counterfactual condition in the analysis of causation. $\ulcorner(\sim P > \sim Q)\urcorner$ is basically a negative condition. We also need a positive condition. It seems obvious that PCQ ($\ulcorner P$ is a cause of $Q\urcorner$) should entail the necessitation conditional $(P >> Q)$, but it does not do so on Lewis's account. My analysis (in Pollock [1976]) built upon this observation, defining causation in terms of the satisfaction of both $\ulcorner(P >> Q)\urcorner$ and $\ulcorner(\sim P > \sim Q)\urcorner$, together with some additional conditions intended to handle epiphenomena, the direction of causation, and other complexities. The resulting analysis was extremely

[2] One might try to avoid these difficulties by insisting that the doorbell's existing and its being the case that either the switch was closed or Caesar crossed the Rubicon are not events. But see the discussion of causal relata in section two.

unwieldy and has since been decisively refuted by counterexamples.[3]

To my mind, one of the main difficulties for any counterfactual analysis of causation is getting causation to come out transitive. No familiar subjunctive conditional is transitive, and so some special maneuvering appears to be required in order to get transitivity. The simplest solution to this problem is that proposed by Lewis. The basic idea is that we use subjunctive conditionals to define a "core causal relation" C_0, and then we identify causation with the ancestral of C_0. This is a "brute force" strategy for obtaining transitivity. It achieves its goal only at the expense of undesirable side effects. In defining C_0 the natural procedure is to conjoin a number of intuitively necessary conditions for causation. If we then define C to be the ancestral of C_0, what were necessary conditions for C_0 will generally fail to be necessary conditions for C. Thus, the intuitively necessary conditions for causation fail to be necessary conditions according to this analysis. We will see an example of this in section three. The only obvious way to avoid this difficulty is to construct an analysis of C in terms of an underlying conditional that is already transitive. This does not seem initially very hopeful because no known nontrivial subjunctive conditional is transitive. The purpose of section three, however, is to construct a strong subjunctive conditional that is transitive and entailed by causation, and is plausibly the conditional underlying causation and in terms of which causation is to be analyzed. This will be called 'the causal conditional'.

The reason transitivity is important is that causation is propagated by causal chains. For example, closing a switch causes a light to come on *by* causing current to flow in the wires, where the latter causes the light to come on. Philosophers have

---

[3] By Glenn Ross [1982]. One of the features of my 1976 analysis was that it did not make causation transitive. I tried to argue that that was a virtue, giving what I took to be counterexamples to the transitivity of causation. But I have since become convinced that those putative counterexamples were specious, so that is another defect of my 1976 analysis.

generally thought of causal chains as simple linear chains, but that is unrealistic. Causal chains can diverge and reconverge. For example, we might have the following causal chain:

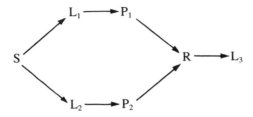

Here closing switch S causes lights L_1 and L_2 to each come on. L_1's coming on activates photocell P_1, and L_2's coming on activates P_2. P_1 and P_2 jointly cause relay R to close, which causes light L_3 to come on. If all this goes according to plan, then closing S causes L_3 to come on. In order for causal chains to work in this way, causation must be not only transitive but also adjunctive, i.e.,

(1.3) If PCQ and PCR then $PC(Q\&R)$.

In the preceding example, transitivity allows us to conclude that SCP_1 and SCP_2 and $(P_1 \& P_2)CL_3$. But in order to conclude that SCL_3, we must also be able to conclude that $SC(P_1 \& P_2)$, and for that we need adjunctivity. This suggests that adjunctivity is as important to causation as transitivity. It will be gratifying then that without any *ad hoc* maneuvering, the causal conditional turns out to be adjunctive.

2. Causal Relata

Philosophers have typically taken causation to be a relation between events. In my opinion, that is incorrect but harmless if we do not bear down too heavily on the notion of an event. Causation should more properly be viewed as a relation between states of affairs. This is best seen by noting that there is no restriction on the logical type of a cause or effect. There can be negative causes ('His not arriving on time caused the

151

party to be delayed'), disjunctive causes ('Its being the case that either switch 1 or switch 2 was closed caused the light to come on'), existential causes ('There being more than twenty people in the elevator caused the cable to snap'), and so on. These are perfectly respectable states of affairs, but they are not what would ordinarily be called 'events'. Events are things like baseball games, duels, and eruptions. Philosophers have often failed to distinguish between events and states of affairs.[4] For example, Davidson [1970] gives the following list of putative events: Sally's third birthday party, the eruption of Vesuvius in A.D. 1906, my eating breakfast this morning, and the first performance of *Lulu* in Chicago. Although the others are events, *my eating breakfast this morning* is a state of affairs. This would not be troublesome were it not that philosophers have repeatedly noted that negations and disjunctions of events (if there are such things) are not usually events and so have concluded that there cannot be negative or disjunctive causes. The above examples demonstrate that such a conclusion is false.

It is clear, I think, that states of affairs are causal relata. But we can also talk about events being causes, such as in 'The rainstorm caused the game to be delayed'. This has suggested to some philosophers that events are the basic causal relata, and talk of states of affairs as causes is to be analyzed in terms of causal relations between events. In fact, however, the logical order is the reverse. Events can be causes only in the same sense that physical objects can be causes. For example, we can say that the tree caused the accident. A physical object can only cause something *by being a certain way*. For instance, the tree might cause the accident by being too close to the road. If x causes something by being F, we can equally say that x's *being* F is the cause, thus reducing causation by physical objects to causation by states of affairs. Now consider events, for example, a duel with swords. We might say that the duel caused women to faint. Ordinarily, when we

---

[4] For discussions of this distinction, see Vendler [1967] and [1967a], Pollock [1976], and Peterson [1981].

say that an event caused something, we have in mind that *the event's occurring* caused it. Thus, we would normally interpret this as meaning that the duel's occurring caused women to faint. But it might have been something else about the duel that caused women to faint. For example, women might be inured to duels, but this one's being exceptionally bloody caused women to faint anyway. The point here is that events are causes only in the sense that physical objects are also causes, and that sense is to be spelled out in terms of causation by states of affairs. States of affairs must be regarded as the most fundamental causal relata. They will be so regarded for the purposes of the present analysis.

3. The Causal Conditional

In constructing a logical analysis, it is customary to make various proposals and test them directly against intuition. I find, however, that most people have quite unclear intuitions about complicated cases of causation, and hence the appeal to intuition tends to be indecisive. Thus, my strategy will be somewhat different. By looking only at simple cases in which our intuitions are reasonably secure, we can defend a few formal principles regarding causation. These formal principles will provide formal constraints on the analysis of causation. My strategy will be to see how far we can get relying almost exclusively on these formal constraints.

The first assumption I will make about causation is an obvious one. In order for one state of affairs to cause another, they must both obtain:

(C1) $PCQ \rightarrow (P \ \& \ Q)$.

The following principle has a distinguished history:

(3.1) $PCQ \rightarrow (\sim P > \sim Q)$.[5]

According to this principle, in order for P to be a cause of Q it must be the case that Q would not have obtained had P not

---

[5] See Lewis [1973] for a discussion of this principle.

obtained. For example, consider a switch that controls a light. We would not agree that the switch's being closed caused the light to be on if the light might have been on anyway.

Although there is a considerable intuitive support for (3.1), there are also examples in which it seems problematic. These involve causal overdetermination. Suppose we have two switches and a light wired together in such a way that the light is on whenever at least one of the switches is closed. Suppose further that both switches are closed. It does not seem unreasonable to insist that the following are true:

(3.2) Switch 1's being closed causes the light to be on.

(3.3) That both switches are closed causes the light to be on.

But it is false that the light would be off if switch 1 were not closed—switch 2 would still be closed and so the light would still be on. It is also false that the light would be off if the switches were not both closed—it would still be on if just one of the switches were closed. These appear to be counterexamples to (3.1). On the other hand, it might be retorted that (3.2) and (3.3) are false and that what causes the light to be on is that at least one of the switches is closed—not that they are both closed and not that a specific one of them is closed. What makes this retort seem reasonable is just (3.1). The cause is not that switch 1 is closed because the light would still be on even if switch 1 were not closed. Similarly, the cause is not that both switches are closed, because the light might still be on even if they were not both closed.

(3.2) and (3.3) seem intuitively reasonable, but so does the rejoinder. What this suggests is that we are confusing two different causal concepts. We can distinguish between *sufficient causes* and *strict causes*. Strict causes satisfy (3.1). Sufficient causes, on the other hand, are states of affairs or conjunctions of states of affairs that would be strict causes if they occurred alone (without any other sufficient causes being present). We can define 'sufficient cause' in terms of 'strict cause' as follows:

154

(3.4) P is a *sufficient cause* of Q iff there is a set X of states of affairs obtaining at the actual world such that (1) P is equivalent to a conjunction of members of X, (2) $\bigvee X$ (the disjunction of X) is a strict cause of Q, and (3) for each R in X, if none of the members of X obtained then R would cause Q were it to obtain, i.e., $\sim \bigvee X > (R > RCQ)$.

I shall assume that strict causation (symbolized by '**C**') satisfies (3.1).[6] (3.1) will not be one of my official assumptions, however, because it follows from either of two stronger assumptions. Let us symbolize $\ulcorner PCQ$ obtains at $w \urcorner$ as $\ulcorner PC_w Q \urcorner$. Recalling that $\| \sim Q \|$ is the set of all $\sim Q$-worlds, by principle (2.4) of Chapter Four, principle (3.1) is equivalent to:

(3.5) If $PC_w Q$ then $\mathbf{M}_w(\sim P) \subseteq \| \sim Q \|$.

I propose that a stronger condition is also satisfied. Consider a simple circuit consisting of a switch and a light wired in series with a power source so that the switch's being closed (P) causes the light to be on (Q). In accordance with (3.1) we have ($\sim P > \sim Q$). Now let R be some irrelevant state of affairs that actually obtains, such as there being a typhoon in Japan. We also have $[\sim(P \vee R) > \sim Q]$, because if the switch were open and there were no typhoon in Japan then the light would be off. But we do not want to affirm that the light's being on is caused by the disjunctive state of affairs that obtains iff either the switch is closed or there is a typhoon in Japan. The second disjunct is irrelevant. What that irrelevancy amounts to is that although one way of having the light off is to have the switch open, adding that there is no typhoon in Japan is a gratuitous additional change that is not required to bring it about that the light is off. This indicates that in order for P to cause Q, the nearest $\sim P$-worlds must not only be

[6] Although (3.1) is suggested by Lewis's analysis, his analysis does not validate (3.1). The difficulty is the general one remarked in section one that necessary conditions for the core relation will not generally be necessary conditions for its ancestral. Lewis's core relation is $\ulcorner P \,\&\, Q \,\&\, (\sim P > \sim Q) \urcorner$, and this of course does satisfy (3.1), but the ancestral does not.

~Q-worlds—they must be nearest ~Q-worlds. This is my second assumption about causation:

(C2) If PC_wQ then $\mathbf{M}_w(\sim P) \subseteq \mathbf{M}_w(\sim Q)$.

In other words, if P causes Q then a minimal change removing the cause is also a minimal change removing the effect. In the case of our switch and light, one way to minimally alter the world so as to have the light off is to minimally alter it so that the switch is open.

My third assumption arises from asking why (C2) and hence (3.1) hold. Consider the light controlled by the single switch again. It seems that the reason the light would be off if the switch were open is that the switch's being open would *cause* the light to be off. I propose in general:

(C3) $PCQ \rightarrow [\sim P > \bar{P}C\bar{Q}]$.

(C2) and (C3) would hold vacuously if $\mathbf{M}_w(\sim P) = \varnothing$. This occurs, for example, if P is necessarily true. The final constraint to be proposed in this section is then that (C2) and (C3) hold nonvacuously:

(C4) If PC_wQ then $\mathbf{M}_w(\sim P) \neq \varnothing$.

(C3) is a "reflection principle". Reflection principles are so called because they can be applied to themselves to yield more complicated principles. By (A7) of modal SS and (C3), we get:

(3.6) $PCQ \rightarrow [\sim P > (P > PCQ)]$.

By another application of (A7) and (C3), we get:

(3.7) $PCQ \rightarrow [\sim P > (P > [\sim P > \bar{P}C\bar{Q}])]$.

By continuing in this manner we obtain all principles of either of the following forms:

(3.8) $PCQ \rightarrow [\sim P > (P > [\sim P > \ldots > (P > PCQ) \ldots])]$.

(3.9) $PCQ \rightarrow [\sim P > (P > [\sim P > \ldots > [\sim P > \bar{P}C\bar{Q}] \ldots])]$.

The nested antecedents in these conditionals involve our moving to a nearest $\sim P$-world, and then a nearest P-world from that, and then a nearest $\sim P$-world from there, and so on. Let us say that such a sequence of worlds is a *P-sequence* and that every world that can be reached in this way is *P-accessible* from the actual world. Precisely:

(3.10) σ is a *P-sequence* iff σ is a sequence of length ω of worlds such that for each i in ω:
(a) if P obtains at σ_i then $\sigma_{i+1} \in \mathbf{M}_{\sigma_i}(\sim P)$;
(b) if $\sim P$ obtains at σ_i then $\sigma_{i+1} \in \mathbf{M}_{\sigma_i}(P)$.

Let $Seq(w,P)$ be the set of all P-sequences starting from w, i.e.,

(3.11) $Seq(w,P) = \{\sigma|\ \sigma \text{ is a } P\text{-sequence and } \sigma_0 = w\}$.

The set of all worlds P-accessible from w is then:

(3.12) $\mathbf{A}_w(P) = \{w^*|\ (\exists \sigma)(\exists i)[\sigma \in Seq(w,P) \text{ and } \sigma_i = w^*]\}$.

More precise versions of (3.8) and (3.9) can now be formulated as follows:

(3.13) If $PC_w Q$ and $w^* \in \mathbf{A}_w(P) \cap \|P\|$ then $PC_{w^*}Q$.

(3.14) If $PC_w Q$ and $w^* \in \mathbf{A}_w(P) \cap \|\sim P\|$ then $\bar{P}C_{w^*}\bar{Q}$.

From (C3) and (C4), we get:

(3.15) If $PC_w Q$ then $\mathbf{A}_w(P) \neq \varnothing$.

Given (3.13) and (3.14) we can immediately obtain from (C2):

(3.16) If $PC_w Q$ and $w^* \in \mathbf{A}_w(P)$, then $\mathbf{M}_{w^*}(P) \subseteq \mathbf{M}_{w^*}(Q)$ and $\mathbf{M}_{w^*}(\sim P) \subseteq \mathbf{M}_{w^*}(\sim Q)$.

We can take the consequents of (3.15) and (3.16) to define a conditional. $(P \twoheadrightarrow Q)$ is the state of affairs that obtains iff the consequents of (3.15) and (3.16) hold:

(3.17) $(P \twoheadrightarrow Q) = \bigvee\{w|\ \mathbf{A}_w(P) \neq \varnothing \text{ and for each } w^* \text{ in } \mathbf{A}_w(P), \mathbf{M}_{w^*}(P) \subseteq \mathbf{M}_{w^*}(Q) \text{ and } \mathbf{M}_{w^*}(\sim P) \subseteq \mathbf{M}_{w^*}(\sim Q)\}$.[7]

---

[7] Recall that the disjunction of a set of possible worlds is a state of affairs that obtains iff one of those worlds obtains.

V. Causation

Less formally, $(P \twoheadrightarrow Q)$ obtains at w iff $\mathbf{A}_w(P) \neq \varnothing$ and for each world w^* that is P-accessible from w, $\mathbf{M}_{w^*}(P) \subseteq \mathbf{M}_{w^*}(Q)$ and $\mathbf{M}_{w^*}(\sim P) \subseteq \mathbf{M}_{w^*}(\sim Q)$. This is the *causal conditional*. It follows from (C1)–(C4) that:

(3.18) $PCQ \rightarrow (P \twoheadrightarrow Q)$.

The causal conditional has an illuminating reformulation:

(3.19) $(P \twoheadrightarrow Q)$ obtains at w iff $Seq(w,P) \neq \varnothing$ and $Seq(w,P) \subseteq Seq(w,Q)$.

$Seq(w,P)$ can be regarded as the set of sequences of worlds that can be reached by manipulating the cause (making minimal changes that impose it and remove it). Thus, what the causal conditional says is that manipulations of the cause are also manipulations of the effect.

It follows immediately from (3.19) that the causal conditional is transitive:

(3.20) $[(P \twoheadrightarrow Q) \& (Q \twoheadrightarrow R)] \rightarrow (P \twoheadrightarrow R)$.

It follows by modal SS that the causal conditional is adjunctive:

(3.21) $[(P \twoheadrightarrow Q) \& (P \twoheadrightarrow R)] \rightarrow [P \twoheadrightarrow (Q \& R)]$.[8]

The causal conditional satisfies the reflection principle for causation:

(3.22) $(P \twoheadrightarrow Q) \rightarrow [\sim P > (\sim P \twoheadrightarrow \sim Q)]$.

Several other noteworthy properties of the causal conditional are as follows:

(3.23) $(P \twoheadrightarrow Q) \leftrightarrow (\sim P \twoheadrightarrow \sim Q)$.

(3.24) $[(P \twoheadrightarrow Q) \& (P \twoheadrightarrow R)] \rightarrow [P \twoheadrightarrow (Q \lor R)]$.

(3.25) $[(P \twoheadrightarrow Q) \& (Q > R)] \rightarrow (P > R)$.

(3.26) $(P \twoheadrightarrow Q) \rightarrow (P >> Q)$.

(3.27) $(\Box P \lor \Box \sim P) \rightarrow \sim (P \twoheadrightarrow Q)$.

---

[8] Specifically, (3.21) follows from the fact that for each P and Q, $\mathbf{M}_w(P) \cap \|P\| \subseteq \mathbf{M}_w(P \& Q)$ and $\mathbf{M}_w(P \lor Q) \subseteq \mathbf{M}_w(P) \cup \mathbf{M}_w(Q)$.

Let us say that P is *causally contingent at* w iff $\mathbf{A}_w(P) \neq \varnothing$. Where '$\Leftrightarrow$' symbolizes nomic equivalence, the following two principles hold if P is causally contingent:

(3.28) $P \twoheadrightarrow P$.

(3.29) $(P \Leftrightarrow Q) \to (P \twoheadrightarrow Q)$.

In general:

(3.30) $(P \Leftrightarrow Q) \to [(P \twoheadrightarrow R) \leftrightarrow (Q \twoheadrightarrow R)]$.

Some principles that do *not* hold are:

$\Box(P \to Q) \to (P \twoheadrightarrow Q)$
$[(P \twoheadrightarrow Q) \; \& \; \Box(Q \to R)] \to (P \twoheadrightarrow R)$
$[(P \twoheadrightarrow R) \; \& \; (Q \twoheadrightarrow R)] \to [(P \vee Q) \twoheadrightarrow R]$
$(P \twoheadrightarrow Q) \to (\sim Q \twoheadrightarrow \sim P)$
$[(P \twoheadrightarrow R) \; \& \; (Q \twoheadrightarrow S)] \to [(P \; \& \; Q) \twoheadrightarrow (R \; \& \; S)]$
$(P \twoheadrightarrow Q) \to [(P \; \& \; R) \twoheadrightarrow Q]$.

We have constructed a transitive and adjunctive conditional that is entailed by causation and that is plausibly the source of the important logical properties of causation. This strongly suggests that causation is to be analyzed in terms of the causal conditional. Such an analysis will be developed in the next two sections.

4. The Role of Time

In attempting to analyze causation in terms of the causal conditional, it might first be suggested that the two relations can be identified for states of affairs that actually obtain:

(4.1) $PCQ \leftrightarrow [P \; \& \; Q \; \& \; (P \twoheadrightarrow Q)]$.

That this is too simple can be seen by considering theorem (3.28) according to which $(P \twoheadrightarrow P)$ holds whenever P is causally contingent (which it normally is). More generally, by theorem (3.29), for causally contingent P:

$(P \Leftrightarrow Q) \to (P \twoheadrightarrow Q)$.

V. Causation

However, nomically equivalent states of affairs do not invariably cause one another, as can be seen by considering a simple example. Suppose there is a kind of particle regarding which there are physical laws requiring it to fluctuate between two states S_1 and S_2 at regular intervals of ϵ seconds. If x is such a particle, x's entering state S_1 at t nomically implies it will enter S_2 at $t+\epsilon$, and x's entering S_2 at $t+\epsilon$ nomically implies it entered S_1 at t. These two states of affairs are thus nomically equivalent. However, although we would agree that x's entering S_1 at t (call this 'P') causes x to enter S_2 at $t+\epsilon$ (Q), we would not agree that x's entering S_2 at $t+\epsilon$ causes x to enter S_1 at t. This shows both that cause and effect are sometimes nomically equivalent and that nomically equivalent states of affairs do not invariably cause one another.

It might be supposed that the preceding difficulty can be avoided by some suitably complex counterfactual analysis of causation. But in fact *no* purely counterfactual analysis can make the required discriminations. It follows from legal conservatism that if P is not counterlegal at w, and P and Q are nomically equivalent at w, then $\mathbf{M}_w(P) = \mathbf{M}_w(Q)$. This implies that no counterfactual condition can distinguish between nomically equivalent states of affairs. Thus, any purely counterfactual analysis of causation must either imply that each of P and Q causes the other in the preceding example or that neither causes the other. But either implication is false. Consequently, although a correct analysis of causation may appeal to counterfactuals, it must also appeal to something else.

Clearly, what distinguishes between cause and effect in the preceding example is temporal precedence. It is the fact that x's entering S_1 at t occurs before x's entering S_2 at $t+\epsilon$ that is responsible for our judging the former to cause the latter but not conversely. This is easily seen by noting that if we reverse the direction of time (i.e., suppose $t+\epsilon$ to be an earlier time than t), we also reverse the direction of causation. Under those circumstances, we would take x's being in S_2 at $t+\epsilon$ to cause x's being in S_1 at t, rather than the other way around. This strongly suggests that what must be added to counterfactual conditions to obtain a correct analysis of causation is a temporal condition. There will be resistance to this move from philosophers who feel that backwards causation should be logically possible or who want to use causation to define the direction of time. I am unmoved by considerations of backwards causation, but I can agree that if it is possible to characterize the direction of time in terms of causation then it would be desirable to have an analysis of causation that does not appeal to temporal precedence. However, the mere fact that that would be desirable is no reason to think it is possible, and I do not see any way to do it. Thus, I shall make free use of temporal relations in analyzing causation.

Whether one state of affairs causes another cannot be relative to a frame of reference. This is an absolute matter independent of frames of reference. Accordingly, the temporal relations involved in the analysis of causation must also be absolute temporal relations and not relative to frames of reference. These are the same relations that played a role in the analysis of counterfactuals. We symbolize ⌜P is absolutely earlier than Q⌝ as ⌜$P < Q$⌝ and ⌜P is absolutely simultaneous with Q⌝ as ⌜$P \approx Q$⌝. Our only assumptions regarding these relations are the following:

(4.2) If $P < Q$ and $Q < R$ then $P < R$.

(4.3) If $P \approx Q$ and $Q < R$ then $P < R$.

(4.4) If $P < Q$ and $Q \approx R$ then $P < R$.

Having decided to take time into account, it is not altogether obvious how to do that. Some states of affairs have natural "dates", but others do not. For example, if a switch's being closed at t causes a light to come on at t^*, then t and t^* are the appropriate dates for these two states of affairs. But what are the appropriate dates for 'My grandfather's having been a horsethief caused me to be embarrassed throughout my later childhood'? In order to sort this out, let us begin by considering the simplest case, which is that of states of affairs that can be regarded as having natural instantaneous dates. The most obvious of these are the simple states of affairs of Chapter Four. Those are states of affairs ascribing logically simple concepts or their negations to n-tuples of objects at specific times. A second category of dated states of affairs are *enumerative states of affairs*, which enumerate the objects exemplifying a simple concept or the negation of a simple concept. More accurately, enumerative states of affairs have the form $\ulcorner a_1,...,a_n$ being the only F's at $t\urcorner$, or more generally, $\ulcorner$The members of X being the only F's at $t\urcorner$, where F is either a simple concept or the negation of a simple concept. I will call simple and enumerative states of affairs *basic states of affairs*. Let **B** be the set of all basic states of affairs, and let $\mathbf{B}_w$ be the set of all basic states of affairs obtaining at a world w.

For basic states of affairs, the temporal condition required for causation seems clear—the cause must precede the effect:

(4.5) If P and Q are basic states of affairs and PCQ then $P < Q$.

The problem now is how to generalize this condition to nonbasic states of affairs. I suggest that the solution lies in observing that in any case of causation involving nonbasic states of affairs, those states of affairs can be regarded as obtaining *because* related sets of basic states of affairs obtain. The obtaining of a nonbasic state of affairs can be regarded as supervenient upon the obtaining of basic states of affairs. For example, the obtaining of *the light's burning steadily from 3 a.m. to 6 p.m.* consists of the obtaining of all events of the form *the light's burning at t* for t between 3 a.m. and 6 p.m. To take another example, if switch 1 is closed and switch 2 is open, then the obtaining of *at least one of the switch's being closed* consists of the obtaining of *switch 1's being closed*. Or if Charlie and Herkimer are the only dragons left in the world, then the obtaining of *all the dragons in the world being airborne at t* consists of the obtaining of *Charlie's being airborne at t* and *Herkimer's being airborne at t* and *Charlie and Herkimer's being the only dragons at t*. In each case, the nonbasic state of affairs is entailed by the set of basic states of affairs upon which it is supervenient.

In Pollock [1976] and [1982] I proposed definitions on the order of:

(4.6) P is supervenient upon X at w iff $X \subseteq \mathbf{B}_w$ and X entails P and no proper subset of X entails P.

However, Glenn Ross has convinced me that such a definition is inadequate.[9] The difficulty is that (4.6) embodies a kind of "limit assumption" according to which if a state of affairs is entailed by some subset X of $\mathbf{B}_w$, there is always a smallest subset of X entailing that state of affairs. There are numerous counterexamples to this assumption. For example, consider ascriptions of velocity. I presume that these are not logically simple. Instead, they supervene upon states of affairs consisting of objects being at various locations at various times. However, velocity at a time t is defined in terms of limits of ratios involving locations and times as those times approach t arbitrarily closely. Where $t_0 < t < t_1$, the set of all actual states of affairs of the form x's *being at location p at t** where $t_0 < t^* < t_1$ entails x's *having velocity v at t*. But there is no minimal set of states of affairs describing x's location at different times that entails its having the velocity it does at t. Thus, it would follow from (4.6) that x's *having velocity v at t* is not supervenient upon any set of basic states of affairs. In order to avoid this sort of difficulty, we must define more simply:

(4.7) P is supervenient upon X at w iff $X \subseteq \mathbf{B}_w$ and X entails P.

This definition allows X to contain much excess baggage not required for the entailment. This will force us to make some of our definitions more complicated than they might otherwise be.

Not all states of affairs are supervenient upon sets of basic states of affairs. For example, a state of affairs consisting of a particular subjunctive generalization being true is not entailed by any set of basic states of affairs. Similarly, a coun-

[9] In Ross [1982].

terfactual state of affairs consisting of one nonactual state of affairs being a counterfactual consequence of another will not be entailed by any set of basic states of affairs that actually obtain. (To get an entailment in this case we must add some subjunctive generalizations.) In all cases, it appears that states of affairs that are not supervenient upon sets of basic states of affairs cannot be causal relata. Possible causal relata are characterized by the following definition:

(4.8) $P \in \mathbf{R}_w$ iff P is supervenient upon some set of basic states of affairs at w.

$\mathbf{R}_w$ is the set of all states of affairs that could be causal relata at the world w.

My proposal is now that the temporal relation required for causation between nonbasic states of affairs can be defined in terms of the temporal relations between the states of affairs upon which the nonbasic states of affairs are supervenient. Let us define:

(4.9) $P <_w Q$ iff $\bar{P}, Q \in \mathbf{R}_w$ and $(\forall w^*)(\forall X)\{$if $w^* \in \mathbf{M}_w(\sim P)$ and Q is supervenient upon X at w, then $(\exists X_0)(\exists Y)[X$ entails $\wedge X_0$ and Q is supervenient upon X_0 at w and $X_0 \subseteq \mathbf{B}_w$ and P is supervenient upon Y at w and $(\forall R)(\forall S)($if $R \in X_0$ and $S \in Y$ and $R \in \mathbf{B}_w$ and $S \in \mathbf{B}_w$ and R and S do not obtain at w^* then $S < R)]\}$.

The final condition I will impose upon causation is:

(C5) If PC_wQ then $P <_w Q$.

To motivate (C5), consider some examples:

Beginning with the simplest case, suppose P and Q are basic states of affairs and P is a cause of Q. Our temporal constraint in this case should be equivalent to the requirement that $P < Q$. We can establish this equivalence if we make the following reasonable assumption about basic states of affairs:

(A1) If $X \subseteq \mathbf{B}_w$ and $P \in \mathbf{B}_w$ and X entails P then $\{Q \mid Q \in X$ and $Q \approx P\}$ entails P.

This is the assumption that basic states of affairs with dates different from that of P cannot contribute to the entailment of P by X. Given (A1), we have the following theorem:

(4.10) If $P,Q \in \mathbf{B}_w$ and $(P \twoheadrightarrow Q)$ obtains at w then $P <_w Q$ iff $P < Q$.

Proof: Suppose $P,Q \in \mathbf{B}_w$ and $(P \twoheadrightarrow Q)$ obtains at w. Then $Seq(w,P) \neq \varnothing$, so there is a w^* in $\mathbf{M}_w(\sim P)$. As $(P \twoheadrightarrow Q)$ obtains at w, $w^* \in \mathbf{M}_w(\sim Q)$. $\{Q\} \subseteq \mathbf{B}_w$ and $\{Q\}$ entails Q, so there is an $X_0 \subseteq \mathbf{B}_w$ such that Q is equivalent to $\bigwedge X_0$, and there is a $Y \subseteq \mathbf{B}_w$ such that Y entails P and $(\forall R)(\forall S)$[if $R,S \in \mathbf{B}_w$ and $R \in X_0$ and $S \in Y$ and R and S do not obtain at w^* then $S < R$]. By (A1), $\{R|\ R \in X_0$ and $R \approx Q\}$ entails Q and $\{S|\ S \in Y$ and $S \approx P\}$ entails P. As P and Q do not obtain at w^*, there is an R in $\{R|\ R \in X_0$ and $R \approx Q\}$ and an S in $\{S|\ S \in Y$ and $S \approx \bar{P}\}$ such that R and S do not obtain at w^*. So $S < R$. As $\bar{P} \approx R$ and $Q \approx S$, $P < Q$.

Conversely, suppose $P < Q$. Suppose $w^* \in \mathbf{M}_w(\sim P)$ and $X \subseteq \mathbf{B}_w$ and X entails Q. Then X entails $\bigwedge\{Q\}$, and $\{Q\}$ entails Q, and $\{P\} \subseteq \mathbf{B}_w$ and $\{P\}$ entails P. P and Q do not obtain at w^*, and $P < Q$, so $(\forall R)(\forall S)$[if $R,S \in \mathbf{B}_w$ and $R \in \{Q\}$ and $S \in \{P\}$ and R and S do not obtain at w^*, then $S < R$]. So $P <_w Q$.

To illustrate (C5) with a slightly more complicated example, consider a switch that controls a light. Suppose the switch was closed just once yesterday, at t, and correspondingly the light came on just once yesterday, at t^*. The switch's having been closed at some time yesterday (P) caused it to be the case that the light came on at some time yesterday (Q). This is a causal relation between nonbasic states of affairs. It seems clear that in this case the temporal relation required for P to cause Q is that t precede t^*, and that is just what (C5) requires. In this case, X_0 is {*the light's coming on at t^**}, and Y is {*the switch's being closed at t*}. The only R is *the light's coming on at t^**, and the only S is *the swtich's being closed at t*. Thus, what is required for $P <_w Q$ is that t precede t^*.

Next, keeping P and Q the same, suppose the switch was

closed several times, at times $t_1,...,t_n$, and the light came on at times $t^*_1,...,t^*_m$. It is tempting to suppose that in order for P to cause Q, for each t_i there must be a corresponding t^*_j such that the switch's being closed at t_i caused the light to come on at t^*_j, but such a supposition is incorrect. For example, the switch might control the light by activating a mechanism that must be reset before the light can be turned on in that way a second time. Then every closing of the switch after the first might be inefficacious in bringing it about that the light comes on. Thus, all that can be required is that for each t^*_j there is a t_i that precedes it. That is precisely what is required for $P <_w Q$ in this case.

In the two preceding examples, nonbasic states of affairs supervene upon unit sets of basic states of affairs, but in general nonbasic states of affairs will supervene upon multimembered sets of basic states of affairs with different dates. For example, consider another pair of switches S_1 and S_2 and lights L_1 and L_2. Suppose S_1 controls L_1 and S_2 controls L_2, and S_1 and S_2 operate independently of each other. Let P_1 be S_1's being closed at t_1, P_2 be S_2's being closed at t_2, Q_1 be L_1's being on at t^*_1, and Q_2 be L_2's being on at t^*_2. We would agree that S_1's being closed at t_1 and S_2 at t_2 causes it to be the case that L_1 is on at t^*_1 and L_2 at t^*_2, i.e., $(P_1 \& P_2)\mathbf{C}(Q_1 \& Q_2)$. It cannot be required that both t_1 and t_2 precede both t^*_1 and t^*_2. It is enough for t_1 to precede t^*_1 and t_2 to precede t^*_2. That is what (4.9) requires for $(P_1 \& P_2) <_w (Q_1 \& Q_2)$. In this case, X_0 is $\{Q_1,Q_2\}$ and Y is $\{P_1,P_2\}$. In some nearest $\sim(P_1 \& P_2)$-worlds P_1 will be false, and in others P_2 will be false, but as P_1 and P_2 are independent of each other, they will never both be false in such a world. Similarly, in some nearest $\sim(P_1 \& P_2)$-worlds Q_1 will be false, and in others Q_2 will be false. P_1 and Q_1 are false in the same nearest $\sim(P_1 \& P_2)$- worlds, and P_2 and Q_2 are false in the same nearest $\sim(P_1 \& P_2)$-worlds. Thus, what (4.9) requires is that $P_1 < Q_1$ and $P_2 < Q_2$, i.e., $t_1 < t^*_1$ and $t_2 < t^*_2$.

Next, let us turn to the logical properties of '$<$'. It is not transitive but the following theorem is easily proven:

4. The Role of Time

(4.11) If $(P \twoheadrightarrow Q)$ obtains at w and $P <_w Q$ and $Q <_w R$, then $P <_w R$.

Proof: Suppose $(P \twoheadrightarrow Q)$ obtains at w and $P <_w Q$ and $Q <_w R$. Suppose $w^* \in \mathbf{M}_w(\sim\bar{P})$. Then as $(P \twoheadrightarrow Q)$ obtains at w, $w^* \in \mathbf{M}_w(\sim Q)$. Suppose $X \subseteq \mathbf{B}_w$ and X entails R. Then there are X_0, Y such that $X_0 \subseteq \mathbf{B}_w$ and $Y \subseteq \mathbf{B}_w$ and X entails $\bigwedge X_0$ and X_0 entails R and Y entails Q and $(\forall A)(\forall B)$[if $A, B \in \mathbf{B}_w$ and $A \in X_0$ and $B \in Y$ and A and B do not obtain at w^* then $B < A$]. As $P < Q$, there are Y_0, Z such that $Y_0 \subseteq \mathbf{B}_w$ and $Z \subseteq \mathbf{B}_w$ and Y entails $\bigwedge Y_0$ and Y_0 entails Q and Z entails P and $(\forall A)(\forall B)$[if $A, B \in \mathbf{B}_w$ and $A \in Y_0$ and $B \in Z$ and A and B do not obtain at w^* then $B < A$]. As Q does not obtain at w^*, there is an A in $\mathbf{B}_w$ such that $A \in X_0$ and A does not obtain at w^*, so $(\forall A)(\forall B)$[if $A, B \in \mathbf{B}_w$ and $A \in X_0$ and $B \in Z$ and A and B do not obtain at w^* then $B < A$]. Hence $P <_w R$.

We also get adjunctivity:

(4.12) If $P <_w Q$ and $P <_w R$ then $P <_w (Q \ \& \ R)$.

Proof: Suppose $P <_w Q$ and $P <_w R$. Suppose $w^* \in \mathbf{M}_w(\sim\bar{P})$ and $X \subseteq \mathbf{B}_w$ and X entails $(Q \ \& \ R)$. Then X entails Q and X entails R, so there are $X_1 \subseteq \mathbf{B}_w$, $X_2 \subseteq \mathbf{B}_w$ such that X entails $\bigwedge X_1$ and X_1 entails Q, and X entails $\bigwedge X_2$ and X_2 entails R, and there are $Y_1 \subseteq \mathbf{B}_w$, $Y_2 \subseteq \mathbf{B}_w$ such that Y_1 entails P and Y_2 entails P and $(\forall A)(\forall B)$[if $A, B \in \mathbf{B}_w$ and $A \in X_1$ and $B \in Y_1$ and A and B do not obtain at w^* then $B < A$] and $(\forall A)(\forall B)$[if $A, B \in \mathbf{B}_w$ and $A \in X_2$ and $B \in Y_2$ and A and B do not obtain at w^* then $B < A$]. Let $X_0 = X_1 \cup X_2$. Then X entails X_0 and X_0 entails $(Q \ \& \ R)$. If there is a B in Y_1 such that for each C in Y_2, $B < C$, then $(\forall A)(\forall B)$[if $A, B \in \mathbf{B}_w$ and $A \in X_0$ and $B \in Y_1$ and A and B do not obtain at w^* then $B < A$]. If instead there is no such B in Y_1 then $(\forall A)(\forall B)$[if $A, B \in \mathbf{B}_w$ and $A \in X_0$ and $B \in Y_2$ and A and B do not obtain at w^* then $B < A$]. So $P <_w (Q \ \& \ R)$.

I have endorsed (C5) as my basic temporal condition on causation, but by virtue of the reflection principles (3.13) and

(3.14), we can obtain a stronger temporal condition:

> (4.13) If PC_wQ then for each $w*$ in $\mathbf{A}_w(P)$: (1) if P obtains at $w*$, then $P <_{w*} Q$; and (2) if P does not obtain at . $w*$, then $P <_{w*} \bar{Q}$.

Let us symbolize the consequent of (4.13) as $\ulcorner P \ll_w Q \urcorner$. Let $(P \ll Q)$ be the state of affairs that obtains at a world w iff $P \ll_w Q$, i.e., $(P \ll Q) = \bigvee\{w|\ P \ll_w Q\}$. We immediately obtain from (4.11):

> (4.14) If $(P \twoheadrightarrow Q)$ obtains at w and $P \ll_w Q$ and $Q \ll_w R$, then $P \ll_w R$.

The adjunctivity of '$\ll$' is not an immediate consequence of our earlier principles. In order to obtain adjunctivity we need both (4.12) and the following principle:

> (4.15) If $P <_w Q$ and $P <_w R$, then $P <_w (Q \vee R)$.

In order to obtain (4.15) we must make an additional assumption about basic states of affairs:

> (A2) If $P,Q \in \mathbf{R}_w$ and P entails Q and $Y \subseteq \mathbf{B}_w$, then $(\exists X)\{X \subseteq \mathbf{B}_w$ and X entails P and X entails $\bigwedge Y$ and $(\forall X_0)[$if $X_0 \subseteq \mathbf{B}_w$ and X entails X_0 and X_0 entails $\bigwedge P$ then $(\exists Y_0)(Y_0 \subseteq \mathbf{B}_w$ and Y entails Y_0 and X_0 entails $\bigwedge Y_0$ and Y_0 entails $Q)]\}$.

Less formally, if P entails Q and Q is supervenient upon Y, then P is supervenient upon some X entailing Y that is such that if P is also supervenient on some X_0 logically weaker than X, then Q is supervenient on some Y_0 logically weaker than both Y and X_0. The rationale for this assumption is as follows. Suppose P entails Q and Q is supervenient on Y. We can always strengthen Y to obtain a set X on which P is supervenient. As we have seen, we cannot require minimality in the definition of supervenience, so Y and X may both contain excess baggage, i.e., P and Q may also be supervenient on smaller sets. If we can trim excess baggage from X to yield a logically weaker set X_0 upon which P is still supervenient, we should be able to trim the same excess baggage from Y to obtain a weaker set Y_0 on which Q is still supervenient. That is just what (A2) tells us.

Given (A2) we can prove (4.15). For this purpose we first need a lemma that we derive from (A1):

(4.16) If X and Y are subsets of $\mathbf{B}_w$ and X entails $\wedge Y$, then for each A in Y that does not obtain at a world w^*, there is an A* in X such that A* $\approx$ A and A* does not obtain at w^*.

Proof: Assume that X and Y are subsets of $\mathbf{B}_w$ and X entails $\wedge Y$. Suppose A$\in X$ and A does not obtain at w^*. As A$\in X$, X entails A, so by (A1), $\{A^*|\ A^*\in X$ and A* $\approx$ A$\}$ entails A. As A does not obtain at w^*, some member of $\{A^*|\ A^*\in X$ and A* $\approx$ A$\}$ does not obtain at w^*.

We can now prove a stronger theorem that has (4.15) as an immediate consequence:

(4.17) If $P <_w Q$ then $P <_w (Q \vee R)$.

Proof: Suppose $P <_w Q$. Suppose $w^*\in \mathbf{M}_w(\sim P)$ and $X \subseteq \mathbf{B}_w$ and X entails $(Q \vee R)$. By (A2), we can strengthen X to X^* in such a way that X^* entails Q and X^* entails $\wedge X$ and
(i) $(\forall X_0)$[if $X_0 \subseteq \mathbf{B}_w$ and X^* entails $\wedge X_0$ and X_0 entails Q then $(\exists Y_0)(Y_0 \subseteq \mathbf{B}_w$ and X entails $\wedge Y_0$ and X_0 entails $\wedge Y_0$ and Y_0 entails $(Q \vee R))$].
As $P <_w Q$, there is an X^*_0 such that $X^*_0 \subseteq \mathbf{B}_w$ and X^* entails $\wedge X^*_0$ and X^*_0 entails Q and there is a Y such that $Y \subseteq \mathbf{B}_w$ and Y entails P and $(\forall A)(\forall B)$[if $A,B\in\mathbf{B}_w$ and $A\in X_0$ and $B\in Y$ and A and B do not obtain at w^* then $B < A$]. Then by (i), there is a Y^*_0 such that $Y^*_0 \subseteq \mathbf{B}_w$ and X entails $\wedge Y^*_0$ and X^*_0 entails $\wedge Y^*_0$ and Y^*_0 entails $(Q \vee R)$. By (4.16), as X^*_0 entails $\wedge Y^*_0$, for each A in Y^*_0 that does not obtain at w^*, there is an A* in Y^*_0 such that A* $\approx$ A and A* does not obtain at w^*. Thus, $(\forall A)(\forall B)$[if $A,B\in\mathbf{B}_w$ and $A\in Y^*_0$ and $B\in Y$ and and A and B do not obtain at w^* then $B < A$]. So $P <_w (Q \vee R)$.

When P and Q are basic states of affairs, the requirement that if PCQ obtains at w then $P \ll_w Q$ should reduce to the requirement that $P < Q$. That it does can be established as follows. First we prove:

(4.18) If $P \in \mathbf{B}_w$ and $w^* \in \mathbf{M}_w(\sim P)$, then $(\exists X)[X \subseteq \mathbf{B}_w$ and X entails $\sim P$ and $(\forall Q)($if $Q \in X$ then $Q \approx P)]$.

Proof: Suppose $P \in \mathbf{B}_w$ and $w^* \in \mathbf{M}_w(\sim P)$. As P is basic, it is either of the form ⌜x's being F at t⌝ (abbreviated: ⌜$[x,F,t]$⌝) or ⌜Y*s containing all F's at t⌝ (abbreviated: ⌜Enum(Y,F,t)⌝).

Suppose $P = $ ⌜x,F,t⌝. As $\sim P$ obtains at w^*, either ⌜$x,\sim F,t$⌝ obtains at w^* or x does not exist at t in w^*. If the former, let $X = \{[x,\sim F,t]\}$. If the latter, choose G such that x is necessarily either G or non-G if x exists. Then for some Y and Z not containing x, Enum(Y,G,t) and Enum$(Z,\sim G,t)$ obtain at w^*, and these jointly entail $\sim P$. So let $X = \{$Enum$(Y,G,t),$Enum$(Z,\sim G,t)\}$.

Suppose $P = $ Enum(Y,F,t). As $\sim P$ obtains at w^*, there is an x not in Y such that $[x,F,t]$ obtains at w^*. Let $X = \{[x,F,t]\}$.

We have as an immediate consequence of (4.18):

(4.19) If $P,Q \in \mathbf{B}_w$ and $w^* \in \mathbf{M}_w(\sim P)$ and $P < Q$, then $P \lll_w Q$.

(4.10) and (4.19) together give us:

(4.20) If $P,Q \in \mathbf{B}_w$ and $(P \twoheadrightarrow Q)$ obtains at w, then $P \lll_w Q$ iff $P < Q$.

5. The Analysis

(C1)–(C5) exhaust the conditions for which I feel we can give an adequate intuitive defense by appealing to simple cases of causation. They jointly imply that if P causes Q at w then the following condition holds:

(5.1) P and Q obtain at w and $(P \twoheadrightarrow_w Q)$ and $P \lll_w Q$.

Furthermore, this condition satisfies (C1)–(C5) (putting it in place of ⌜PCQ⌝), so it follows that this is the strongest condition that (C1)–(C5) imply causation to entail. I propose this as our analysis of causation:

Analysis: $PCQ = [P \ \& \ Q \ \& \ (P \twoheadrightarrow Q) \ \& \ (P \lll Q)]$.

On the basis of this analysis, (C1)–(C5) become theorems. In addition, causation is provably transitive and adjunctive:

(5.2) $[PCQ \ \& \ QCR] \rightarrow PCR$.

(5.3) $[PCQ \ \& \ PCR] \rightarrow PC(Q \ \& \ R)$.

For basic states of affairs, the analysis reduces to the simpler:

(5.4) If P and Q are basic states of affairs then:
$PCQ = [P \ \& \ Q \ \& \ (P \twoheadrightarrow Q) \ \& \ (P < Q)]$.

Thus, we have an analysis of causation from which its normal logical properties follow in a natural way without any *ad hoc* maneuvering. I take this to constitute strong confirmation for the analysis. It also constitutes a further illustration of the usefulness of possible worlds in philosophical analysis.

VI
Formal Semantics

1. Introduction

The semantical theories we have been considering thus far in this book are *realistic semantical theories*. That is, they consist of analyses framed directly in terms of possible worlds. *Formal semantical theories* have also played an important role in contemporary philosophical logic. Various formal semantics have been proposed for modal logic, for counterfactuals, for indexicals and token reflexives, and so on. But it has never been entirely clear what the point of such a formal semantics is. It is generally supposed that by constructing a formal semantics for a logical concept, one has thereby analyzed it or in some sense elucidated it. But it is not at all obvious just how a formal semantics is supposed to accomplish this. The purpose of this chapter is to determine when a formal semantics is reasonable, and what philosophical conclusions we can draw from it.

To appreciate the depth of our problem, let us consider a concrete example of a formal semantics—that designed for non-quantificational modal logic.[1] As always in formal semantics, we begin by constructing a logical notation. For this purpose we begin with a set *At* of *atomic formulas*, and the logical constants $\neg$, $\wedge$, and $\Box$. We define $\vee$, $\rightarrow$, $\leftrightarrow$, and $\Diamond$ in the usual ways. We define an *assignment* to be a function G mapping *At* into $\{0,1\}$. A *model* is an ordered pair $\langle G,K \rangle$ where K is a set of assignments and $G \in K$. We define *truth in a model* recursively as follows:

(1.1) Definition of *truth in* $\langle G,K \rangle$:
    (a) if $p \in At$ then p is true in $\langle G,K \rangle$ iff $G(p) = 1$;

---

[1] Non-quantificational modal logic is what would more conventionally be called 'propositional modal logic'.

(b) $\neg p$ is true in $\langle G,K\rangle$ iff p is not true in $\langle G,K\rangle$;
(c) $(p \wedge q)$ is true in $\langle G,K\rangle$ iff p and q are both true in $\langle G,K\rangle$;
(d) $\Box p$ is true in $\langle G,K\rangle$ iff p is true in every $\langle H,K\rangle$ for $H \in K$.

A formula is *valid* iff it is true in every model.

The preceding is the simplest semantics for non-quantificational modal logic. The set of formulas valid on this semantics comprises S5. S5 can be axiomatized as follows:

(1.2) Axioms and Rules for S5:
   (A1) all truth-functionally valid formulas
   (A2) $\Box p \rightarrow p$
   (A3) $\Box(p \rightarrow q) \rightarrow (\Box p \rightarrow \Box q)$
   (A4) $\Diamond\Box p \rightarrow \Box p$
   (R1) *modus ponens*: If $\vdash p$ and $\vdash(p \rightarrow q)$ then $\vdash q$.
   (R2) *necessitation*: If $\vdash p$ then $\vdash \Box p$.[2]

S5 is generally favored as the appropriate logic when $\Box$ is taken to symbolize logical necessity, and we have seen that it can be justified by appealing to the characterization of necessity in terms of possible worlds. But there are other respected non-quantificational modal logics, principally M and S4. S4 results from replacing (A4) by the weaker axiom

(A5) $\Box p \rightarrow \Box\Box p$

and M is obtained by deleting (A4) from S5 altogether. Formal semantics have also been constructed for M and S4. For this purpose we revise the definition of a model, taking a *model* to be a triple $\langle G,K,R\rangle$ where K is a set of assignments, $G \in K$, and R is a relation defined on K, i.e., $R \subseteq K \times K$. R is called 'the accessibility relation'. Truth in a model is defined as before with the exception of the clause for $\Box$:

(1.3) Definition of *truth in* $\langle G,K,R\rangle$:
   (a) if $p \in At$ then p is true in $\langle G,K,R\rangle$ iff $G(p) = 1$;
   (b) $\neg p$ is true in $\langle G,K,R\rangle$ iff p is not true in $\langle G,K,R\rangle$;

[2] A different axiomatization of S5 was given in Chapter Three.

(c) $(p \wedge q)$ is true in $\langle G,K,R \rangle$ iff p and q are both true in $\langle G,K,R \rangle$;

(d) $\Box p$ is true in $\langle G,K,R \rangle$ iff p is true in every $\langle H,K,R \rangle$ such that HRG.

In other words, $\Box p$ is true in $\langle G,K,R \rangle$ iff p is true in every $\langle H,K,R \rangle$ where H is accessible from G. We get different modal logics by making different assumptions about R. $\langle G,K,R \rangle$ is an *M-model* iff R is reflexive; an *S4-model* iff R is transitive and reflexive; and an *S5-model* iff R is reflexive, transitive, and symmetric (i.e., an equivalence relation). A formula is *M-valid* iff it is true in every *M*-model, *S4-valid* iff it is true in every S4-model, and *S5-valid* iff it is true in every S5-model. It then turns out that a formula is a theorem of *M* iff it is *M*-valid, a theorem of S4 iff it is S4-valid, and a theorem of S5 iff it is S5-valid.

Kripke's discovery of these formal semantics for *M*, S4, and S5 is generally considered one of the great achievements of modern logic. That achievement made modal logic respectable for the first time in the eyes of most philosophers. Prior to 1959, modal logic was viewed with considerable suspicion and most philosophers were loathe to use it in doing serious philosophy. Since 1959, modal logic has become a standard tool of philosophy and has been embraced by all but a few diehards. Just how did the discovery of these formal semantics accomplish this?

These formal semantics are labeled 'possible worlds semantics'. In $\langle G,K,R \rangle$, K is supposed to represent the set of all possible worlds, and G is supposed to represent the actual world. Necessity is then identified with 'truth at all possible worlds', and we get clause (d) of either (1.1) or (1.3). It seems likely that in his original paper Kripke intended this to be no more than a heuristic aid in understanding the formal semantics, but it is now generally felt that these formal semantics represent the notion of truth at all possible worlds in some very literal sense. There is, however, considerable difficulty in understanding the kind of representation involved. First, what is the accessibility relation supposed to be doing? As far as I can see, it is no more than a technical trick to enable us to get M and S4. No one has ever given a plausible account of its intuitive significance. Perhaps what this shows is that we should eschew the accessibility relation, embracing the formal semantics based upon the simpler models $\langle G,K \rangle$ and resting content with S5. But it is still far from clear how these models represent truth at all possible worlds. For example, $\langle G,\{G\} \rangle$ is a model, but how can this represent truth at all possible worlds? It is surely a necessary truth that there are more possible worlds than the actual world. This might suggest that instead of allowing K to be just *any* set of assignments, we should require K to be the set of *all* assignments. But it turns out that if we make such a requirement, we no longer get S5. Instead we get a totally unreasonable modal logic. For example, if p is atomic, one of the theorems of this modal logic is $\diamond p$ (but this need not be a theorem if p is not atomic).[3] The upshot of this is that we seem unable, at this point, to give any simple answer to the question of how this formal semantics represents the notion of truth at all possible worlds, and the philosophical significance of the semantics is left in doubt. Perhaps all the semantics amounts to is a mathematical characterization of the theorems of the modal logic, devoid of philosophical significance. But if that is true, logicians have been pulling the wool over the eyes of their colleagues for years by convincing them they were doing something philosophically important. As I am still doing logic, the reader will surmise that I believe there is more to formal semantics than the skeptical view I have just suggested, but the true significance of formal semantics involves a long story.

I was recently surprised to discover that there are logicians who do not believe that formal semantics stands in need of any justification or foundations. They regard formal semantics as a "philosophical accomplishment in its own right". Such a view strikes me as absurd. One thing that has become apparent in recent years is that we can construct formal seman-

---

[3] This modal logic was endorsed by Carnap [1947], but it has fallen into general disrepute.

tics to yield virtually any logical theory, regardless of whether the logical theory has anything to antecedently recommend it. Obviously, the existence of the semantics does not automatically lend the theory the respectability it originally lacked. The semantics can only do that if it is itself, in some sense, reasonable. It is precisely the criterion for the reasonableness of a semantics that this chapter aims to uncover.

2. Logical Validity

Let us begin by asking the most basic question of all regarding the nature of formal semantics. When we do formal semantics, we construct systems of logical notation and then define the notion of logical validity for formulas of our notation. What is the significance of logical validity supposed to be? I do not think there is any single right answer to this question. One could be doing different things in constructing semantical theories, and accordingly, logical validity may differ in significance from one semantical theory to another. The simplest possibility is that our logical notation may allow us to symbolize various *propositional forms*. For example, the propositions $(\varphi \lor \sim\varphi)$ and $(\theta \lor \sim\theta)$ have the same form, which we might describe as $(X \lor \sim X)$. Formally, propositional forms can be viewed as functions from propositional constituents to propositions. For example, we can identify the form $(X \lor \sim X)$ with that function on propositions that assigns to a proposition φ the proposition $(\varphi \lor \sim\varphi)$. A proposition *has* a certain form iff it is in the range of that form. If formulas of our logical notation are taken to symbolize propositional forms, a formula being logically valid might be intended to capture the notion of every proposition of that form being necessarily true. This is probably the simplest and most obvious notion of logical validity.[4]

A second possibility is that our logical notation might symbolize *statemental forms* rather than propositional forms. These are functions from statemental constituents to statements. Then

---

[4] I proposed this as an analysis of logical validity in Pollock [1967a].

logical validity might be intended to capture the notion of every statement of that form being (either internally or externally) necessary. A third possibility is that our logical notation might be intended to symbolize the forms of states of affairs, and a formula would be logically valid iff every state of affairs of that form is necessary. A fourth possibility is that our logical notation might symbolize sentence forms. In this case, a formula's being valid might be intended to capture the notion of a formula's being such that every sentence of that form is analytic (or internally necessary, or externally necessary, or weakly analytic). It is apparent that formal semantics and the resulting logical theories can be intended to serve different purposes, and it is important to distinguish between different kinds of semantical theories in terms of the purposes they are intended to serve.

2.1 *Propositional Logics*

Propositional logics are logics whose formulas are intended to express the forms of propositions. The *language* of a propositional logic will consist of an ordered pair $\langle F, \pi \rangle$ where F is the set of *formulas* and π is a function that assigns to each p in F the propositional form $\pi(p)$ that p expresses. Propositional forms are functions, and the different argument places in a propositional form will typically have different domains. For example, in the first-order propositional form $(X:y)$, the instances of X are one-place concepts and the instances of y are propositional designators. These different domains are made up of different classes of propositions and propositional constituents. For each such class we require our language to contain a corresponding class of variables. For example, the predicate calculus (construed as a propositional logic) contains sentence letters that serve as variables ranging over propositions, n-place relation symbols that serve as variables ranging over n-place concepts, and individual constants that serve as variables ranging over propositional designators. These variables are, somewhat perversely, called 'nonlogical constants'. We require each formula p to contain a nonlogical constant of the appropriate type for each argument place of $\pi(p)$. Thus, for example, $\ulcorner(\bigwedge x)(Fx \rightarrow Fa)\urcorner$ expresses the propositional form $(\forall x)((X{:}x) \rightarrow (X{:}y))$ where instances of X are one-place concepts and instances of y are propositional designators. As in the propositional and predicate calculi, our languages are generally constructed so that $\pi(p)$ can be read off from the syntactic structure of p. Frequently F will be defined recursively by reference to a larger class of expressions not all of which express propositional forms. For example, we have the distinction between open formulas and closed formulas in first-order logic.

The range of $\pi(p)$ is the set of propositions of the form expressed by p. We can define different concepts of validity in each of the following ways:

(2.1) A formula p is (1) valid$_N$, (2) valid$_A$, or (3) valid$_T$ iff for every proposition φ of the form expressed by p, φ is (1) necessary, (2) *a priori*, or (3) true.

We obtain three different kinds of propositional logics corresponding to the three different kinds of validity. It is interesting to note that for most classical propositional logics, such as the truth-functional and predicate calculi, the three kinds of validity appear to coincide, and hence logicians have not found it necessary to clearly distinguish between them. In higher-order logic, however, there is the distinct possibility that validity$_N$ and validity$_A$ will diverge with respect to formulas expressing principles of elementary number theory (which might be necessary but not *a priori*). And in first-order modal logic there is only one proposition of the form expressed by the formula $\ulcorner \neg(\bigvee_k x)\Diamond\neg(\bigvee y)\ y = x \urcorner$ (which says that there do not exist k contingent objects). Thus, this formula is valid$_T$ iff that proposition is true. Hence such a formula can be valid$_T$ without being valid$_N$ or valid$_A$. This suggests that for most purposes validity$_N$ is the most interesting of these three concepts.

A fruitful reformulation of our concepts of validity proceeds in terms of *interpretations* of a language. These are functions that assign propositions to formulas in such a way that the proposition assigned is always of the form expressed by the formula. Interpretations accomplish this by assigning propositions and propositional constituents to the nonlogical constants in the formula. Let us define an interpretation to be any function that assigns to each nonlogical constant a proposition or propositional constituent of the appropriate type. For example, in the predicate calculus an interpretation will assign n-ary concepts to n-place relation symbols, propositional designators to individual constants, and so on. Given an interpretation μ and a formula p whose nonlogical constants are $c_1,\ldots,c_n$, the proposition assigned to p by μ (symbolized: $\ulcorner\mu(p)\urcorner$) is $\pi(p)(\mu(c_1),\ldots,\mu(c_n))$. In other words, $\mu(p)$ is the proposition that results from applying the propositional form expressed by p to the interpretation of the nonlogical constants in p.

Given a characterization of the set of all interpretations and a specification of what propositions each interpretation assigns to each formula, we can define π in terms of interpretations. $\pi(p)$ is the function that determines the value of $\mu(p)$ given the value of $\mu(c)$ for each nonlogical constant c occurring in p, so:

(2.2) If $p\in F$ and $c_1,\ldots,c_n$ are the nonlogical constants occurring in p, listed in order of their initial occurrence, then $\pi(p) = \{\langle\langle\mu(c_1),\ldots,\mu(c_n)\rangle,\mu(p)\rangle|\ \mu$ is an interpretation$\}$.

This is the way we will normally define π. When π is defined in this way, interpretations satisfy two conditions that will be of importance:

(2.3) If μ is an interpretation, then for each formula p, $\mu(p)$ is of the form $\pi(p)$.

(2.4) If φ is a proposition of the form expressed by p, then there is an interpretation μ such that $\varphi = \mu(p)$.

Given these two principles, our concepts of validity can be reformulated in terms of interpretations:

(2.5) A formula p is (1) valid$_N$, (2) valid$_A$, or (3) valid$_T$ iff for every interpretation μ, $\mu(p)$ is (1) necessary, (2) *a priori*, or (3) true.

With the help of the notion of an interpretation, we can also define *consistency* and *logical consequence*:

(2.6) If X is a set of formulas:
  (a) X is *consistent$_N$* iff there is an interpretation μ such that $\Diamond_{X,\mu}$(for each q in X, $\mu(q)$ is true);
  (b) X is *consistent$_A$* iff there is an interpretation μ such that there is no *a priori* argument allowing us to derive a contradiction from the set of propositions $\{\mu(q)| \; q{\in}X\}$;
  (c) X is *consistent$_T$* iff there is an interpretation μ such that for each q in X, $\mu(q)$ is true.

(2.7) If X is a set of formulas and p a formula:
  (a) $X \Rightarrow_N p$ iff for every interpretation μ, $\Box_{X,\mu}$[if for each q in X, $\mu(q)$ is true, then $\mu(p)$ is true];
  (b) $X \Rightarrow_A p$ iff for every interpretation μ, there is an *a priori* argument allowing us to derive $\mu(p)$ from $\{\mu(q)|q{\in}X\}$;
  (c) $X \Rightarrow_T p$ iff for every interpretation μ, if for each q in X, $\mu(q)$ is true, then $\mu(p)$ is true.

2.2 *Statemental Logics*

Statemental logics differ from propositional logics in that their formulas are intended to express the forms of statements, these being defined as functions from statements and statemental constituents to statements. The language of a statemental logic will consist of an ordered pair $\langle F,\sigma \rangle$ where F is the set of formulas and σ is a function that assigns to each formula p the statemental form $\sigma(p)$ that p expresses. In light of the distinction between internal and external necessity for statements, we can define four kinds of validity for statemental logics:

(2.8) A formula p is (1) valid$_N$, (2) valid$_I$, (3) valid$_A$, or (4) valid$_T$ iff for every statement ψ of the form expressed by p, ψ is (1) externally necessary, (2) internally necessary, (3) *a priori*, or (4) true.

We can define the notion of an *interpretation* as we did for propositional logics and use that to define consistency$_N$, consistency$_A$, consistency$_T$, $\not\Rightarrow_N$, $\not\Rightarrow_A$, and $\not\Rightarrow_T$. There is, however, no obvious way to define consistency$_I$ or $\not\Rightarrow_I$.

2.3 *SOA Logics*

SOA logics are logics of states of affairs. We would like to develop SOA logics on analogy to propositional and statemental logics, but there is an immediate obstacle to doing so. Whereas the notion of the form of a proposition or of a statement makes literal sense because of their having structure and constituents, we cannot make analogous sense of the notion of the form of a state of affairs. This is particularly true in light of our taking equivalent states of affairs to be identical. Instead, in defining the notion of the form of a state of affairs, we must be guided by our desire to interpret existing logical theories in terms of states of affairs. For this purpose we will presumably want closed formulas to express states of affairs, predicates and open formulas to express properties, and individual constants to express (or denote) individuals. This suggests defining an *SOA form* to be a function from individuals, properties, and states of affairs, to states of affairs. The language of an SOA logic will then consist of an ordered pair $\langle F, v \rangle$ where F is the set of (closed) formulas and v is a function that assigns to each p in F the SOA form $v(p)$ that p expresses. As states of affairs are not (except indirectly) objects of belief, apriority is inapplicable to states of affairs. We have only one concept of necessity for states of affairs, so we obtain just two concepts of validity for SOA logics:

(2.9) A formula p is (1) valid$_N$ or (2) valid$_O$ iff for every state of affairs S of the form expressed by p, S (1) is necessary or (2) obtains.

We can define the notion of an *interpretation* as before and use that to define *consistency$_N$, consistency$_O$,* $\not\Rightarrow_N$, and $\not\Rightarrow_O$.

2.4 *Linguistic Logics*

In motivating first-order logic, it is not uncommon to find logicians telling us, on the one hand, that formulas express propositions and, on the other hand, that individual constants express proper names. Such an account is incoherent. If formulas express propositions, then individual constants, as parts of formulas, must express propositional constituents. Proper names are constituents of sentences—not propositions. What is happening here is that two kinds of logics—propositional logics and linguistic logics—are being confused with each other. Linguistic logics are interestingly different from propositional, statemental, and SOA logics. The formulas of a linguistic logic express the forms of sentences of a language, not in the sense of mirroring their syntactic structure, but in the sense of expressing what I will call their *semantical form*. Typically, sentences are built out of smaller meaningful parts, and the *S*-intension of the entire sentence is a function of the *S*-, *D*-, and *A*-intensions of those parts. This is the doctrine of *semantical compositionality*.[5] The function determining the *S*-intension of the sentence on the basis of the intensions of its parts is its *semantical form*. Sentences with different parts may have the same semantical form. For example, every sentence of the syntactic form ⌜*p* and *q*⌝ has the semantical form **K** that assigns to the *S*-intensions of sentences *p* and *q* the *S*-intension of their conjunction ⌜*p* and *q*⌝. The semantical form **K** can be defined explicitly as follows:

(2.10) If Δ_1 and Δ_2 are *S*-intensions, $\mathbf{K}(\Delta_1, \Delta_2)$ is that *S*-intension Δ such that for any assignment π of values to the pragmatic parameters, $\Delta(\pi) = (\Delta_1(\pi) \ \& \ \Delta_2(\pi))$.

In general, a semantical form is any function from *S*-, *D*-, and *A*-intensions to *S*-intensions. The language of a linguistic logic is then an ordered pair $\langle F, \lambda \rangle$ where F is the set of formulas and λ is a function that assigns to each formula *p* the semantical form $\lambda(p)$ expressed by *p*. The range of $\lambda(p)$ is a set

---

[5] For an extended discussion of compositionality, see Pollock [1982], 262–280.

of *S*-intensions—functions from pragmatic parameters to statements. These are the *S*-intensions *having the form expressed by p*. On analogy to a statement's being the sense of a sentence (relative to a particular assignment of values to the pragmatic parameters), let us say that a statement ψ is a *possible sense of* a formula *p* iff ψ is a possible value for one of the *S*-intensions having the form expressed by *p*, i.e., iff ψ∈range(∪(range(λ(*p*)))). We can then define the following notions of validity for linguistic logics:

(2.11) A formula *p* is (1) valid$_N$, (2) valid$_I$, (3) valid$_A$, or (4) valid$_T$ iff for every statement ψ that is a possible sense of *p*, ψ is (1) externally necessary, (2) internally necessary, (3) *a priori*, or (4) true.

Regarding languages as abstract entities that exist necessarily, and assuming that every semantical form can be possessed by some sentence in some language, we can relate our notions of validity to languages as follows:

(2.12) A formula *p* is (1) valid$_N$, (2) valid$_I$, (3) valid$_A$, or (4) valid$_T$ iff for every language **L** and sentence *q* of **L**, if *q* has the semantical form λ(*p*) then every statement expressible by *q* is (1) externally necessary, (2) internally necessary, (3) *a priori*, or (4) true;[6] i.e., *q* is (1) externally necessary, (2) internally necessary, (3) analytic, or (4) weakly analytic.

These four notions of validity are interestingly different. For example, if λ(*p*) is the semantical form of the sentence 'I exist', then *p* is valid$_T$ but not valid$_N$, valid$_I$, or valid$_A$.

There is another way of formulating our concepts of validity for linguistic logics. This is to employ a concept of an interpretation akin to that employed in talking about propositional, statemental, and SOA logics. For linguistic logics, an interpretation will assign intensions (*S*-, *A*-, or *D*-) to the nonlogical constants of a formula, and then will assign an *S*-intension to the entire formula in terms of the intensions assigned to the

---

[6] ψ is expressible by *q* iff ψ is in the range of the *S*-intension of *q*.

nonlogical constants. If μ is an interpretation and p is a formula whose nonlogical constants are $c_1,\ldots,c_n$, then $\mu(p) = \lambda(p)(\mu(c_1),\ldots,\mu(c_n))$.

If μ is an interpretation and p a formula, $\mu(p)$ is an S-intension—a function from pragmatic parameters to statements. Taken together, an interpretation μ and an assignment π of values to the pragmatic parameters will determine a statement corresponding to each formula—the statement $\mu(p)(\pi)$. For notational convenience, let us write this as $\ulcorner(\mu/\pi)(p)\urcorner$. We can characterize our four notions of validity for linguistic logics as follows:

(2.13) A formula p is (1) valid$_N$, (2) valid$_I$, (3) valid$_A$, or (4) valid$_T$ iff for every interpretation μ and assignment π of values to the pragmatic parameters, $(\mu/\pi)(p)$ is (1) externally necessary, (2) internally necessary, (3) *a priori*, or (4) true.

We can define notions of consistency and logical consequence corresponding to validity$_N$, validity$_A$, and validity$_T$ just as we did for propositional, statemental, and SOA logics.

3. Formal Semantical Theories

Minimally, a formal semantics for a logical theory is a mathematical (e.g., a set-theoretic) characterization of the set of valid formulas for that theory. The minimal purpose of such a semantics is to make the study of validity amenable to a precise mathematical investigation by characterizing it in a purely mathematical way.[7] Frequently, however, a formal semantics is supposed to do more. It is often thought that a formal semantics gives us insight into the logical concepts them-

---

[7] An even weaker purpose for a formal semantics is to give a characterization of the set of provable formulas of some axiomatized logical theory. However, such theories are generally intended to capture the set of valid formulas in one of the above senses, and are only really interesting insofar as they do so. Thus, for the most part the pursuit of formal semantics for such theories is only of interest when it coincides with what is described here as the minimal purpose of a formal semantics.

selves, or even that the formal semantics provides us with an analysis of the logical concepts. This claim is particularly prevalent in connection with so-called "possible worlds semantics". We have already seen reason to be suspicious of the heuristic basis of the standard possible worlds semantics for modal logic. It is not at all obvious initially that it will yield the right set of valid formulas. But even if it does, why should we think that this sort of semantics does anything beyond characterizing validity mathematically? Why should we suppose that there is any sense in which it provides us with an actual analysis of our logical concepts?

In order to answer these questions, I shall describe the way in which I think possible worlds semantics *ought* to work. It is an open question whether this is really what is going through the minds of logicians who constructed such semantics, but many of the semantics that have been constructed will meet the conditions imposed below.

Between propositional, statemental, SOA, and linguistic logics, we have thirteen different kinds of validity and correspondingly thirteen different kinds of logic. Possible worlds semantics may differ for each kind of logic, and may not be amenable to all. We cannot possibly discuss all of these kinds of logic at this time, so I will confine my attention to validity$_N$ in each case. Validity$_N$ for propositional, statemental, and SOA logics is basically similar, enabling us to discuss possible worlds semantics for all three kinds of logic at once. Possible worlds semantics for linguistic logics, however, will function in a more complicated way, and will be discussed separately.

3.1 *Propositional, Statemental, and SOA Logics*

Suppose we have a propositional, statemental, or SOA logic whose language is $\langle F, \rho \rangle$. A formula p is valid$_N$ iff it is "necessarily true under every interpretation", i.e., for every interpretation μ, $\mu(p)$ is (externally) necessary. A possible worlds semantics seeks to capture this characterization of validity by defining the notions of a *model* and *truth in a model*. Models are set-theoretic structures, and truth in a model is a set-theoretic concept. Models are thought of as simultaneously interpreting the language and describing a possible world at which to evaluate the truth of the proposition, statement, or state of affairs resulting from the interpretation. The precise definition of 'model' will depend upon what logical theory is being investigated, but however it is defined, we will arrive at a definition of what it is for a formula to be true in a model. If a formula p is true in a model M, M is said to be a model *of p*. We define *semantical validity* (in constrast to validity$_N$) as follows:

(3.1) $\models p$ (p is semantically valid) iff every model is a model of p.

Our semantics is *adequate* iff validity$_N$ and semantical validity coincide for all formulas of the language.

A formal semantics is also used to study logical consequence. To this end we define a model of a *set* of formulas to be any model that is a model of all the formulas in the set. If Γ is a set of formulas, we define:

(3.2) Γ is *satisfiable* iff Γ has at least one model.

(3.3) $\Gamma \models p$ (Γ *semantically implies p*) iff every model of Γ is a model of p.

Let us say that our semantics is *strongly adequate* just in case logical consequence and semantical implication coincide, i.e., for any formula p and set Γ of formulas, $\Gamma \Rrightarrow_N p$ iff $\Gamma \models p$. Equivalently, for a language containing negation:

(3.4) A semantics is strongly adequate iff for any set Γ of formulas, Γ is satisfiable iff Γ is consistent$_N$.

Trivially:

(3.5) If a semantics is strongly adequate then it is adequate.

A semantics should be at least adequate, and preferably strongly adequate. How does the construction of a possible worlds semantics ensure this?

The standard view of possible worlds semantics is that models are formal surrogates of possible worlds, but that appears to be a mistake. Instead, a model should be regarded as a formal surrogate simultaneously of an interpretation and a possible world. It takes both to yield a truth value for a formula. Let us define the *surrogate relation* as follows:

(3.6) $M \simeq \langle w,\mu \rangle$ iff M is a model and w is a possible world and μ is an interpretation and for every formula p, M is a model of p iff $\mu(p)$ is true at w.

Thus, truth in a model can be taken to correspond to truth under an interpretation at a possible world. A reasonable semantics should satisfy the following conditions:

(A1) For each possible world w and interpretation μ, there is a model M such that $M \simeq \langle w,\mu \rangle$.

(A2) For each model M there is an interpretation μ and possible world w such that $M \simeq \langle w,\mu \rangle$.

The following theorem might be regarded as *The Fundamental Theorem of Possible Worlds Semantics*:

(3.7) If our language contains negation, a semantics for it is strongly adequate iff (A1) and (A2) hold.

Proof: Suppose (A1) and (A2) hold, and Γ is a set of formulas. By (A1), if Γ is consistent$_N$ then Γ is satisfiable; and by (A2), if Γ is satisfiable then Γ is consistent$_N$. So by (3.4), the semantics is strongly adequate.

Conversely, suppose (A1) fails; i.e., for some $\langle w,\mu \rangle$, there is no model M such that $M \simeq \langle w,\mu \rangle$. Let $\Gamma = \{p|\ \mu(p)$ is true at $w\}$. For each formula p, either p or $\neg p$ is in Γ. Thus if there is a model M of Γ, $\Gamma = \{p|\ p$ is true in $M\}$, and hence $M \simeq \langle w,\mu \rangle$. Thus Γ has no model, i.e., Γ is unsatisfiable. But for each p in Γ, $\mu(p)$ is true in w, so $\Diamond_{\mu,\Gamma}$(for each p in Γ, $\mu(p)$ is true), i.e., Γ is consistent$_N$. Thus by (3.5), the semantics is not strongly adequate.

Suppose instead that (A2) fails, i.e., there is a model M for which there is no $\langle w,\mu \rangle$ such that $M \simeq \langle w,\mu \rangle$. Let $\Gamma = \{p|\ p$ is true in $M\}$. If there is a $\langle w,\mu \rangle$ such that for each p in Γ, $\mu(p)$ is true at w, then $M \simeq \langle w,\mu \rangle$ (because for each

p, either p or $\neg p$ is in Γ). Thus there is no such $\langle w,\mu \rangle$. Hence for each μ, there is no world w such that each $\mu(p)$ for p in Γ is true at w. That is, for each interpretation μ, $\sim\Diamond_{\mu,\Gamma}$(for each p in Γ, $\mu(p)$ is true), i.e., Γ is inconsistent$_N$. So Γ is satisfiable but inconsistent$_N$, and hence by (3.5), the semantics is not strongly adequate.

Theorem (3.7) provides the cornerstone for possible worlds semantics.

If our concern is just with adequacy rather than strong adequacy, we can make do with a weaker principle than (A2):

(A3) For each formula p, if p is satisfiable then there is an interpretation μ and possible world w such that $\mu(p)$ is true at w.

We easily prove:

(3.8) If our language contains negation and (A1) and (A3) hold then our semantics is adequate.

We will establish below that (A1) and either (A2) or (A3) are true of the standard formal semantics for most popular logical theories. It follows that those semantics do succeed in characterizing validity. But what can be made of the claim that possible worlds semantics do more than just characterize validity? For example, suppose we have a semantics for a language containing a subjunctive conditional '>'. Is there any sense in which the semantics can be regarded as providing an analysis of the conditional? There are different senses of 'analysis', but I would propose that the sense germane to a logical operator like '>' is:

(3.9) An analysis of '>' is a statement of truth conditions for propositions (or statements, or states of affairs) of the form $(\varphi > \theta)$ in terms of the truth conditions for φ and the truth conditions for θ.

Such a statement of truth conditions for a proposition $(\varphi > \theta)$ will have the form

(3.10) $(\forall\varphi)(\forall\theta)(\forall w)$[if w is a possible world then $(\varphi > \theta)$ is true at w iff $R(\varphi,\theta,w)$]

where $\ulcorner R(\varphi,\theta,w)\urcorner$ expresses a relation between φ and θ that we already understand. Now suppose we construct a logical theory whose language $\langle F,\kappa \rangle$ enables us to express the propositional form (or statemental form, or SOA form) $(X > Y)$. That is, there is a formula $p_>$ in F such that $\kappa(p_>) = (X > Y)$. Suppose further that we have a strongly adequate semantics for this language. By theorem (3.7), (A1) and (A2) hold, and (A1) and (A2) jointly imply:

(3.11) $(\forall\varphi)(\forall\theta)(\forall w)$[if w is a possible world then $(\varphi > \theta)$ is true at w iff there is an interpretation μ and model M such that $\mu(p_>) = (\varphi > \theta)$ and $p_>$ is true in M and $M \simeq \langle w,\mu \rangle$].

(3.11) appears to be an analysis of the form of (3.10). Thus, it appears that our formal semantics provides us with an analysis of '$>$'. However, this analysis will be circular if the surrogate relation '$\simeq$' is defined as in (3.6). In order to generate a noncircular analysis from (3.11), we must have an alternative characterization of the surrogate relation. Such a characterization of the surrogate relation is not part of the formal semantics, although it seems likely that the inventors of a formal semantics generally have a characterization of the surrogate relation at least vaguely in mind as a heuristic guide in the construction of the semantics.

Once we have coupled the formal semantics with an independent characterization of the surrogate relation, we are no longer doing formal semantics. We have, in effect, turned our formal semantics into a realistic semantics. For example, suppose our formal semantics for '$>$' proceeds in terms of models of the form $\langle G,K,R \rangle$ where K is a set of valuations, $G \in K$, and R is a ternary relation between members of K. It will normally be explained that R represents the "nearness" relation between possible worlds, however that is spelled out (e.g., in terms of minimal change, or in terms of comparative similarity). The effect of this is to turn (3.11) into an analysis of counterfactuals in terms of the nearness relation, and hence is equivalent to the realistic semantics for counterfactuals based upon the same choice of the nearness relation. Thus, I think it must be concluded that it is at least an exaggeration to claim that formal semantics provides us with analyses of logical concepts. Formal semantics might provide useful tools for the construction of realistic semantics, but they appear to do little more.

3.2 *Linguistic Logics*

Possible worlds semantics for linguistic logics also proceed by defining a set of models and a notion of truth in a model. The models for linguistic logics may, however, be more complicated than those for propositional, statemental, and SOA logics. In the latter logics, formulas are evaluated in terms of just two parameters—an interpretation μ and a world w. Thus, models are formal surrogates for pairs $\langle w, \mu \rangle$. But in order to assign a truth value to a formula of a linguistic logic, we need a third bit of information. An interpretation μ only provides us with an S-intension for p. In order to evaluate p at a world w, we must also have an assignment π of values to the pragmatic parameters so that we can obtain a particular statement from the S-intension of p. Thus, models in linguistic logics become formal surrogates for the ordered triples $\langle w, \mu, \pi \rangle$.

Linguistic logics constitute a relatively new subject matter and have not been studied with any generality. Van Fraassen [1977] has examined a very restricted class of such logics in which the only pragmatic parameter is the possible world at which a statement is made. Kaplan ([1976] and [1979]) has investigated a linguistic logic with a somewhat more liberal class of pragmatic parameters. Some of the work on tense logic could be interpreted as dealing with linguistic logics. But little work has been done on the general nature of linguistic logics. We can, however, modify the results of section 3.1 to apply to linguistic logics. As before, we define:

(3.12) $\models p$ iff p is true in every model.

(3.13) A semantics is *adequate* iff for every formula p, p is valid$_N$ iff $\models p$.

(3.14) If Γ is a set of formulas, M is a model of Γ iff every member of Γ is true in M.

(3.15) Γ is *satisfiable* iff Γ has a model.

(3.16) If p is a formula and Γ a set of formulas, $\Gamma \models p$ iff every model of Γ is a model of p.

(3.17) A semantics is strongly adequate iff for every formula p and set Γ of formulas, $\Gamma \Rightarrow_N p$ iff $\Gamma \models p$.

We can try to prove the adequacy of semantics for linguistic logics by proceeding much as we did for propositional and statemental logics. Let us define:

(3.18) $M \simeq \langle w, \mu, \pi \rangle$ iff M is a model and w is a possible world and μ is an interpretation and π is an assignment of values to the pragmatic parameters and for each formula p, p is true in M iff $(\mu/\pi)(p)$ is true at w.

If our semantics is reasonable, we should have both:

(AL1) For every possible world w, interpretation μ, and assignment π of values to the pragmatic parameters, there is a model M such that $M \simeq \langle w, \mu, \pi \rangle$.

(AL2) For every model M, there is a possible world w, interpretation μ, and assignment π of values to the pragmatic parameters such that $M \simeq \langle w, \mu, \pi \rangle$.

As before:

(3.19) If our languages contain negation, a semantics for it is strongly adequate iff (AL1) and (AL2) hold.

Most standard logical theories can be regarded as linguistic logics as well as propositional, statemental, or SOA logics, and their adequacy or strong adequacy as a linguistic logic

VI. Formal Semantics

often goes hand-in-hand with their adequacy or strong adequacy as a statemental logic. Let us define:

(3.20) If $\langle F,\sigma \rangle$ is a statemental logic and $\langle F,\lambda \rangle$ is a linguistic logic with the same set of formulas, they *agree* iff for every p in F:
(a) for each interpretation μ for $\langle F,\sigma \rangle$ there is an interpretation η for $\langle F,\lambda \rangle$ and a pragmatic assignment π such that $\mu(p) = (\eta/\pi)(p)$; and
(b) for each interpretation η for $\langle F,\lambda \rangle$ and pragmatic assignment π there is an interpretation μ for $\langle F,\sigma \rangle$ such that $\mu(p) = (\eta/\pi)(p)$.

Roughly, to say that $\langle F,\sigma \rangle$ and $\langle F,\lambda \rangle$ agree is to say that each formula p expresses the same range of statements whether we construe it as part of the statemental logic or part of the linguistic logic. Obviously:

(3.21) If $\langle F,\sigma \rangle$ and $\langle F,\lambda \rangle$ agree then any formula p is valid$_N$ for $\langle F,\sigma \rangle$ iff it is valid$_N$ for $\langle F,\lambda \rangle$.

An immediate corollary of (3.21) is:

(3.22) If $\langle F,\sigma \rangle$ and $\langle F,\lambda \rangle$ agree then a semantics is adequate for one iff it is adequate for the other.

We can also define a stronger sense of agreement:

(3.23) If $\langle F,\sigma \rangle$ is a statemental logic and $\langle F,\lambda \rangle$ is a linguistic logic with the same set of formulas, they *agree uniformly* iff:
(a) for each interpretation μ of $\langle F,\sigma \rangle$ there is an interpretation η of $\langle F,\lambda \rangle$ and a pragmatic assignment π such that for every p in F, $\mu(p) = (\eta/\pi)(p)$; and
(b) for each interpretation η of $\langle F,\lambda \rangle$ and pragmatic assignment π there is an interpretation μ of $\langle F,\sigma \rangle$ such that for every p in F, $\mu(p) = (\eta/\pi)(p)$.

To say that $\langle F,\sigma \rangle$ and $\langle F,\lambda \rangle$ agree uniformly is to say, roughly, that each *set* of formulas expresses the same range of sets of

192

statements whether we regard the formulas as part of the statemental logic or part of the linguistic logic. Obviously:

(3.24) If $\langle F,\sigma \rangle$ and $\langle F,\lambda \rangle$ agree uniformly then if Γ is a set of formulas and p a formula, $\Gamma \Mapsto_N p$ in $\langle F,\sigma \rangle$ iff $\Gamma \Mapsto_N p$ in $\langle F,\lambda \rangle$.

An immediate corollary of (3.24) is:

(3.25) If $\langle F,\sigma \rangle$ and $\langle F,\lambda \rangle$ agree uniformly then a semantics is strongly adequate for one iff it is strongly adequate for the other.

In light of (3.22) and (3.24), even if a semantics was designed for statemental logics rather than linguistic logics, it will often be adequate or strongly adequate for the latter as well. We will find that this is true of all the standard semantics for truth-functional and first-order nonmodal and modal logic. On the other hand, there are also semantics that appear to be designed explicitly for linguistic logics. The models in the semantics of Kamp [1971], van Fraassen [1977], and Kaplan [1979] all contain an element mirroring the pragmatic assignment and have a more exotic structure than do classical models. I will illustrate this by constructing a simple linguistic logic distilled out of Kaplan's more complicated logic of demonstratives.[8] In order to keep the illustration as simple as possible, let us begin by considering a first-order modal logic *without quantifiers* but with individual constants. By avoiding quantifiers, we can keep the definition of 'truth in a model' relatively simple.[9] The models for this non-quantificational modal language are those of Kripke [1963]. Such a model is a quintuple $\langle w_0, \mathbf{W}, \mathbf{U}, \mathbf{D}, \mu \rangle$ where $\mathbf{W}$ is a set (the set of "worlds"); $w_0 \in \mathbf{W}$; $\mathbf{U}$ is a set (the set of all "possible objects"); $\mathbf{D}$ is a function that assigns to each w in $\mathbf{W}$ a subset of $\mathbf{U}$ (the *domain* of w) in such a way that $\mathbf{U} = \bigcup_{w \in \mathbf{W}} \mathbf{D}(w)$;

---

[8] This is taken from Kaplan [1976], 74–84. Kaplan's logic goes considerably further than the simple logic described here. Kaplan includes an array of modal operators, tense operators, and his 'dthat' operator.

[9] The semantics for a full first-order modal logic with quantifiers will be discussed in section eight.

and μ is a function that to each individual constant c assigns a member of U (the *denotation* of c) and to each pair $\langle w,R \rangle$ where $w \in W$ and R is an n-place relation symbol assigns some set of ordered n-tuples of members of U. $\mu(w,R)$ is the *extension* of R at w, i.e., the set of all n-tuples of "possible objects satisfying R at w". Truth in a model is defined recursively as follows:

(3.26) (a) $\ulcorner Ra_1...a_n \urcorner$ is true in $\langle w_0,\mathbf{W},\mathbf{U},\mathbf{D},\mu \rangle$ iff $\langle \mu(a_1),...,\mu(a_n) \rangle \in \mu(R,w_0)$;

(b) $\ulcorner \neg p \urcorner$ is true in $\langle w_0,\mathbf{W},\mathbf{U},\mathbf{D},\mu \rangle$ iff p is not true in $\langle w_0,\mathbf{W},\mathbf{U},\mathbf{D},\mu \rangle$;

(c) $\ulcorner (p \wedge q) \urcorner$ is true in $\langle w_0,\mathbf{W},\mathbf{U},\mathbf{D},\mu \rangle$ iff p and q are both true in $\langle w_0,\mathbf{W},\mathbf{U},\mathbf{D},\mu \rangle$;

(d) $\ulcorner \Box p \urcorner$ is true in $\langle w_0,\mathbf{W},\mathbf{U},\mathbf{D},\mu \rangle$ iff for every w in $\mathbf{W}$, p is true in $\langle w,\mathbf{W},\mathbf{U},\mathbf{D},\mu \rangle$.

Following Kaplan (roughly), we extend this language by adding the privileged constants 'I' and '$here$' and the privileged relation symbols 'E' ('exists') and 'L' ('is located at'). Then we revise the definition of a model by saying that a model is an ordered pair $\langle \langle w_0,\mathbf{W},\mathbf{U},\mathbf{D},\mu \rangle, \langle s,p \rangle \rangle$ where $\langle w_0,\mathbf{W},\mathbf{U},\mathbf{D},\mu \rangle$ is a Kripke-model and:

(a) $s,p \in \mathbf{D}(w_0)$;
(b) for each w in $\mathbf{W}$, $\mu(w,L) \subseteq \mathbf{D}(w) \times \mathbf{D}(w)$;
(c) for each w in $\mathbf{W}$, $\mu(w,E) = \mathbf{D}(w)$;
(d) for each w in $\mathbf{W}$, $\mu(w,I) = s$;
(e) for each w in $\mathbf{W}$, $\mu(w,here) = p$.
(f) $\langle s,p \rangle \in \mu(w_0,L)$.[10]

Truth in a model is then defined recursively pretty much as before:

(3.27) (a) $\ulcorner Ra_1...a_n \urcorner$ is true in $\langle \langle w_0,\mathbf{W},\mathbf{U},\mathbf{D},\mu \rangle, \langle s,p \rangle \rangle$ iff $\langle \mu(a_1),...,\mu(a_n) \rangle \in \mu(R,w_0)$;

(b) $\ulcorner \neg p \urcorner$ is true in $\langle \langle w_0,\mathbf{W},\mathbf{U},\mathbf{D},\mu \rangle, \langle s,p \rangle \rangle$ iff p is not true in $\langle \langle w_0,\mathbf{W},\mathbf{U},\mathbf{D},\mu \rangle, \langle s,p \rangle \rangle$;

---

[10] Additional constraints might reasonably be added, but this is sufficient for our present purposes, which are purely illustrative.

(c) $\ulcorner(p{\wedge}q)\urcorner$ is true in $\langle\langle w_0,\mathbf{W},\mathbf{U},\mathbf{D},\mu\rangle,\langle s,p\rangle\rangle$ iff p and q are both true in $\langle\langle w_0,\mathbf{W},\mathbf{U},\mathbf{D},\mu\rangle,\langle s,p\rangle\rangle$;

(d) $\ulcorner\Box p\urcorner$ is true in $\langle\langle w_0,\mathbf{W},\mathbf{U},\mathbf{D},\mu\rangle,\langle s,p\rangle\rangle$ iff for every w in $\mathbf{W}$, p is true in $\langle\langle w_0,\mathbf{W},\mathbf{U},\mathbf{D},\mu\rangle,\langle s,p\rangle\rangle$.

$\langle s,p\rangle$ plays the role of pragmatic parameters in this semantics. The novelty of this semantics is illustrated by the fact that $\ulcorner E(I)\urcorner$ ('*I* exist') and $\ulcorner L(I,here)\urcorner$ ('I am here') are both valid, but neither $\ulcorner\Box E(I)\urcorner$ nor $\ulcorner\Box L(I,here)\urcorner$ are valid. The suggestion is that this semantics (perhaps with some added constraints) captures validity$_T$ rather than one of the stronger kinds of validity. One invariably makes a true statement by saying either 'I exist' or 'I am here', but the statement one makes is not necessary.

For the most part, linguistic logics and their semantics have been constructed in connection with rather difficult philosophical problems concerning the philosophy of language, time, etc. This makes these semantics hard to evaluate, because their adequacy generally turns upon questions regarding time, demonstratives, and so on, for which there is no general agreement. To avoid becoming enmeshed in those substantive questions, I will not directly discuss any of these semantical theories in the present book, but the reader may find it interesting to apply the present framework to them himself.

4. Truth-Functional Logic

In the last section, a framework was established within which to study various formal semantical theories. Beginning in this section, that framework will be applied to some well-known logical theories. In the present section I will consider truth-functional logic (i.e., the propositional calculus), alternatively as a propositional logic, a statemental logic, an SOA logic, and a linguistic logic. The discussion of truth-functional logic is actually rather trivial, but it will serve as a good introduction to the investigation of more complex theories.

Let us begin by considering truth-functional logic as a propositional logic. The language is $\langle F,\pi\rangle$ where the set of for-

VI. Formal Semantics

mulas F is constructed in the usual way from a denumerable set At of atomic formulas and π is the obvious assignment of propositional forms to formulas. A *model* is a function mapping the set of atomic formulas into $\{0,1\}$. Truth in a model is defined in the usual way. In truth-functional logic, all formulas are built exclusively out of atomic formulas, and the latter express propositions, so an *interpretation* is any function assigning propositions to atomic formulas. If μ is an interpretation, μ assigns propositions to molecular formulas recursively as follows:

(a) $\mu(\neg p) = \sim\mu(p)$;
(b) $\mu(p \wedge q) = \mu(p)\&\mu(q)$.

The characterization of the surrogate relation in truth-functional logic is extremely simple. We prove by induction on the length of a formula:

(4.1) $M \simeq \langle w,\mu \rangle$ iff for every atomic formula p, $M(p) = 1$ iff $\mu(p)$ is true at w.

We can use (4.1) to prove that the semantics for truth-functional logic is strongly adequate. To this end we prove (A1) and (A2):

(A1) For each possible world w and interpretation μ, there is a model M such that $M \simeq \langle w,\mu \rangle$.

Proof: For each atomic formula p, define: $M(p) = 1$ iff $\mu(p)$ is true at w. Then by (4.1), $M \simeq \langle w,\mu \rangle$.

(A2) For each model M there is an interpretation μ and possible world w such that $M \simeq \langle w,\mu \rangle$.

Proof: Let w be the actual world, and for each atomic formula p, if $M(p) = 1$ let $\mu(p)$ be the proposition that $2+2 = 4$, and if $M(p) = 0$ let $\mu(p)$ be the proposition that $2+2 = 5$. Then by (4.1), $M \simeq \langle w,\mu \rangle$.

It follows that truth-functional logic, construed as a propositional logic, is strongly adequate. If we reconstrue it as a statemental logic or an SOA logic, nothing much changes.

The only difference is that an interpretation becomes a function assigning either statements or states of affairs to atomic formulas. Strong adequacy is still established in precisely the same manner.

It is also possible to regard truth-functional logic as a linguistic logic. In that case we take formulas to express semantical forms. We can define the conjunction $\mathbf{K}(\Delta_1,\Delta_2)$ of two S-intensions as in (2.10), and we can define the negation of an S-intension analogously:

> (4.2) If Δ is an S-intension, $\mathbf{N}(\Delta)$ is that S-intension such that for any pragmatic assignment π, $\mathbf{N}(\Delta)(\pi) = \sim\Delta(\pi)$.

Then an interpretation η assigns S-intensions to the atomic formulas directly and assigns S-intensions to the molecular formulas recursively as follows:

> (a) $\eta(\neg p) = \mathbf{N}(\eta(p))$;
> (b) $\eta(p \wedge q) = \mathbf{K}(\eta(p),\eta(q))$.

It is easy to see that this linguistic logic agrees uniformly with truth-functional logic construed as a statemental logic. To this end we must establish two simple theorems:

> (4.3) For each statemental interpretation μ of truth-functional logic there is a linguistic interpretation η and a pragmatic assignment π such that for every formula p, $\mu(p) = (\eta/\pi)(p)$.

Proof: For each atomic formula q, we let $\eta(q)$ be the constant-valued S-intension Δ such that for every pragmatic assignment π, $\Delta(\pi) = \mu(q)$. It is then trivial to prove by induction on the length of a formula p that $\mu(p) = (\eta/\pi)(p)$.

Equally trivially:

> (4.4) For each linguistic interpretation η and pragmatic assignment π there is a statemental interpretation μ such that for every formula p, $\mu(p) = (\eta/\pi)(p)$.

It then follows by (3.25) that our semantics is strongly adequate for truth-functional logic construed as a linguistic logic.

Precisely the same argument will serve to show that first-order logic, non-quantificational modal logic, and first-order modal logic construed as statemental logics agree uniformly with themselves construed as linguistic logics; so in each case, the adequacy or strong adequacy of the semantics for the linguistic logic follows from the adequacy or strong adequacy of the semantics for the statemental logic.

5. First-Order Logic

When we turn to first-order logic, the situation becomes considerably more complicated. We can consider first-order logic with or without individual constants. Our logical constants will consist of the existential quantifier ($\lor x$), the truth functions $\land$ and $\lnot$, and identity $=$. We define the universal quantifier ($\land x$), and the truth functions $\lor$, $\rightarrow$, and $\leftrightarrow$ in the usual manner. We define the set F of closed formulas and the set WFF of open-or-closed formulas in the normal way. In first-order logic, a *model* is an ordered pair $\langle D, \mu \rangle$ where D is a nonempty set and μ is a function that assigns extensions to the relation symbols and denotations to the individual constants (if there are any). In this language, only the closed formulas are formulas in the sense of section three, i.e., only the closed formulas express propositional forms (or statemental forms or SOA forms). This creates difficulties for giving a recursive definition of truth. These difficulties are circumvented by introducing the notion of an *assignment* that is a function σ assigning elements of D to individual variables. This can be regarded as a purely technical trick to enable us to define truth (perhaps we should call it something else) recursively for all formulas (open as well as closed) relative to $\langle \langle D, \mu \rangle, \sigma \rangle$. To this end we define:

(5.1) If x is an individual variable and σ and σ^* are assignments, $\sigma \mathrel{\underset{x}{\cong}} \sigma^*$ iff σ and σ^* agree on their assignments to all individual variables except possibly x.

The individual constants and individual variables jointly comprise the *individual symbols* of our first-order language. The *denotation* of an individual symbol x in $\langle\langle D,\mu\rangle,\sigma\rangle$ is $\mu(x)$ if x is an individual constant, and it is $\sigma(x)$ if x is an individual variable. Then we define:

(5.2) If $\langle D,\mu\rangle$ is a model and σ is an assignment, truth relative to $\langle\langle D,\mu\rangle,\sigma\rangle$ is defined recursively as follows:
(a) if R is an n-place relation symbol and $x_1,\ldots,x_n$ are individual symbols whose denotations are $a_1,\ldots,a_n$ respectively, then $\ulcorner Rx_1,\ldots,x_n\urcorner$ is true in $\langle\langle D,\mu\rangle,\sigma\rangle$ iff $\langle a_1,\ldots,a_n\rangle\in\mu(R)$;
(b) $\ulcorner x = y\urcorner$ is true in $\langle\langle D,\mu\rangle,\sigma\rangle$ iff x and y have the same denotation in $\langle\langle D,\mu\rangle,\sigma\rangle$;
(c) $\ulcorner\neg p\urcorner$ is true in $\langle\langle D,\mu\rangle,\sigma\rangle$ iff p is not true in $\langle\langle D,\mu\rangle,\sigma\rangle$;
(d) $\ulcorner p\wedge q\urcorner$ is true in $\langle\langle D,\mu\rangle,\sigma\rangle$ iff p and q are both true in $\langle\langle D,\mu\rangle,\sigma\rangle$;
(e) $\ulcorner(\vee x)p\urcorner$ is true in $\langle\langle D,\mu\rangle,\sigma\rangle$ iff there is an assignment σ^* such that $\sigma \underset{x}{\approx} \sigma^*$ and p is true in $\langle\langle D,\mu\rangle,\sigma^*\rangle$.

We can then define truth in a model for closed formulas as follows:

(5.3) A formula p is true in a model $\langle D,\mu\rangle$ iff there is an assignment σ such that p is true in $\langle\langle D,\mu\rangle,\sigma\rangle$.

The reason this definition works is that for closed formulas, every choice of an assignment yields the same truth value.

Unlike the propositional calculus, it makes a difference whether we construe first-order logic as a propositional logic, a statemental logic, an SOA logic, or a linguistic logic, so we will consider each of these alternatives separately.

5.1 Propositional First-Order Logic

We have specified the syntax of our first-order language, but we have not yet specified how it is to be interpreted. The same set of formulas can be combined with different functions

π assigning propositional forms to yield different languages $\langle F, \pi \rangle$, and this will give us different logical theories. We will define π as in (2.2) by specifying the class of interpretations. It is clear how most of the details of the specification of the class of interpretations should go: '$\wedge$' should symbolize conjunction, '$\neg$' should symbolize negation, '$=$' should symbolize identity, and relation symbols should symbolize concepts. There are, however, several options regarding the interpretation of the quantifiers, and there are problems concerning the role of individual constants. Let us begin by supposing that our language does not contain individual constants. In that case, interpretations are characterized recursively as follows:

(a) If R is an n-place relation symbol, $\eta(R)$ is an n-place concept;

(b) $\eta(Rx_1, \ldots, x_n) = \eta(R)$;

(c) $\eta(x = y)$ is identity;

(d) if p is any formula, $\eta(\neg p) = \sim \eta(p)$;

(e) if p and q are formulas, $\eta(p \wedge q) = \eta(p) \& \eta(q)$.[11]

(f) —clause for quantifiers—

To complete this, we must fill out clause (f), explaining how quantifiers are to be interpreted.

In interpreting quantifiers, we must ask what they are to range over. They might be taken to range over everything there is, or only over some restricted universe of discourse. This will be reflected by differences in π, and the formal semantics we described above might be adequate for some of these choices of π and not for others. Let us examine the alternatives:

(1) The simplest choice is to have the quantifiers range over everything in the world. On this alternative, in constructing an interpretation $\eta(p)$ of a formula p, a quantifier is translated directly into a quantifier in the proposition, i.e., we have the following clause (f):

[11] This presupposes some convention regarding how the argument places in concepts are associated with the variables occurring free in an open formula, but I will leave that to the reader.

(f_1) if p is an open formula then $\eta((\bigvee x)p) = (\exists x)\eta(p)$.[12]

Let us call the resulting choice of π 'π_1'. To assess the adequacy of our formal semantics for $\langle F,\pi_1 \rangle$, consider (A1) and (A2).

(A1) requires that for each $\langle w,\eta \rangle$ there is a model M that is a surrogate of it. This would be unproblematic if there were always a set of all objects over which unrestricted quantifiers range, i.e., a universal set; but according to the received view on set theory, there is no such set.[13] Fortunately, we can establish (A1) in another way. Given a set $\mathbf{R}$ of axioms and rules of inference, if $\Gamma \subseteq F$ and $p \in F$, let us say that $\Gamma \vdash p$ (p is *derivable from* Γ) iff there are $q_1,...,q_n$ in Γ such that $\ulcorner(q_1 \wedge ... \wedge q_n) \rightarrow p\urcorner$ is a theorem (i.e., provable using $\mathbf{R}$). $\mathbf{R}$ is *sound* iff every theorem of $\mathbf{R}$ is valid$_N$. There exist any number of sets $\mathbf{R}$ of axioms and rules of inference for first-order logic that are *strongly complete* in the sense that for any $\Gamma \subseteq F$ and $p \in F$, $\Gamma \vdash p$ iff $\Gamma \models p$. Furthermore, it is readily proven by induction on the length of a proof in $\mathbf{R}$ that every theorem is valid$_N$ and hence $\mathbf{R}$ is sound. As $\mathbf{R}$ is sound it follows that if $\Gamma \vdash p$ and η is an interpretation, then if all the propositions in $\{\eta(q)|\ q \in \Gamma\}$ are true at a world w, $\eta(p)$ is also true at w; i.e., $\mathbf{R}$ is *truth preserving*. Now consider a world w and an interpretation η, and let $\Gamma = \{p|\ \eta(p)$ is true at $w\}$. Γ is consistent, so we cannot obtain a contradiction from Γ using truth preserving rules of inference, and hence we cannot derive a contradiction from Γ using $\mathbf{R}$. By strong completeness, Γ has a model M. For every formula p, either p or $\neg p$ is in Γ, so $\Gamma = \{p|\ p$ is true in $M\}$. Hence $M \simeq \langle w,\eta \rangle$. Therefore, (A1) holds. Note that this argument can be replicated for any logical theory having a

---

[12] Again, this presupposes some convention associating variables in formulas with argument places in concepts.

[13] One is tempted to reason that, in light of the Skolem-Löwenheim theorem, we can always cut down the range of the quantifiers and obtain a model of any infinite cardinality without affecting the truth of any formula in the model. But such reasoning is invalid. The Skolem-Löwenheim theorem is not applicable unless our quantifiers range over a set of objects initially, and the problem we are trying to avoid is that they do not.

formal semantics for which there exists a strongly complete system of sound axioms and rules.

Although (A1) holds for $\langle F, \pi_1 \rangle$, (A2) and (A3) both fail. The difficulty is that there are infinitely many necessary entities (e.g., numbers), and so every possible world contains infinitely many objects. Consequently, no model with a finite domain can be a surrogate of any possible world. Thus the semantics is inadequate. The semantics makes formulas like $\ulcorner (\vee y)(\wedge x) \; y = x \urcorner$ satisfiable (in a model with a one-element domain), but for $\langle F, \pi_1 \rangle$ the negations of such formulas are valid$_N$.

It is obvious how to alter the semantics in order to meet this difficulty. We simply require that models have infinite domains. If we do this the set $\mathbf{R}$ of rules of inference is no longer strongly complete, and so our defense of (A1) collapses. It can be resurrected by strengthening $\mathbf{R}$, but even then it is unclear whether (A2) or (A3) holds. Furthermore, even if our modified semantics is adequate for $\langle F, \pi_1 \rangle$, the resulting set of valid formulas is not the same as the set of theorems for classical first-order logic (although the fragment without identity is the same). It is essential for obtaining classical first-order logic that we have models with finite domains. For example, on our modified semantics, $\models \neg(\vee x)(\wedge y) \; y = x$.

(2) If we are to obtain classical first-order logic, we must adopt an interpretation of the quantifiers that legitimizes models with finite domains. The obvious way to do this is to interpret quantifiers as ranging over restricted universes of discourse. On this proposal, for each interpretation η there is a concept α_η such that in constructing the interpretation $\eta(p)$ of a formula p, quantifiers in p are translated into quantifiers in propositions *relativized to* α_η. In other words, we have the following clause (f):

(f_2) if p is an open formula then $\eta((\vee x)p) = (\exists x)[(\alpha_\eta : x) \; \& \; \eta(p)]$.

Let π_2 be the resulting assignment of propositions to formulas.

The standard formal semantics for first-order logic is again inadequate for $\langle F, \pi_2 \rangle$. This time the difficulty is that there are

202

interpretations η that relativize the quantifiers to concepts α_η whose extensions are empty in some worlds. Consequently, $\ulcorner(\forall x)(Fx \vee \neg Fx)\urcorner$ is not valid$_N$ for $\langle F, \pi_2 \rangle$, but it is semantically valid. Again, it is obvious how to alter our formal semantics in order to meet this difficulty, viz., by admitting models with empty domains. With this alteration, (A1) holds. (A1) can be established as before, using a modified set of rules **R**.

Turning to (A2), it can be established as follows. (A2) requires that every model M is the surrogate of some $\langle w, \eta \rangle$. Two models are *elementarily equivalent* iff they make the same formulas true. Elementarily equivalent models are surrogates for the same $\langle w, \eta \rangle$'s. By the Skolem-Löwenheim theorem, every model is elementarily equivalent to a countable model, so to establish (A2) we need only show that every countable model is a surrogate of some $\langle w, \eta \rangle$. We describe a possible world w by supposing that substances in w are infinitely divisible, so for any object it is possible to have any finite number of pieces of that object. We suppose further that there exists in w a set S of billiard balls having the same cardinality as the domain of our model M, and for each natural number n, there exists a carton (something like an egg carton) C_n consisting of n cells arranged linearly and numbered 1 through n. Pieces of the billiard balls can be fitted into the cells of the cartons. We define our interpretation η as follows. Consider an enumeration of the relation symbols: for each $n > 0$, let R_n^i be the ith n-place relation symbol. Consider a denumerable set of distinct temporal instants t_i. We let α_η be the concept expressed by 'is a billiard ball', and for each i, $\eta(R_n^i)$ is the concept expressed by 'at some time between t_i and t_{i+1}, a piece of x_1 occupies the first cell in C_n and ... and a piece of x_n occupies the nth cell in C_n'. The point of this construction is that the concepts thus expressed by the relation symbols are logically independent of one another and can have any extensions within S that we like. Thus, regardless of the extensions of the relation symbols in M, it is possible for there to be a world w of the preceding sort such that $M \simeq \langle w, \eta \rangle$.[14]

---

[14] Note that there is no obvious way to accommodate this construction to $\langle F, \pi_1 \rangle$ so that the quantifiers range over more than just contingent objects.

As (A1) and (A2) hold for this semantics, it is strongly adequate for $\langle F,\pi_2 \rangle$. But it should be emphasized that the resulting set of valid formulas is not the same as the set of theorems of classical first-order logic. For example, $\ulcorner (\lor x)(Fx \lor \neg Fx) \urcorner$ is not valid. The logic we get in this way is a "free logic".

(3) There is a contrived choice of π that gives us classical first-order logic. Once again, we take the quantifiers to range over restricted universes of discourse. For each interpretation η, there is a concept α_η in terms of which we interpret the quantifiers. But now, rather than simply relativizing the quantifiers to α_η, we relativize the quantifiers to α^*_η defined as follows:

$$\alpha^*_\eta = [(\alpha_\eta:x) \ \& \ (\exists y)(\alpha_\eta:y)] \lor [(x = \varnothing) \ \& \ \sim(\exists y)(\alpha_\eta:y)].$$

Assuming that the empty set exists necessarily, this ensures that the quantifiers range over a nonempty universe of discourse. If the extension of α^*_η has nothing else in it, it contains the empty set. Let us call this choice of π 'π_3'.

This procedure suffices to obtain classical first-order logic, but it is *ad hoc*. If we have to work this hard to get classical first-order logic, one cannot help but wonder why we should want it so badly. The choice of either π_1 or π_2 is much more natural. If we really want to relativize quantifiers to arbitrary universes of discourse, we should adopt π_2. If instead the thought is that we are going to be dealing with numbers or some other universe of discourse that cannot be empty, we will almost invariably know that such a universe is infinite, and then the choice of π_1 becomes appropriate.

In discussing the interpretation of the quantifiers, we have been assuming that our language does not contain individual constants. Now let us reverse that assumption and see what difference it makes. What role should individual constants play in a propositional logic? It is frequently claimed that individual constants symbolize either proper names or arbitrary singular terms, but that is to confuse propositional logics with linguistic logics. The formulas of a propositional logic symbolize propositional forms. As such, it makes no sense to talk about individual constants symbolizing linguistic items. Within propositional logics there appear to be just two choices regarding individual constants. We can either include them as constituents of formulas that express propositional forms, or we can relegate them exclusively to those formulas that (like open formulas) do not express propositional forms but are included in the language merely as a technical convenience for defining truth for those formulas that do express propositional forms. In the latter case, individual constants would be treated like free variables were treated before—as convenient devices for the interpretation of quantifiers in our formal semantics. On the other hand, if individual constants are to be constituents of formulas expressing propositional forms, there would seem to be only one choice regarding how an interpretation should treat an individual constant. Individual constants denote individuals, so they must be interpreted in terms of propositional constituents that designate individuals. In other words, interpretations must assign propositional designators to individual constants.

Which way we interpret individual constants makes a difference to the resulting logical theory. If we treat them merely as devices for calculating truth values, their treatment is the classical one, and as they are not constituents of formulas expressing propositional forms, the logical theory is the same as before. But if we take individual constants to symbolize propositional designators, our models must allow individual constants to lack denotations because propositional designators may fail to designate. This in turn requires us to re-examine the definition of truth for atomic formulas. If a constant c lacks a denotation, how do we compute the truth value of $\ulcorner Fc \urcorner$? Given that an interpretation can assign any one-place concept to F, there cannot be a standard way of doing this. Some concepts α are such that if δ has no designatum then $(\alpha{:}\delta)$ is automatically false, but others (e.g., the concept of not existing) make $(\alpha{:}\delta)$ automatically true, and still others treat different nondesignating designators differently. For an example of the latter, let α be the counterfactual concept $[(\exists y)\, y \approx x > x \approx \delta]$.

Then $(\alpha{:}\delta)$ is true even if δ does not designate, but if δ^* is some other nondesignating designator, $(\alpha{:}\delta^*)$ will usually be false. These complexities can only be accommodated by altering the formal semantics. Specifically, the truth value of an atomic formula can no longer be determined by the extension of the relation symbols and the denotations of the individual constants. A more complex definition of truth is required. This is most easily handled within first-order modal logic. But notice that even given a suitable revision of the semantics the resulting logic will be nonclassical. For example, $\ulcorner Fa \rightarrow (\bigvee x)Fx \urcorner$, which is a theorem of classical first-order logic, will not be valid.

5.2 *Statemental First-Order logic and Linguistic First-Order Logic*

Next consider what happens when we view first-order logic as a statemental logic. If our language does not contain individual constants, it appears that everything we said about propositional first-order logic can be repeated for statemental first-order logic. If our language does contain individual constants and we interpret them as expressing statemental designators, the situation becomes even more complicated than in propositional first-order logic. The difficulty is that the standard symbolism in first-order logic does not allow us to make some necessary distinctions. For example, in Chapter Two we discussed the difference between the statements $(x \approx y{:}\partial,\partial)$ and $(x \approx x{:}\partial)$, arguing that both are externally necessary but only the latter is internally necessary and *a priori*. Similar remarks can be made about the statements

$$([(A{:}x) \vee \sim(A{:}y)]{:}\partial,\partial)$$

and

$$([(A{:}x) \vee \sim(A{:}x)]{:}\partial).$$

But in each of these cases, whereas we have two different statements to be symbolized, we have only a single formula that is a candidate for symbolizing both, viz., $\ulcorner c = c \urcorner$ and $\ulcorner Fc \vee \overset{\text{\tiny 1}}{\neg} Fc \urcorner$. Thus, if we are to study first-order statemental

206

logic with individual constants, we must enrich the syntax of our formal language. I will not pursue that here, however.

Obviously, linguistic first-order logic agrees uniformly with statemental first-order logic, so any conclusions we can draw about the adequacy or strong adequacy of the latter generalize immediately to the former.

5.3 *SOA First-Order Logic*

Construing first-order logic as an SOA logic, an interpretation assigns properties to relation symbols and open formulas, individuals to individual constants, and states of affairs to closed formulas. This treatment of individual constants is made possible by the fact that properties operate directly on individuals to produce states of affairs, unlike concepts and attributes, which only operate on individuals via designators designating those individuals. Nondenoting individual constants cease to be a problem in SOA logics, because the constants are interpreted directly in terms of individuals and hence cannot fail to denote. This makes individual constants behave much more like they are supposed to behave in the standard semantics for first-order logic. As we will see in the next paragraph, however, there is a residual difficulty concerning individual constants.

Just as for propositional first-order logic, we have different options regarding the interpretation of the quantifiers. The most natural interpretation of the quantifiers is analogous to π_2 for propositional first-order logic. That is, an interpretation η assigns some property α_η to which it relativizes quantifiers. Let us call the resulting language '$\langle F, \rho_2 \rangle$'. As in the case of propositional first-order logic, the standard semantics must be modified to allow for empty domains if it is to be adequate for $\langle F, \rho_2 \rangle$. This, however, creates difficulties for the interpretation of individual constants. How are they to be interpreted in any empty domain? They cannot be assigned denotations from the domain, because there are no denotata to be assigned. And if we allow individual constants to go without denotata in models with empty domains, we again have the problem of stating truth conditions. Because of these considerations, I will confine my attention here to SOA first-order logic without individual constants. We can then establish the strong adequacy of our semantics using precisely the same argument we used in connection with $\langle F, \pi_2 \rangle$. It is worth observing, however, that it is much easier to establish strong adequacy for SOA logics than for propositional logics. Specifically, it is much easier to establish (A2). In propositional first-order logic we had to construct elaborate interpretations in order to obtain surrogates for arbitrary models, but in SOA first-order logic it is absolutely trivial to find an interpretation that is a surrogate of a model. Suppose our model is $\langle D, \mu \rangle$. D is a set of individuals, and to each n-place relation symbol R, μ assigns a set $\mu(R)$ of ordered n-tuples of members of D. Let our interpretation η assign to R the property of *being an ordered n-tuple that is a member of* $\mu(R)$. That is (recalling that n-place properties are functions from n-tuples to states of affairs), $\eta(R)$ is that property that assigns to an n-tuple $\langle x_1, \ldots, x_n \rangle$ the necessary state of affairs if $\langle x_1, \ldots, x_n \rangle \in \mu(R)$, and assigns the contradictory state of affairs otherwise. Similarly, let η relativize quantifiers to the property of *being a member of D*; i.e., $\alpha_\eta(x)$ is the necessary state of affairs if $x \in D$, and $\alpha_\eta(x)$ is the contradictory state of affairs otherwise. It is then trivial to verify by induction on the length of a formula that:

(5.4) (a) If p is a closed formula then $\eta(p)$ obtains iff p is true in $\langle D, \mu \rangle$; and

   (b) if p is an n-formula (i.e., a formula in which n variables occur free), an n-tuple $\langle x_1, \ldots, x_n \rangle$ has the property $\eta(p)$ iff $\langle x_1, \ldots, x_n \rangle$ satisfies p in $\langle D, \mu \rangle$.[15]

The greater ease with which we can find surrogates for models in SOA logics will be even more significant when we turn to modal logic. Because of the difficulty in finding surrogates for models, I have been unable to establish strong adequacy for either non-quantificational or first-order propositional or

---

[15] This theorem also tells us that in constructing $\langle w, \eta \rangle$ for a model, we can always let w be the actual world. It follows from this that validity$_N$ and validity$_O$ for SOA first-order logic coincide.

statemental modal logic, but I am able to establish the strong adequacy of both SOA non-quantificational modal logic and SOA first-order modal logic. It appears that in many ways the standard formal semantics are better suited for SOA logics than they are for either propositional or statemental logics.

6. Non-Quantificational Modal Logic

Non-quantificational modal logic is what might more conventionally be called 'propositional modal logic'. However, we want to talk about 'propositional non-quantificational modal logic', 'statemental non-quantificational modal logic', and so on. It would be unduly confusing to talk instead about 'propositional propositional modal logic', 'statemental propositional modal logic', etc. The language of non-quantificational modal logic is that of truth-functional logic augmented with a *de dicto* modal operator $\diamond$ symbolizing possibility. The semantics is that discussed in section one. As I have already endorsed S5, there is no point in considering the versions of the semantics that incorporate the accessibility relation. *Models* will be taken to be ordered pairs $\langle G,K \rangle$ where K is a set of valuations (functions mapping the atomic formulas into $\{0,1\}$) and $G \in K$. Truth in a model is defined as in section one.

6.1 *Propositional Non-Quantificational Modal Logic*

In propositional non-quantificational modal logic, interpretations assign propositions to atomic formulas and interpret formulas in terms of propositional forms. To assess the adequacy of our formal semantics, we attempt to establish (A1) and (A2). (A1) can be established just as it was for first-order logic. S5 is strongly complete for our formal semantics, and we have endorsed S5, so we know that all inferences in accordance with S5 are sound. If η is an interpretation and w is a possible world, let $\Gamma = \{p \mid \eta(p)$ is true at $w\}$. Γ is consistent, so we cannot obtain a contradiction from Γ using sound inferences and hence cannot obtain a contradiction from Γ within S5. By the strong completeness of S5, it follows that Γ has a model M, and hence $M \simeq \langle w,\eta \rangle$. Therefore, (A1) holds.

(A2) is considerably more problematic. Consider the following principle:

(6.1) If K is any nonempty set of valuations, there is an interpretation η such that:
  (1) if $H \in K$ then there is a world w_H such that for each atomic formula p, $H(p) = 1$ iff $\eta(p)$ is true at w_H; and
  (2) if $H \notin K$ then there is no such world w_H.

To establish (A2) for non-quantificational modal logic, it suffices to establish (6.1). This is proven as follows. First, we prove the following simple lemma by induction on the length of formulas:

(6.2) If η is an interpretation and w and w^* are worlds and for every atomic formula q, $\eta(q)$ is true at w iff $\eta(q)$ is true at w^*, then for every formula q, $\eta(q)$ is true at w iff $\eta(q)$ is true at w^*.

Given lemma (6.2), we prove the following theorem:

(6.3) If $\langle G,K \rangle$ is a model and η an interpretation such that
  (1) if $H \in K$ then there is a world w_H such that for each atomic formula p, $H(p) = 1$ iff $\eta(p)$ is true at w_H; and
  (2) if $H \notin K$ then there is no such world w_H; then $\langle G,K \rangle \simeq \langle w_G, \eta \rangle$.

Proof by induction on the length of a formula. This is trivial for all but the case of $\ulcorner \Diamond p \urcorner$. If $\ulcorner \Diamond p \urcorner$ is true in $\langle G,K \rangle$ then for some H in K, p is true in $\langle H,K \rangle$, so by the induction hypothesis, there is an H in K such that $\eta(p)$ is true at w_H, and hence $\eta(\Diamond p)$ is true at w_G. Conversely, suppose $\eta(\Diamond p)$ is true at w_G. Then $\eta(p)$ is true at some world w. Define the valuation H by specifying that for each atomic formula q, $H(q) = 1$ iff $\eta(q)$ is true at w. By supposition then $H \in K$, and by (6.2) $\eta(p)$ is true at w_H. By the induction hypothesis, p is true in $\langle H,K \rangle$, so $\ulcorner \Diamond p \urcorner$ is true in $\langle G,K \rangle$.

Consequently, if (6.1) holds then (A2) holds.

Unfortunately, I have been unable to establish (A2) either by proving (6.1) or by any other means, and hence unable to use theorem (3.7) to establish the strong adequacy of the formal semantics for S5. We can, however, employ theorem (3.7) in a different way to show that our semantics is adequate. This is done by narrowing the language. Our language is $\langle F, \pi \rangle$. For each p in F, let F_p be the set of formulas containing no atomic formulas (i.e., sentence letters) not contained in p. Then consider the restricted language $\langle F_p, \pi \rangle$. A valuation for $\langle F_p, \pi \rangle$ is finite because the restricted language contains only finitely many atomic formulas. If G is a valuation for $\langle F, \pi \rangle$, let G_p be that subset of G that is a valuation for $\langle F_p, \pi \rangle$, and for a set K of valuations, let $K_p = \{G_p | \ G \in K\}$. Then if $\langle G, K \rangle$ is a model for $\langle F, \pi \rangle$, $\langle G_p, K_p \rangle$ is a model for $\langle F_p, \pi \rangle$, and we readily prove by induction on the length of a formula of F_p that:

(6.4) If $q \in F_p$ then q is true in $\langle G, K \rangle$ iff q is true in $\langle G_p, K_p \rangle$.

Consequently, the strong adequacy of the formal semantics for $\langle F_p, \pi \rangle$ (for each formula p) implies the adequacy of the semantics for $\langle F, \pi \rangle$. Furthermore, (6.1) is easily established for $\langle F_p, \pi \rangle$. If $p_1, \ldots, p_n$ are the atomic parts of p (listed in some fixed order), a *Boolean conjunction* for F_p is a conjunction of the form $\ulcorner (\neg) p_1 \wedge \ldots \wedge (\neg) p_n \urcorner$ where each negation can be either present or absent. Because $\langle F_p, \pi \rangle$ has only finitely many atomic formulas, each valuation G corresponds to a unique Boolean conjunction B_G that, in effect, just lists the truth values of the p_i in G. B_G is the unique Boolean conjunction that is true in G. Let $C = \{B_G | \ G \in K_p\}$. C is finite, so suppose $C = \{C_0, \ldots, C_k\}$ for some k. For each $i < k$, let φ_i be the proposition that there exist exactly i red objects, and let φ_k be the proposition that there exist at least k red objects. This has the result that the propositions φ_i are consistent but pairwise inconsistent, and $(\varphi_0 \vee \ldots \vee \varphi_k)$ is necessary. To construct an interpretation η satisfying (6.1), for each atomic formula p_j we let $\eta(p_j)$ be the disjunction of all the φ_i such that p_j occurs unnegated in C_i. Then we establish two facts about this interpretation:

VI. Formal Semantics

(a) For each i, $\eta(C_i)$ is equivalent to φ_i;
(b) if B is a Boolean conjunction not in C then $Nec(\sim\eta(B))$.

We establish (a) as follows. If p_j occurs unnegated in C_i, then $\eta(p_j)$ is a disjunction one of whose disjuncts is φ_i, so φ_i entails $\eta(p_j)$. If p_j occurs negated in C_i, then $\eta(p_j)$ is a disjunction none of whose disjuncts is φ_i, and hence as the φ_j are pairwise inconsistent, φ_i entails $\sim\eta(p_j)$. Thus, $\eta(C_i)$ is a conjunction each conjunct of which is entailed by φ_i, and hence φ_i entails $\eta(C_i)$. Now consider φ_j for $j \neq i$. As above, φ_j entails $\eta(C_j)$. But C_i is inconsistent with C_j, so φ_j entails $\sim\eta(C_i)$, and hence $\eta(C_i)$ entails $\sim\varphi_j$. Thus, $\eta(C_i)$ entails $(\sim\varphi_0 \ \& \ ... \ \& \ \sim\varphi_{i-1} \ \& \ \sim\varphi_{i+1} \ \& \ ... \ \& \ \sim\varphi_k)$. But $Nec(\varphi_0 \vee ... \vee \varphi_k)$, so $\eta(C_i)$ entails φ_i. Consequently, $\eta(C_i)$ is equivalent to φ_i.

Turning to (b), suppose B is a Boolean conjunction not in C. Different Boolean conjunctions are inconsistent with one another, so for each i, $\eta(B)$ entails $\sim\eta(C_i)$, and hence $\eta(B)$ entails $(\sim\varphi_0 \ \& \ ... \ \& \ \sim\varphi_k)$. As $Nec(\varphi_0 \vee ... \vee \varphi_k)$, $Nec(\sim\eta(B))$.

(a) and (b) together imply that (6.1) holds for $\langle F_p,\pi \rangle$. Consequently, (A2) holds for $\langle F_p,\pi \rangle$ and hence our formal semantics is strongly adequate for $\langle F_p,\pi \rangle$. It follows that our semantics is adequate for $\langle F,\pi \rangle$. However, the strong adequacy of the semantics for $\langle F,\pi \rangle$ remains an open question.

We are now in a position to resolve one of the puzzles propounded in section one regarding the formal semantics for non-quantificational modal logic. The puzzle consisted of noting that we can have models like $\langle G,\{G\} \rangle$ where the set of valuations intended to represent the set of all possible worlds is very small. This is puzzling because the set of all possible worlds is infinite. The first step in resolving this puzzle consists in observing that, contrary to what is normally claimed, valuations do not really correspond to possible worlds. Rather, they correspond to pairs $\langle w,\eta \rangle$ of possible worlds and interpretations. Furthermore, two different pairs $\langle w,\eta \rangle$ and $\langle w^*,\eta \rangle$ will correspond to the same valuation if they make the same formulas true. Finally, we note that it is possible to construct an interpretation η for non-quantificational modal logic that makes every formula either necessarily true or necessarily false.

6. Non-Quantificational Modal Logic

For such an interpretation η, the worlds in the pairs ⟨w,η⟩ are irrelevant to the determination of the truth values of formulas. Thus, there is just one valuation G corresponding to such an interpretation regardless of what world we pair the interpretation with, and hence the appropriate model for such a pair ⟨w,η⟩ will be ⟨G,{G}⟩.

6.2 Statemental and Linguistic Non-Quantificational Modal Logic

The heuristic idea behind the formal semantics for non-quantificational modal logic is the identification of necessity with truth at all possible worlds. We have seen, however, that statemental modal operators must express internal necessity rather than external necessity, and internal necessity does not coincide with truth at all possible worlds. Thus, we would naturally expect that the semantics is not adequate for statemental modal logic. It is somewhat surprising then that the semantics is adequate despite the failure of its heuristic basis. We showed above that S5's holding for propositional modal logic entails that S5 also holds for statemental modal logic.[16] It follows that (A1) holds for statemental modal logic. In establishing the adequacy of S5 for propositional modal logic, what we showed was that if p is any formula that is not a theorem of S5 then we can construct a proposition φ that is a counterexample to p; i.e., φ has the form expressed by p, but φ is not necessary. The propositions φ are constructed out of the propositions φ_i together with the logical operators &, ~, and ◇. The propositions φ_i are about how many red objects there are and have the important characteristic that they are also statements. For statements that are also propositions, internal and external necessity coincide and the modal operator can be regarded as expressing both. Consequently, the proposition φ that is a counterexample to p is also a statement, and so it follows that (A3) holds for statemental non-quantificational modal logic. Therefore, our semantics is adequate for

---

[16] See section four of Chapter Three.

213

statemental non-quantificational modal logic. This shows how unimportant the heuristic basis of the semantics actually is.

Clearly, statemental non-quantificational modal logic agrees uniformly with linguistic non-quantificational modal logic, so our semantics is adequate for the latter as well.

6.3 SOA Non-Quantificational Modal Logic

In SOA non-quantificational modal logic, our language is $\langle F, \rho \rangle$ where ρ assigns SOA forms to formulas. An interpretation assigns states of affairs to formulas. It was argued in Chapter Three that S5 holds for SOA modal operators, so we can establish (A1) for $\langle F, \rho \rangle$ just as we did for propositional and statemental non-quantificational modal logic. When we turn to (A2), however, things become interestingly different. We were unable to establish (A2) for either propositional or statemental modal logic, and hence had to settle for adequacy rather than strong adequacy. But in SOA modal logic, we can prove strong adequacy. This can be done very simply by adapting the argument used in section 6.1 to prove the strong adequacy of $\langle F_p, \pi \rangle$. Unlike the case of propositions and statements, we have infinite conjunctions and disjunctions of states of affairs. As a result, we can form infinite Boolean conjunctions of states of affairs. Of course, our language contains only finite conjunctions, so we must modify the argument slightly. In order to prove (6.1), let K be a nonempty set of valuations. The cardinality of K is less than or equal to $2^{\aleph_0}$. Choose a set S of pairwise inconsistent states of affairs such that the cardinality of S is the same as that of K and such that $\bigvee S$ is necessary, and let f be a one-one mapping of K onto S. For example, if the cardinality of K is $2^{\aleph_0}$, the members of S might have the form x *and* y *being separated by* r *meters* where r is a real number. We construct an interpretation η satisfying (6.1) as follows. For each atomic formula p, let $\eta(p) = \bigvee \{ f(G) \mid G \in K$ and $G(p) = 1 \}$. For each G in K, the *Boolean conjunction of states of affairs corresponding to* G is $B_G = \bigvee \{ \eta(p) \mid p \in At$ and $G(p) = 1 \}$ & $\bigvee \{ \sim\eta(p) \mid p \in At$ and $G(p) = 0 \}$. Then we establish as before:

(a) For each G in K, $f(G) = B_G$;[17]
(b) if G is a valuation not in K then $\text{Nec}(\sim B_G)$.

(a) and (b) imply (6.1), from which (A2) follows for $\langle F, \rho \rangle$. Thus, our formal semantics is strongly adequate for $\langle F, \rho \rangle$.

It is very interesting that we can establish strong adequacy for SOA non-quantificational modal logic, but not for propositional or statemental modal logic. This turns upon the fact that we have greater freedom in constructing states of affairs than we do in constructing propositions and statements. In particular, we can form infinite conjunctions and disjunctions of states of affairs. We will find that something analogous is true in first-order modal logic. This suggests that standard formal logics may be more naturally construed as SOA logics than as propositional or statemental logics. Such an interpretation at least makes the semantics more natural.

7. First-Order Modal Logic

What is normally called 'first-order modal logic' might more properly be called 'first-order *de re* modal logic'. Our logical notation is that of first-order logic without identity or individual constants, but with an added *de re* modal operator $\square$. Identity could be added to our notation at the expense of only slightly greater complexity, but the addition of individual constants would involve us in all of the same difficulties as in nonmodal first-order logic. Furthermore, for propositional and statemental first-order logic where individual constants would be taken to symbolize propositional and statemental designators, there is the additional problem noted in Chapter Three that the syntax must be enriched to distinguish between '$\square$' and '$\square_a$' and the semantics complicated accordingly.

Our formal semantics is that of Kripke [1963] and is constructed as follows. A *model* is an ordered quintuple $\langle w, \mathbf{W}, \mathbf{U}, \mathbf{D}, \mu \rangle$ where $\mathbf{W}$ is a set (the set of "worlds"); $w \in \mathbf{W}$; $\mathbf{U}$ is a (possibly empty) set (the set of all "possible objects");

---

[17] Recall that equivalent states of affairs are identical.

D is a function that assigns to each w in **W** a subset of **U** (the *domain* of w, i.e., the set of objects "existing in w") in such a way that $\mathbf{U} = \bigcup_{w \in \mathbf{W}} \mathbf{D}(w)$; and μ is a function that, to each pair $\langle w, R \rangle$ where $w \in \mathbf{W}$ and R is an n-place relation symbol, assigns some set of ordered n-tuples of members of **U**. $\mu(w,R)$ is the *extension* of R at w, i.e., the set of all n-tuples of "possible objects satisfying R at w". Note that it is not required that the extension of R at w be included in the domain of w. An *assignment* relative to $\langle w, \mathbf{W}, \mathbf{U}, \mathbf{D}, \mu \rangle$ is a function mapping the set Vr of individual variables into **U**. If $x \in$ Vr and σ and σ^* are assignments, $\sigma \underset{x}{\approx} \sigma^*$ iff σ and σ^* make the same assignments to all variables except possibly x. If $\langle w, \mathbf{W}, \mathbf{U}, \mathbf{D}, \mu \rangle$ is a model for which $\mathbf{U} \neq \varnothing$ and σ is an assignment relative to $\langle w, \mathbf{W}, \mathbf{U}, \mathbf{D}, \mu \rangle$, truth relative to $\langle \langle w, \mathbf{W}, \mathbf{U}, \mathbf{D}, \mu \rangle, \sigma \rangle$ is defined recursively as follows:

(7.1) (a) $\ulcorner Rx_1 \ldots x_n \urcorner$ is true in $\langle \langle w, \mathbf{W}, \mathbf{U}, \mathbf{D}, \mu \rangle, \sigma \rangle$ iff $\langle \sigma(x_1), \ldots, \sigma(x_n) \rangle \in \mu(w,R)$;

 (b) $\ulcorner \neg p \urcorner$ is true in $\langle \langle w, \mathbf{W}, \mathbf{U}, \mathbf{D}, \mu \rangle, \sigma \rangle$ iff p is not true in $\langle \langle w, \mathbf{W}, \mathbf{U}, \mathbf{D}, \mu \rangle, \sigma \rangle$;

 (c) $\ulcorner (p \wedge q) \urcorner$ is true in $\langle \langle w, \mathbf{W}, \mathbf{U}, \mathbf{D}, \mu \rangle, \sigma \rangle$ iff p and q are both true in $\langle \langle w, \mathbf{W}, \mathbf{D}, \mathbf{U}, \mu \rangle, \sigma \rangle$;

 (d) $\ulcorner (\vee x) p \urcorner$ is true in $\langle \langle w, \mathbf{W}, \mathbf{U}, \mathbf{D}, \mu \rangle, \sigma \rangle$ iff there is a σ^* such that $\sigma^* \underset{x}{\approx} \sigma$ and $\sigma^*(x) \in \mathbf{D}(w)$ and p is true in $\langle \langle w, \mathbf{W}, \mathbf{U}, \mathbf{D}, \mu \rangle, \sigma^* \rangle$;

 (e) $\ulcorner \Box p \urcorner$ is true in $\langle \langle w, \mathbf{W}, \mathbf{U}, \mathbf{D}, \mu \rangle, \sigma \rangle$ iff for every w^* in **W**, p is true in $\langle \langle w^*, \mathbf{W}, \mathbf{U}, \mathbf{D}, \mu \rangle, \sigma \rangle$.

As in nonmodal first-order logic, the assignment of denotations to individual variables is just a technical trick employed in order to define truth for closed formulas (F being the set of closed formulas). Closed formulas are the only formulas that express propositional, statemental, or SOA forms. Open formulas are here called '*wff*s' rather than 'formulas'. We then define truth in a model as follows:

(7.2) If $p \in F$ and $\langle w, \mathbf{W}, \mathbf{U}, \mathbf{D}, \mu \rangle$ is a model for which $\mathbf{U} \neq \varnothing$, p is true in $\langle w, \mathbf{W}, \mathbf{U}, \mathbf{D}, \mu \rangle$ iff there is an assignment σ relative to $\langle w, \mathbf{W}, \mathbf{U}, \mathbf{D}, \mu \rangle$ such that p is true in $\langle \langle w, \mathbf{W}, \mathbf{U}, \mathbf{D}, \mu \rangle, \sigma \rangle$.

If $\mathbf{U} = \varnothing$ then there are no assignments relative to $\langle w, \mathbf{W}, \mathbf{U}, \mathbf{D}, \mu \rangle$, and so truth must be defined differently. In that case, we rule that all existential generalizations are false and compute the truth values of compound formulas built out of existential generalizations as in non-quantificational modal logic.

An *n-formula* is a *wff* in which n different variables have free occurrences. We define *satisfaction* as follows:

(7.3) If p is an *n*-formula and $\langle w, \mathbf{W}, \mathbf{U}, \mathbf{D}, \mu \rangle$ is a model then $\langle a_1, \ldots, a_n \rangle$ *satisifes* p in $\langle w, \mathbf{W}, \mathbf{U}, \mathbf{D}, \mu \rangle$ iff, if $x_1, \ldots, x_n$ are the variables occurring free in p listed in order of their initial occurrence in p then there is an assignment σ relative to $\langle w, \mathbf{W}, \mathbf{U}, \mathbf{D}, \mu \rangle$ such that $\sigma(x_1) = a_1$ and ... and $\sigma(x_n) = a_n$ and p is true in $\langle \langle w, \mathbf{W}, \mathbf{U}, \mathbf{D}, \mu \rangle, \sigma \rangle$.

This treatment of variables and quantification deserves comment. It is frequently "explained", in a heuristic way, that $\mathbf{U}$ represents the set of all possible objects—different ones of which are actual in different possible worlds—and the variables range over all of the possible objects. Taken literally, that is nonsense. There are no merely possible objects, and so there can be no set of all possible objects. It is tempting to try to make sense of this in terms of the possibilistic quantifiers and possibilistic set theory of Chapter Three, but even that will not work. Not only is there no actual set of all possible objects—there can be no possible set of all possible objects. Possible sets are actual sets in other possible worlds. Therefore, to suppose there is a possible set of all possible objects is to suppose that there is a world at which the set of all possible objects is an actual set. We have seen that a set cannot exist without all of its members existing, so this supposition requires there to be a world at which all possible objects exist. We have already noted that such a supposition is unreasonable. To the contrary, it would seem to be a necessary truth that at any world it is possible for there to be something that does not actually exist;

i.e., $\ulcorner\lozenge(\exists x){\sim}\mathbf{A}(x\text{ exists})\urcorner$ is necessary. Thus, we cannot take the heuristic explanation of this semantics too literally.

A second nonsensical claim that is often made about this semantics is that it treats variables as rigid designators. Variables are not designators, rigid or limp. It should be emphasized once more that the assignment of denotations to variables is just a technical trick that facilitates the definition of truth for closed formulas. All it does is provide us with an elegant way of talking about the satisfaction of open formulas by sequences of objects. At the expense of further definitional complexity, we could eliminate all talk of assignments, instead providing a recursive definition for the notion of an n-tuple of objects satisfying an open formula in a model, and then define truth in terms of satisfaction.

Kripke [1963] presents a version of quantified S5, which I have been calling 'KS5'. KS5 is strongly complete for this formal semantics. If p is any *wff*, we define a *closure* of p to be any (closed) formula obtained by prefixing universal quantifiers and necessity signs, in any order, to p. The axioms of KS5 are then all closures of *wff*s of the following forms:

(A0) truth-functional tautologies

(A1) $\Box p \rightarrow p$

(A2) $\Box(p \rightarrow q) \rightarrow (\Box p \rightarrow \Box q)$

(A3) $p \rightarrow (\wedge x)p$ (provided x does not occur free in p)

(A4) $(\wedge x)(p \rightarrow q) \rightarrow [(\wedge x)p \rightarrow (\wedge x)q]$;

(A5) $(\wedge y)[(\wedge x)p \rightarrow \mathrm{Sb}(y/x)p]$ (where $\mathrm{Sb}(y/x)p$ results from replacing all free occurrences of x in p by y, and y does not occur in p)

(A6) $\lozenge p \rightarrow \Box\lozenge p$

The only rule of inference is *modus ponens* for '$\rightarrow$'. Universal generalization and necessitation are derived rules of KS5.[18]

7.1 *Propositional First-Order Modal Logic*

In propositional first-order modal logic, formulas express propositional forms. Interpretations assign concepts to relation

---

[18] I presented a different axiomatization of KS5 in Chapter Three.

symbols and open formulas and they assign propositions to (closed) formulas. As in nonmodal first-order logic, we have several options regarding the interpretation of the quantifiers. I will only pursue the one that seems to me to be the most natural. I will take an interpretation η to assign a concept α_η to which the quantifiers will be relativized. This is option (b) of section (5.1). Let $\langle F,\pi \rangle$ be the language resulting from this choice of interpretations.[19]

Turning to questions of adequacy and strong adequacy, we can prove (A1) for $\langle F,\pi \rangle$ in the same way we have proven it for all of the other logical theories we have encountered so far. Inspection reveals that the axioms of KS5 are all true and the only rule of inference is truth preserving, so it follows as before from the strong completeness of KS5 that (A1) holds for $\langle F,\pi \rangle$.

(A2) is problematic for first-order modal logic for the same reason it was problematic for non-quantificational modal logic. I have been unable to prove it and consequently unable to establish the strong adequacy of our formal semantics. However, we can prove (A3) instead and thereby establish the adequacy of the semantics. (A3) requires:

[19] In my opinion, the next most reasonable choice of interpretations would require that $\Diamond(\exists x)x$ exemplifies α_η. This is more reasonable than the analogous requirement in nonmodal first-order logic that $(\exists x)x$ exemplifies α_η, because this is at least a logical constraint rather than a contingent constraint. If we modify the semantics by requiring that $\mathbf{U} \neq \varnothing$, we can prove the adequacy of this semantics as below. For that purpose we make use of the strongly complete version of S5 presented in Fine [1978].

It is of interest that the decision to relativize quantifiers rather than have them range over absolutely everything makes a difference to the logic. In connection with possibilistic set theory, I urged that given any two possible objects, there is a world at which they both exist, i.e.,

$\Box(\forall x)\Box(\forall y)\Diamond(x$ exists and y exists$)$.

If quantifiers were not relativized to concepts, that would make the following valid:

$\Box(\wedge x)(\wedge y)\Box Fxy \rightarrow \Box(\wedge x)\Box(\wedge y)\Box Fxy$.

This is not a theorem of KS5. Nor should it be if quantifiers are interpreted as relativized to arbitrary concepts.

(A3) For each formula p, if p is satisfiable then there is an interpretation η and a possible world w such that $\eta(p)$ is true at w.

The proof of (A3) is rather involved and will occupy us for the next several pages.

Given our set F of first-order modal formulas, we can construct a corresponding set $F_\square$ of nonmodal first-order formulas by (1) adding a predicate 'W' ('is a possible world'), (2) adding a binary relation '$E(i,x)$' ('x exists in world i'), (3) adding a place to each relation symbol (so that two-place relation symbols become three-place, etc.), and (4) adding an individual constant '$@$' (to denote the actual world). Formulas of F can then be translated into formulas of $F_\square$ that intuitively "say the same thing" in the following recursive manner:

(7.4) $t(\ulcorner Rx_1 \ldots x_n \urcorner) = \ulcorner Rx_1 \ldots x_n @ \urcorner$;

$t(\ulcorner \neg p \urcorner) = \ulcorner \neg t(p) \urcorner$;

$t(\ulcorner (p \wedge q) \urcorner) = \ulcorner (t(p) \wedge t(q)) \urcorner$;

$t(\ulcorner \square p \urcorner) = \ulcorner (\wedge x)[W(x) \to \mathrm{Sb}(x/@)t(p)] \urcorner$ (where x is some variable not occuring free in p);

$t(\ulcorner (\vee x)p \urcorner) = \ulcorner (\vee x)[E(@,x) \wedge t(p)] \urcorner$.

Given a model $\langle w, \mathbf{W}, \mathbf{U}, \mathbf{D}, \mu \rangle$ for F, we can construct a first-order model for $F_\square$ that preserves truth under the translation t. Let us define:

(7.5) If $\langle w, \mathbf{W}, \mathbf{U}, \mathbf{D}, \mu \rangle$ is a model for F, $\langle \mathbf{D}, \xi \rangle$ is the *first-order model derived from* $\langle w, \mathbf{W}, \mathbf{U}, \mathbf{D}, \mu \rangle$ iff:

(a) $\mathbf{D} = \mathbf{U} \cup \mathbf{W}$;

(b) $\xi(@) = w$;

(c) $\xi(W) = \mathbf{W}$;

(d) $\xi(E) = \{\langle i,x \rangle | \ i \in \mathbf{W} \text{ and } x \in \mathbf{D}(i)\}$;

(e) if R is an n-place relation symbol, $\xi(R) = \{\langle x_1, \ldots, x_n \rangle | \ i \in \mathbf{W} \text{ and } \langle x_1, \ldots, x_n \rangle \in \mu(i,R)\}$.

(7.6) If $\langle \mathbf{D}, \xi \rangle$ is a first-order model for $F_\square$ and $i \in \mathbf{W}$, $\xi^{(i)}$ is just like ξ except that $\xi(@) = i$.

We then have the following simple lemma:

(7.7) If $\langle w,\mathbf{W},\mathbf{U},\mathbf{D},\mu\rangle$ is a model for F and $\langle \mathbf{D},\xi\rangle$ is the first order model derived from $\langle w,\mathbf{W},\mathbf{D},\mathbf{U},\mu\rangle$ then:
  (a) for any p in F and i in $\mathbf{W}$, p is true in $\langle i,\mathbf{W},\mathbf{U},\mathbf{D},\mu\rangle$ iff $t(p)$ is true in $\langle \mathbf{D},\xi^{(i)}\rangle$;
  (b) for any n-formula p of F and for any i in $\mathbf{W}$, if $x_1,\ldots,x_n\in\mathbf{U}$ then $\langle x_1,\ldots,x_n\rangle$ satisfies p in $\langle i,\mathbf{W},\mathbf{U},\mathbf{D},\mu\rangle$ iff $\langle x_1,\ldots,x_n,i\rangle$ satisfies $t(p)$ in $\langle \mathbf{D},\xi^{(i)}\rangle$.

The translation of first-order modal formulas into first-order nonmodal formulas enables us to use certain facts about nonmodal first-order logic in establishing (A3). Let us say that a model $\langle \mathbf{D},\xi\rangle$ is *generated by* an interpretation η iff (1) $\mathbf{D}$ is the extension of α_η; (2) for each individual constant c, $\xi(c)$ is the object denoted by $\eta(c)$; and (3) for each relation symbol R, $\xi(R)$ is the extension of $\eta(R)$. An *arithmetical interpretation* of $F_\Box$ is an interpretation η such that: for each n-place relation symbol R of $F_\Box$, $\eta(R)$ is an n-place concept definable in the language of first-order arithmetic; for the sole individual constant '$@$', $\eta(@)$ is a propositional designator that is a definite description definable in the language of first-order arithmetic; and quantifiers are relativized to the concept $\mathbf{N}$ of *being a natural number*. Then an *arithmetical model* for $F_\Box$ is a first-order model $\langle \omega,\xi\rangle$ that is generated by an arithmetical interpretation η for $F_\Box$. The following theorem is due to Kreisel [1950]:

(7.8) If p is a formula of $F_\Box$ and p has a model then p has an arithmetical model.

We now prove (A3) as follows. Suppose $p\in F$ and p has a model. By (7.7), $t(p)$ has a model, so by (7.8), $t(p)$ has an arithmetical model $\langle \omega,\xi_0\rangle$. If $\xi_0(W) = \omega$, let $\xi = \xi_0$. If $\xi_0(W) \neq \omega$, then we construct a new model $\langle \omega,\xi\rangle$ in the following way. Let w_0 be the first number in ξ_0, and then define:

  (a) $\xi(W) = \omega$;
  (b) $\xi(@) = \xi_0(@)$;
  (c) $\xi(E) = \xi_0(E) \cup \{\langle i,x\rangle|\ i\notin\xi_0(W)$ and $\langle w_0,x\rangle\in\xi_0(E)\}$;
  (d) if R is an n-place relation symbol of F, $\xi(R) = \xi_0(R) \cup \{\langle x_1,\ldots,x_n,i\rangle|\ i\notin\xi_0(W)$ and $\langle x_1,\ldots,x_n,w_0\rangle\in\xi_0(R)\}$.

The effect of this construction is to make all natural numbers not in $\xi_0(W)$ duplicates of w_0 when viewed as possible worlds. It is then trivial to prove by induction on the length of q:

(7.9) (a) If $q \in F$ then $t(q)$ is true in $\langle \omega, \xi \rangle$ iff $t(q)$ is true in $\langle \omega, \xi_0 \rangle$; and

(b) if q is an n-formula of F and σ is an n-tuple, σ satisfies $t(q)$ in $\langle \omega, \xi \rangle$ iff σ satisfies $t(q)$ in $\langle \omega, \xi_0 \rangle$.

$\langle \omega, \xi \rangle$ is an arithmetical model because $\langle \omega, \xi_0 \rangle$ is, so let α be an arithmetical interpretation of $F_\square$ that generates $\langle \omega, \xi \rangle$. Let β be the concept expressed by $\ulcorner x$ is finite and there are exactly x red objects in the world, or $x = 0$ and there are infinitely many red objects in the world$\urcorner$, and for each natural number i let δ_i be a propositional designator that is necessarily such that it designates i.[20] Where $i = \xi(@)$, let $\delta_i = \alpha(@)$. Clearly, for each i, the proposition $(\beta : \delta_i)$ is possible. Furthermore, $(\exists i)[(\mathbf{N}:i) \ \& \ (\beta:i)]$ is necessary. For each $i \in \omega$, construct the interpretation α_i of $F_\square$ that is just like α except that $\alpha(@) = \delta_i$.

Our proof of (A3) will turn upon the fact that as the α_i are arithmetical interpretations, for any closed formula q, $\alpha_i(q)$ is true iff it is necessarily true, and for any open formula q, σ exemplifies $\alpha_i(q)$ iff σ is necessarily such that it exemplifies $\alpha_i(q)$. Using this fact we prove the crucial lemma of our adequacy theorem:

(7.10) (a) If $q \in F$ then $\diamondsuit(\exists i)[((\beta:\delta_i) \ \& \ \alpha_i(t(q)))$ is true] iff $(\exists i)[\alpha_i(t(q))$ is true]; and

(b) if q is an n-formula of F and σ an n-tuple of natural numbers, $\diamondsuit(\exists i)[(\beta:\delta_i)$ is true and σ exemplifies $\alpha_i(t(q))]$ iff $(\exists i)[\sigma$ exemplifies $\alpha_i(t(q))]$.

Proof: We will only explicitly consider the case of n-formulas, the case of closed formulas being analogous. α_i is an arithmetical interpretation, so either $\square_{\sigma,i}(\sigma$ exemplifies $\alpha_i(q))$ or $\square_{\sigma,i}(\sigma$ does not exemplify $\alpha_i(q))$. If $\diamondsuit(\exists i)[(\beta:\delta_i)$ is

---

[20] Such designators are readily available. For example, δ_0 might be the definite description 'the smallest natural number', δ_1 might be 'the smallest natural number larger than 0', and so on.

true and σ exemplifies $\alpha_i(t(q))$], then for some $i\in\omega$, $\Diamond_{\sigma,i}(\sigma$ exemplifies $\alpha_i(t(q)))$. Conversely, if σ exemplifies $\alpha_i(t(q))$, then $\Box_{\sigma,i}(\sigma$ exemplifies $\alpha_i(t(q)))$. $\Diamond[(\beta{:}\delta_i)$ is true], so by S5, $\Diamond[(\beta{:}\delta_i)$ is true and σ exemplifies $\alpha_i(t(q))$]. Hence $\Diamond(\exists i)[(\beta{:}\delta_i)$ is true and σ exemplifies $\alpha_i(t(q))$].

Next, let us enrich the language $F_\Box$ by adding an individual constant k_j for each $j\in\omega$ and letting $\alpha_i(k_j) = \delta_j$. Then an obvious lemma that we will use below is:

(7.11) (a) If $q\in F$ then $\alpha_i(\mathrm{Sb}(k_j/@)t(q)$ is true iff $\alpha_j(t(q))$ is true; and

(b) if q is an n-formula of F and σ is an n-tuple of natural numbers, then σ exemplifies $\alpha_i(\mathrm{Sb}(k_j/@)t(q)$ iff σ exemplifies $\alpha_j(t(q))$.

Next construct the interpretation η of F as follows. Let τ be the propositional designator $\imath i(\beta{:}i)$. η relativizes quantifiers to $(\alpha(E){:}\tau,x)$, and for each n-place relation symbol R of F, $\eta(R) = (\alpha(R){:}x_1,\ldots,x_n,\tau)$. Note that $\mathrm{Nec}((\bigvee x)\ x \approx \tau)$. We then prove:

(7.12) (a) If $q\in F$ then $\eta(q)$ is true iff $(\exists i)[((\beta{:}\delta_i)\&\alpha_i(t(q)))$ is true]; and

(b) if q is an n-formula of F and σ is an n-tuple then σ exemplifies $\eta(q)$ iff $(\exists i)[(\beta{:}\delta_i)$ is true and σ exemplifies $\alpha_i(t(q))$].

Proof by induction on the length of q (we only explicitly discuss the case of n-formulas, the case of closed formulas being analogous):

(i) Suppose $q = \ulcorner Rx_1\ldots x_n\urcorner$. σ exemplifies $\eta(R_1\ldots x_n)$ iff σ exemplifies $(\alpha(R){:}x_1,\ldots,x_n,\tau)$, iff σ exemplifies $(\exists i)[(\beta{:}i)$ & $(\alpha(R){:}x_1,\ldots,x_n,i)]$, iff $(\exists i)[(\beta{:}\delta_i)$ is true and σ exemplifies $(\alpha(R){:}x_1,\ldots,x_n,\delta_i)]$, iff $(\exists i)[(\beta{:}\delta_i)$ is true and σ exemplifies $\alpha_i(t(Rx_1\ldots x_n))]$.

(ii) and (iii), the cases of negation and conjunction, are trivial.

(iv) Suppose $q = \ulcorner\Diamond r\urcorner$. Then:

σ exemplifies $\eta(\Diamond r)$

iff σ exemplifies $\Diamond\eta(r)$

iff $\Diamond$ σ exemplifies $\eta(r)$

iff $\Diamond(\exists i)((\beta{:}\delta_i)$ is true and σ exemplifies $\alpha_i(t(r)))$

iff $(\exists i)$ σ exemplifies $\alpha_i(t(r))$ (by (7.10))

iff $(\exists j)$ σ exemplifies $\alpha_j(t(r))$

iff $(\exists j)[\sigma$ exemplifies $\alpha_j(t(r))$ and $(\exists i)((\beta{:}\delta_i)$ is true)]

iff $(\exists i)(\exists j)[(\beta{:}\delta_i)$ is true and σ exemplifies $\alpha_i(\mathrm{Sb}(k_j/@)t(r))]$ (by (7.11))

iff $(\exists i)((\beta{:}\delta_i)$ is true and $(\exists j)[(\alpha(W){:}\delta_j$ is true and σ exemplifies $\alpha_i(\mathrm{Sb}(k_j/@)t(r))])$ (because $\xi(W) = \omega)$

iff $(\exists i)(\sigma$ exemplifies $(\exists j)[(\alpha(W){:}j)$ & $\alpha_i(\mathrm{Sb}(k_j/@)t(r))]$ and $(\beta{:}\delta_i)$ is true)

iff $(\exists i)(\sigma$ exemplifies $\alpha_i((\exists j)[\mathrm{W}j$ & $\mathrm{Sb}(k_j/@)t(r)]$ & $(\beta{:}\delta_i)$ is true)

iff $(\exists i)[\sigma$ exemplifies $\alpha_i(t(\Diamond r))$ & $(\beta{:}\delta_i)$ is true].

(v) Suppose $q = \ulcorner(\exists x)r\urcorner$. If x is the kth variable to occur free in r, listed in order of occurrence, let $\sigma^\frown\langle j\rangle$ be the result of inserting j between the $(k-1)$th and the kth place in the sequence σ. Then:

σ exemplifies $\eta((\exists x)r)$

iff $(\exists j)[j$ exemplifies $(\alpha(E){:}\tau,x)$ & $\eta(t(r))]$

iff $(\exists j)(j$ exemplifies $(\alpha(E){:}\tau,x)$ & $\sigma^\frown\langle j\rangle$ exemplifies $\eta(t(r))]$

iff $(\exists j)(j$ exemplifies $(\alpha(E){:}\tau,x)$ & $(\exists i)[(\beta{:}\delta_i)$ is true and $\sigma^\frown\langle j\rangle$ exemplifies $\alpha_i(t(r))])$

iff $(\exists i)(\exists j)(j$ exemplifies $(\alpha(E){:}\delta_i,x)$ and $(\beta{:}\delta_i)$ is true and $\sigma^\frown\langle j\rangle$ exemplifies $\alpha_i(t(r))])$

iff $(\exists i)((\beta{:}\delta_i)$ is true and $(\exists j)[j$ exemplifies $(\alpha(E){:}\delta_i,x)$ and $\sigma^\frown\langle j\rangle$ exemplifies $\alpha_i(t(r))])$

iff $(\exists i)((\beta{:}\delta_i)$ is true and $(\exists j)[j$ exemplifies $\alpha_i(E(@,x))$ and $\sigma^\frown\langle j\rangle$ exemplifies $\alpha_i(t(r))])$

iff $(\exists i)((\beta{:}\delta_i)$ is true and σ exemplifies $(\exists j)[(\alpha_i(E(@,j)$ & $t(r)])$

iff $(\exists i)[(\beta{:}\delta_i)$ is true and σ exemplifies $\alpha_i(t((\exists x)r))]$.

Finally, we can conclude that (A3) is true. Recalling that p is the formula with which we began and that $\langle\omega,\xi\rangle$ is a model of $t(p)$, we have:

(7.13) There is a world w such that $\eta(p)$ is true at w.

Proof: Let $i = \alpha(@)$. Then $\alpha(t(p)) = \alpha_i(t(p))$, so $\alpha_i(t(p))$ is true and hence necessary. $(\beta{:}\delta_i)$ is possibly true, so $[(\beta{:}\delta_i)$ & $\alpha_i(t(p))]$ is possibly true. Then by (7.12), $\eta(p)$ is possibly true, i.e., there is a world at which $\eta(p)$ is true.

By virtue of theorem (7.13), the formal semantics for first-order modal logic is adequate for $\langle F, \pi \rangle$. This is true despite the fact that the semantics makes heuristic use of such problematic notions as "the set of all possible objects". We have not, however, succeeded in establishing that the semantics is strongly adequate. The obstacle to converting our argument into a proof of strong adequacy is the use of Kreisel's theorem (7.8). Kreisel's theorem gives us an arithmetical model for just the single formula $t(p)$. If Kreisel's theorem gave us an arithmetical model for the entire set $\{t(q) \mid q$ is true in $M\}$ (where M is the model for F with which we began), our argument would generate a proof of strong adequacy. However, it is not true that every satisfiable set of formulas has an arithmetical model, so strong adequacy cannot be proven in this way. Let us say that a set of integers is arithmetical iff it is the extension of some monadic concept definable in the language of first-order arithmetic. A set of formulas is arithmetical iff the set of its Gödel numbers is arithmetical. Kreisel's theorem is not applicable to arbitrary sets of formulas, but it is applicable to arithmetical sets of formulas, with the result that we can prove the following as above:

(7.14) If Γ is an arithmetical set of formulas and Γ is satisfiable, then there is an interpretation η and a world w such that for every p in Γ, $\eta(p)$ is true in w.

Combining this with (A1) we obtain:

(7.15) If Γ is an arithmetical set of formulas, then Γ is satisfiable iff Γ is consistent$_N$.

This is weaker than strong adequacy, which would require the analogous principle for non-arithmetical sets of formulas as well. Our inability to prove strong adequacy indicates that we must beware what our formal semantics tells us about the semantical implication relation. Semantical implication may not coincide with logical consequence. However, as we almost always deal with arithmetical sets of formulas, this may not be as much of a problem as it first appears.

For future reference, let us take note of precisely how Kreisel's theorem is used in the proof of adequacy. Kreisel's theorem is used to give us an arithmetical model, and the significance of the model being arithmetical is that it is generated by a corresponding arithmetical interpretation α such that $\alpha(t(p))$ is true. The only fact that we use about the interpretation's being arithmetical is that for each formula q of $F_\square$, necessarily, $\alpha(q)$ is true iff $\alpha(q)$ is necessary, and for each open formula q of $F_\square$ and each sequence σ, necessarily, σ exemplifies $\alpha(q)$ iff σ is necessarily such that it exemplifies $\alpha(q)$). Let us call this the *noncontingency condition*. Any other interpretation that satisfied the noncontingency condition would work equally well. Let $M_\square$ be the model of $F_\square$ derived from our model M of F. If we could find some interpretation α^* that (1) generates $M_\square$, and (2) satisfies the noncontingency condition, then we could prove (7.12) for α^*. By (7.7) and the fact that α^* generates $M_\square$, we have:

(7.16) For each $p \in F$, p is true in M iff $\alpha^*(t(p))$ is true.

We have proven (7.12), so it is necessarily true. Consequently, letting i be the denotation of '@' in $M_\square$ we have for any Γ:

$\square$[if $(\beta{:}\delta_i)$ is true then $(\forall q \in \Gamma)(\eta(q)$ is true iff $\alpha^*(t(q))$ is true)].

Letting $\Gamma = \{q \mid q$ is true in $M\}$, this entails:

$\square$[if $(\beta{:}\delta_i)$ is true then $((\forall q \in \Gamma)\ \eta(q)$ is true iff $(\forall q \in \Gamma)$ $\alpha^*(t(q))$ is true)].

$(\beta{:}\delta_i)$ is possibly true, so $\lozenge[(\forall q \in \Gamma)\ \eta(q)$ is true iff $(\forall q \in \Gamma)$ $\alpha^*(t(q))$ is true]. By the noncontingency condition,

$\square[(\forall q \in \Gamma)\ \alpha^*(t(q))$ is true iff $\square(\forall q \in \Gamma)\ \alpha^*(t(q))$ is true],

so by S5, $\lozenge[(\forall q \in \Gamma)\ \eta(q)$ is true] iff $(\forall q \in \Gamma)\ \alpha^*(t(q))$ is true, i.e., there is a possible world w such that $M \simeq \langle w, \eta \rangle$. Unfortunately, I see no way to construct such an interpretation for propositional first-order modal logic. However, when we consider SOA first-order modal logic, we will be able to construct such an interpretation, and so it will follow that this semantics is strongly adequate for SOA first-order modal logic.

7.2 *Statemental and Linguistic First-Order Modal Logic*

Despite the fact that the semantics for first-order modal logic is based intuitively upon the identification of necessity with truth at all possible worlds, inspection of the preceding argument reveals that we have nowhere used that identification. Furthermore, the propositions upon which the constructions are based are all statements as well. Consequently, the preceding argument can be applied without change to establish that our semantics is also adequate for statemental first-order modal logic. Clearly, statemental first-order modal logic agrees uniformly with linguistic first-order modal logic, so it follows that our semantics is also adequate for the latter.

7.3 *SOA First-Order Modal Logic*

SOA first-order modal logic is basically similar to propositional first-order modal logic, the difference being the same as the difference between SOA first-order logic and propositional first-order logic. We can prove (A1) just as we did for propositional first-order modal logic. The major difference emerges when we consider (A2), which we could not prove for propositional first-order modal logic but which we can prove for SOA first-order modal logic. Let M be a model for F. It was remarked above that for the purpose of proving (A2) it suffices to find an interpretation α^* that (1) generates $M_\square$ and (2) satisfies the noncontingency condition. Because of the greater ease in constructing properties and states of affairs, such an interpretation is easily constructed for SOA logic. The interpretation is the same as that used in section 5.3 for proving the strong adequacy of SOA first-order logic. To '@' we let α^* assign the denotation of '@' in $M_\square$. To each n-place relation symbol R of $F_\square$ we let α^* assign the property of *being*

227

an n-tuple in the extension of R in $M_\square$. That is (recalling that *n*-place properties are functions from *n*-tuples to states of affairs), $\alpha^*(R)$ is that property that assigns to each *n*-tuple σ the tautologous state of affairs if σ satisfies R in $M_\square$ and the contradictory state of affairs otherwise. So constructed, α^* clearly satisfies the noncontingency condition and generates $M_\square$. It follows that (A2) holds and our semantics is strongly adequate for SOA first-order modal logic.

The greater ease with which we can construct interpretations for SOA logics is extremely interesting. Traditional conceptions of logic viewed it as studying "laws of thought" or, more recently, relations between propositions. But set-theoretic semantics are better tailored to SOA logics. The reason is that such semantics define models to be any sets satisfying certain formal constraints. If every set were the extension of a concept, such models could always be described intensionally in terms of concepts (as in the case of arithmetical models), and such descriptions could be turned into interpretations for propositional logics. But there is no reason to think that every set is the extension of a concept and, I would suppose, considerable reason to be suspicious of such a claim. Thus, it is quite natural to suspect that set-theoretic models may outstrip propositional interpretations, and hence set-theoretic semantics may not be strongly adequate for propositional logics. On the other hand, the concept of a property was defined sufficiently broadly that every set is the extension of a property, and so it is a simple matter to generate SOA interpretations from set-theoretic models.

8. Assessment of Formal Semantics

We are now in a position to answer the rather general question with which we began this chapter. Formal semantics does have a limited philosophical significance, although it does not have the all-pervasive significance sometimes attributed to it by logicians. To begin with, formal semantics attempts to characterize with mathematical precision the sets of formulas that are valid for the different concepts of validity we have been able to make precise. The extent to which a particular semantics accomplishes this can be objectively evaluated, and we have done that for a number of the most popular formal semantical theories.

It is often alleged that formal semantics provide us with analyses of logical concepts. That is not entirely accurate. A formal semantics by itself cannot provide us with an analysis. It can do that, however, when it is coupled with a characterization of the surrogate relation. Such a characterization cannot be purely mathematical. It must proceed by relating the mathematical concept of a model to the philosophical concepts of an interpretation and a possible world. The effect of this is to turn the formal semantics into a realistic semantics.

Perhaps the greatest obstacle to understanding the heuristic claims often made about possible worlds semantics is that they generally involve the misconception that models are formal surrogates for possible worlds. They are not. Rather, they are surrogates for ordered pairs $\langle w, \eta \rangle$ of possible worlds and interpretations (or in linguistic logics, for the triples $\langle w, \eta, \pi \rangle$). This is of considerable importance. It is this that legitimizes models like $\langle G, \{G\} \rangle$. Given the framework established in this chapter, I believe we are finally in a position to make clear sense of what is going on in formal semantics and formal logic.

References

Ackermann, Diana
  1979 Proper names, propositional attitudes and non-descriptive connotations. *Philosophical Studies* 35, 55–70.
  1979a Proper names, essences, and intuitive beliefs. *Theory and Decision* 11, 5–26.
  1980 Thinking about an object: comments on Pollock. *Midwest Studies in Philosophy* 5, 501–508.

Adams, Robert M.
  1974 Theories of actuality. *Nous* 8, 211–231.
  1979 Primitive thisness and primitive identity. *Journal of Philosophy* 76, 5–26.
  1981 Actualism and thisness. *Synthese* 49, 3–42.

Bell, J. L., and A. B. Slomson
  1969 *Models and Ultraproducts*. Amsterdam: North Holland.

Bennett, Jonathan
  1983 Even if. *Linguistics and Philosophy* 5, 403–418.

Black, Max
  1952 The identity of indiscernibles. *Mind* 61, 153–164.

Bowie, G. Lee
  1979 The similarity approach to counterfactuals: some problems. *Nous* 13, 477–498.

Carnap, Rudolph
  1942 *Introduction to Semantics*. Cambridge: Harvard University Press.
  1943 *Formalization of Logic*. Cambridge: Harvard University Press.

1947 *Meaning and Necessity*. Chicago: University of Chicago Press.

Cartwright, Richard
1962 Propositions. In *Analytic Philosophy*, edited by Ronald Butler, 81–103. New York: Barnes and Noble.

Chisholm, Roderick
1976 *Person and Object*. London: Allen & Unwin.

Crossley, J. N., and I. L. Humberstone
1977 The logic of "actually". *Reports on Mathematical Logic* 8, 11–29.

Davidson, Donald
1970 The individuation of events. In *Essays in Honor of Carl Hempel*, edited by Nicholas Rescher, 216–234. Dordrecht: Reidel.

Davidson, Donald, and Gilbert Harman, eds.
1972 *Semantics of Natural Language*. Dordrecht: Reidel.

Donnellan, Keith
1972 Proper names and identifying descriptions. In Davidson and Harman [1972], 356–379.

Fine, Kit
1975 Review of Lewis [1973]. *Mind* 84, 451–458.
1978 Model theory for modal logic. *Journal of Philosophical Logic* 7, 125–156, 277–306; 10, 293–308.

Hughes, G. E., and M. J. Cresswell
1968 *An Introduction of Modal Logic*. London: Metheun.

Kamp, Hans
1971 Formal properties of "now". *Theoria* 37, 277–273.

References

Kaplan, David
1976 *Demonstratives*, mimeographed.
1981 On the logic of demonstratives. *Journal of Philosophical Logic* 8, 81–98.

Kim, Jaegwon
1973 Causes and counterfactuals. *Journal of Philosophy* 70, 570–572.

Kreisel, George
1950 Note on arithmetical models for consistent formulae of the predicate calculus. *Fundamentae mathematica* 37.

Kripke, Saul
1959 A completeness theorem in modal logic. *The Journal of Symbolic Logic* 24, 1–14.
1963 Semantical considerations on modal logic. *Acta Philosophica Fennica* 16, 83–94.
1972 Naming and necessity. In Davidson and Harman [1972], 253–355.

Lewis, C. I.
1946 *An Analysis of Knowledge and Valuation*. LaSalle: Open Court.

Lewis, David
1968 Counterpart theory and quantified modal logic. *Journal of Philosophy* 65, 113–126.
1972 Completeness and decidability of three logics of counterfactual conditionals. *Theoria* 37, 74–85.
1972a General semantics. In Davidson and Harman [1972], 169–218.
1973 *Counterfactuals*. Cambridge: Harvard University Press.
1973a Causation. *Journal of Philosophy* 90, 556–567.
1979 Counterfactual dependence and time's arrow. *Nous* 13, 455–476.

1981   Ordering semantics and premise semantics for counterfactuals. *Journal of Philosophical Logic* 10, 217–
234.

Loewer, Barry
1979   Cotenability and counterfactual logics. *Journal of
Philosophical Logic* 8, 99–115.

McMichael, Alan
1983   A problem for actualism about possible worlds. *Philosophical Review* 92, 49–56.

Montague, Richard
1963   Syntactical treatments of modality, with corollaries
on reflexion principles and finite axiomatizability.
Acta Philosophica Fennica 16, 153–167.
1969   On the nature of certain philosophical entities. Re-
printed in Thomason [1974], 148–187.
1970   Universal grammar. *Theoria* 36, 373–398.
1973   The proper treatment of quantification in ordinary
English. In *Approaches to Natural Language*, edited
by J. Hintikka, J. Moravcsik, and P. Suppes, 221–
242. Dordrecht: Reidel.

Nute, Donald
1981   Introduction. *Journal of Philosophical Logic* 10, 127–
148.
1984   Conditional logic. In *Handbook of Philosophical Logic*
2, edited by Dov Gabbay and Franz Guenthner, 387–
439. Dordrecht: Reidel.

Otte, Richard
1982   Modality as a metalinguistic predicate. *Philosophical Studies* 41, 153–160.

Peterson, Philip
1981   What causes effects? *Philosophical Studies* 39, 107–
140.

References

Plantinga, Alvin
1974 *The Nature of Necessity*. Oxford: Oxford University Press.
1976 Actualism and possible worlds. *Theoria* 42, 139–160.
1979 De Essentia. *Grazer Philosophische Studien* 7/8, 101–122.
1983 On existentialism. *Philosophical Studies* 44, 1–21.

Pollock, John
1967 The logic of logical necessity. *Logique et analyse* 10, 307–323.
1967a Logical validity in modal logic. *The Monist* 51, 128–135.
1974 *Knowledge and Justification*. Princeton: Princeton University Press.
1975 Four kinds of conditionals. *American Philosophical Quarterly* 12, 51–60.
1976 *Subjective Reasoning*. Dordrecht: Reidel.
1976a The "possible worlds" analysis of counterfactuals. *Philosophical Studies* 29, 469–476.
1980 Thinking about an object. *Midwest Studies in Philosophy* 5, 487–500.
1981 A refined theory of counterfactuals. *Journal of Philosophical Logic* 10, 239–266.
1982 *Language and Thought*. Princeton: Princeton University Press.
1983 A theory of direct inference. *Theory and Decision* 15, 29–96.
1984 Plantinga on possible worlds. In *Profiles: Plantinga*, edited by J. Tomberlin and Peter van Inwagen. Dordrecht: Reidel.

Putnam, Hilary
1975 The meaning of "meaning". In *Boston Studies in the Philosophy of Science*, vol. 2, edited by R. Cohen and M. Wartofsky, 205–222. Atlantic Highlands, N.J.: Humanities Press.

Quine, W. V. O.
1953   Three grades of modal involvement. *Proceedings of the XI International Congress in Philosophy* 14, 65–81. Brussels.

Ross, Glenn
1982   *Counterfactuals and Causes*. Doctoral dissertation, University of Arizona.

Skyrms, Brian
1978   An immaculate conception of modality. *Journal of Philosophy* 75, 368–387.

Stalnaker, Robert
1968   A theory of conditionals. *American Philosophical Quarterly*, monograph series 2, 98–112.
1981   A defense of conditional excluded middle. In *Ifs*, edited by William Harper, Robert Stalnaker, and Glenn Pearce, 87–106. Dordrecht: Reidel.

Strawson, P. F
1950   On referring. *Mind* 59, 320–344.

Swain, Marshall
1978   A counterfactual analysis of event causation. *Philosophical Studies* 34, 1–20.

Tichý, Pavel
1984   Subjunctive conditionals: two parameters vs. three. *Philosophical Studies* 45, 47–180.

Thomason, Richmond
1974   *Formal Philosophy: Selected Papers of Richard Montague*. New Haven: Yale University Press.

van Fraassen, Bas
1977   The only necessity is verbal necessity. *Journal of Philosophy* 74, 71–85.

References

Vendler, Zeno
1967   Causal relations. *Journal of Philosophy* 64, 704–711.
1967a *Linguistics in Philosophy*. Ithaca: Cornell University Press.

Wittgenstein, Ludwig
1921   Tractatus Logico-Philosophicus, new translation by D. F. Pears and B. F. McGuiness. London: Routledge and Kegan Paul.

Index

Index

Fine, Kit, 137n, 219n
first-order logic, 198ff
first-order modal logic, 215ff
formal semantical theories, 184ff
formal semantics, 2, 172ff
free logics, 204
functions-in-extension, 73
functions-in-intension, 73
Fundamental Theorem of Possible
  Worlds Semantics, 187

general assertions, 47
generalized consequence principle
  (GCP), 113, 130

haecceities, 47
hereditary designators, 29
historical antecedents, 120
historical connection theory, 20
Humberstone, I. L., 86n

indexed difference, 115
indexicality, 37
individual constants, 204ff
individual symbols, 199
infinite conjunction of states of affairs, 58
infinite disjunction of states of affairs, 61
internal necessity, 29, 39
interpretations, 178

Kamp, Hans, 193
Kaplan, David, 1, 23, 190, 193,
  194
Kim, Jaegwon, 149
Kreisel, George, 221, 225
Kripke, Saul, 1, 11, 12n, 20, 23,
  25, 31, 43, 52, 70, 72, 82, 82n,
  193, 215, 218
KS5, 82, 108, 218

legal conservatism, 116ff
Lewis, C. I., 57n
Lewis, David, 1, 2, 43, 49n, 64,

110, 111n, 115, 117, 128,
  130ff, 147n, 148, 149, 153n,
  155n
limit assumption (LA), 130ff
linguistic first-order logic, 206
linguistic first-order modal logic,
  227
linguistic logics, 182ff, 190ff
linguistic non-quantificational
  modal logic, 213
Loewer, Barry, 134
logical analyses, 78
logical consequence, 180
logical designators, 14
logical interchange, 141
logical validity, 176

M, 173
McKay, Tom, 24
McMichael, Alan, 84, 98n
maximal similarity, 128ff
meaning: of a predicate, 38; of a
  sentence, 36; of a singular term,
  38
meso-states, 104
minimal changes, 115, 128ff
miracles, 139
modal operators, 13,32
modal SS, 128
models, 2, 185; first-order logic,
  198; first-order modal logic,
  215; non-quantificational modal
  logic, 172, 193; truth-functional
  logic, 196
Montague, Richard, 1, 40, 72

n-formulas, 217
nearest possible worlds, 114
necessary truth, 12ff; as an operator, 13
necessitation, rule of, 67n, 173
necessitation conditionals, 111,
  149
nomic equivalence, 26, 81, 159
nomic implication, 118

238

Index

Definitions of Symbols

240

Library of Congress Cataloging in Publication Data

Pollock, John L.
The foundations of philosophical semantics.

Includes bibliographical references and index.
1. Semantics (Philosophy) I. Title.
B820.P58   1984   149'.946   83-43088
ISBN 0-691-07283-3 (alk. paper)